Hymns for Today's Church

COMPLETE WORDS EDITION

D1395934

Hymns for Today's Church

COMPLETE WORDS EDITION

Consultant Editor: Michael Baughen,
Bishop of Chester

Hodder & Stoughton

LONDON SYDNEY AUCKLAND TORONTO

British Library Cataloguing in Publication Data

Hymns for today's church. —— Words ed.,
    New ed.
    1. Hymns, English
    I. Baughen, Michael
    264'.2   BV459

ISBN 0-340-41254-2

CONTENTS

INDEX SECTION

INSIDE BACK COVER

Prayers and The Apostles' Creed

FOREWORD

This new edition of *Hymns for Today's Church* is entirely compatible with the second Music Edition. It includes such revisions of words as were recommended to us by authors, and those thought necessary in the light of our slowly evolving language. Further important adjustments have been made in response to the call for inclusive language from English-speaking churches throughout the world.

While the numbering scheme remains the same, twenty-two new texts have been appended. These comprise more hymns in traditional form, standard hymns in revised form, additional canticle versions and two songs previously omitted.

The Editors' prefaces, and the Consultant Editor's Preface to the Second Edition may be found in the Music Edition. Similarly, the complete indexes are available there.

Also from Jubilate Hymns, published by Hodder and Stoughton

Hymns for Today's Church – Music Edition
Hymns for Today's Church – Melody Edition
Carols for Today – Music Editions
Carols for Today – Words Edition
Church Family Worship
Carols for Christmas – Carol selection from *Hymns for Today's Church*

LEGAL INFORMATION

Copyright

The Editors' use of copyright is to safeguard the interests of authors, composers, copyright holders and, in the case of Jubilate Hymns copyrights, of our publishers.

Reprinting

Those seeking to reprint hymns in this book which are the property of Jubilate Hymns Ltd., or of author or composer members of Jubilate Hymns (indicated by †), may write to The Copyright Secretary, Jubilate Hymns Ltd., c/o 47 Bedford Square, London WC1P 3DP. Alternatively, these items may be used under the scheme operated by the Christian Music Association, Glyndley Manor, Stone Cross, Eastbourne, East Sussex BN24 5BS. Addresses of other authors can also be supplied. In all cases please enclose a reply-paid envelope. Hymns copyrighted Stainer & Bell Ltd. may not be reprinted or photocopied under any blanket licensing scheme but should be cleared individually with Stainer & Bell.

Recording and Broadcasting

Jubilate Hymns Ltd., as well as most author or composer members, are also members of the Performing Right Society and the Mechanical Copyright Protection Society.

Prayers

The Confession is from the ASB 1980 © Central Board of Finance of the Church of England. The text of the Apostles' Creed is that of the International Consultation on English Texts (ICET). The Lord's Prayer is adapted from the ICET version.

Reproduction in North America

The following copyright holders have agents to control their copyrights in North America:

Oxford University Press – Hope Publishing Company, Carol Stream, Illinois 60188 or O.U.P. Inc., 200 Madison Avenue, New York 10016. (Please note: 'God is love' is still in copyright in North America.)

Stainer & Bell – Galaxy Music Corporation, 131 West 86th Street, New York 10024 (except for items by F. Kaan and F. Pratt Green, which are controlled by Hope Publishing Co.).

Thankyou Music – 'I will sing' – Celebration, 809 Franklin Ave., PO Box 309, Aliquippa, Pennsylvania 15001.

continued overleaf

Josef Weinberger – E. B. Marks c/o Freddy Bienstok Enterprises, 1619 Broadway, New York 10019.

Word Music (UK) – 'Father we adore you' – Maranatha Music, PO Box 1396, Costa Mesa, California 92628. 'Freely, freely,' 'Holy, holy,' 'Come together' (music) – Lexicon Music Inc., PO Box 2222, 3547 Old Conejo Road, Newbury Park, California 91320.

All items by Bishop Timothy Dudley-Smith and all items (marked †) by Jubilate authors and musicians, including Word & Music, are controlled in North America by Hope Publishing Company, Carol Stream, Illinois 60188.

Hymns for Today's Church

1
G. B. Timms
© Oxford University Press

1 Father eternal, Lord of the ages,
  you who have made us,
        you who have called us:
  look on your children gathered before you;
  worship they bring you, Father of all.

2 Jesus our Saviour, born of a virgin,
  truth from high heaven you came to teach us;
  you are the way that leads to the Father:
  be now our life, both here and above.

3 Spirit all-holy, Spirit of mercy,
  bind us in one with Christ and the Father;
  give us all joy and peace in believing,
  firm on the rock of faith in our God.

4 Father eternal, Jesus redeemer,
  Spirit all-holy, Trinity perfect;
  Unity endless, Love everlasting:
  praise evermore we offer to you.

2
D. T. Niles
in © Christian Conference of Asia Hymnal

1 Father in heaven,
  grant to your children
  mercy and blessing,
  songs never ceasing;
  love to unite us,
  grace to redeem us,
        Father in heaven,
        Father, our God.

2 Jesus redeemer,
  may we remember
  your gracious passion,
  your resurrection:
  worship we bring you,
  praise we shall sing you,
        Jesus redeemer,
        Jesus, our Lord.

3 Spirit descending,
  whose is the blessing,
  strength for the weary,
  help for the needy:
  sealed in our sonship,
  yours be our worship,
        Spirit descending,
        Spirit adored.

3
from the Latin
A. E. Alston

1 Father most holy, merciful and loving,
  Jesus, redeemer, ever to be worshipped,
  life-giving Spirit, comforter most gracious,
  God everlasting:

2 Three in a gracious unity unbroken,
  one perfect Godhead, bound in love unfailing,
  light of the angels, helper of the needy,
        hope of all living:

3 Let all creation honour its creator,
  let every creature praise you without ceasing!
  We too would bring our songs
        of true devotion:
        hear in your mercy!

4 Lord God Almighty, to your name be glory,
  One in Three persons, over all exalted;
  to you belong all honour, praise, and blessing,
        now and for ever.

4
© Christopher Idle†

1 My Lord of light who made the worlds,
  in wisdom you have spoken;
  but those who heard your wise commands
  your holy law have broken.

2 My Lord of love who knew no sin,
  a sinner's death enduring:
  for us you wore a crown of thorns,
  a crown of life securing.

3 My Lord of life who came in fire
  when Christ was high ascended:
  your burning love is now released,
  our days of fear are ended.

4 My Lord of lords, one Trinity,
  to your pure name be given
  all glory now and evermore,
  all praise in earth and heaven.

5
after Patrick, Cecil F. Alexander
© in this version Jubilate Hymns†

1 I bind myself to God today,
  the strong and holy Trinity,
  to know his name and make him known,
  the Three-in-One and One-in-Three.

2 I bind myself to God for ever,
  to Jesus in his incarnation,
  baptized for me in Jordan river
  and crucified for my salvation;
  he burst the prison of his tomb,
  ascended to the heavenly throne,
  returning at the day of doom:
  by faith I make his life my own.

3 I bind myself to God today,
   to his great power to hold and lead,
   his eye to watch me on my way,
   his ear to listen to my need;
   the wisdom of my God to teach,
   his hand to guide, his shield to ward,
   the word of God to give me speech,
   his heavenly host to be my guard.

4   Christ be with me, Christ within me,
   Christ behind me, Christ before me,
   Christ to seek me, Christ to win me,
   Christ to comfort and restore me;
   Christ beneath me, Christ above me,
   Christ in quiet, Christ in danger,
   Christ sustaining all who love me,
   Christ uniting friend and stranger!

5 I bind myself to God today,
   the strong and holy Trinity,
   to know his name and make him known,
   the Three-in-One and One-in-Three;
   from him all nature has creation,
   eternal Father, Spirit, Word:
   praise God, my strength and my salvation;
   praise in the Spirit through Christ the Lord!
      Amen.

6   from the Lenten Triodion of the Orthodox Church
     © Michael Saward†

1 O Trinity, O Trinity,
    the uncreated One;
  O Unity, O Unity
    of Father, Spirit, Son:
  you are without beginning,
  your life is never ending;
    and though our tongues
    are earthbound clay,
    light them with flaming fire today.

2 O Majesty, O Majesty,
    the Father of our race;
  O Mystery, O Mystery,
    we cannot see your face:
  your justice is unswerving,
  your love is overpowering;
    and though . . .

3 O Virgin-born, O Virgin-born,
    of humankind the least;
  O Victim torn, O Victim torn,
    both spotless lamb and priest:
  you died and rose victorious,
  you reign above all-glorious;
    and though . . .

4 O Wind of God, O Wind of God,
    invigorate the dead;
  O Fire of God, O Fire of God,
    your burning radiance spread:
  your fruit our lives renewing,
  your gifts, the church transforming;
    and though . . .

5 O Trinity, O Trinity,
    the uncreated One;
  O Unity, O Unity
    of Father, Spirit, Son:
  you are without beginning,
  your life is never-ending;
    and though . . .

7   R. Heber
    (see also traditional version, 594)

1 Holy, holy, holy, Lord God almighty!
   early in the morning
     our song of praise shall be:
  Holy, holy, holy! – merciful and mighty,
  God in three persons, glorious Trinity.

2 Holy, holy, holy! All the saints adore you
  casting down their golden crowns
     around the glassy sea,
  cherubim and seraphim
     falling down before you:
  you were and are, and evermore shall be!

3 Holy, holy, holy!
     Though the darkness hide you,
  though the sinful human eye
     your glory may not see,
  you alone are holy, there is none beside you,
  perfect in power, in love and purity.

4 Holy, holy, holy, Lord God almighty!
  all your works shall praise your name,
     in earth and sky and sea:
  Holy, holy, holy! – merciful and mighty,
  God in three persons, glorious Trinity.

8   © Michael Perry†

1 Praise the Father, God of justice:
  sinners tremble at his voice,
  crowns and creatures fall before him,
  saints triumphantly rejoice.

2 Praise the Son, who comes with burning,
  purging sin and healing pain,
  by whose cross and resurrection
  we have died to rise again.

3 Praise the Spirit: power and wisdom,
   peace that like a river flows,
   word of Christ and consolation,
   life by whom his body grows.

4 Praise the Father, Son and Spirit,
   One-in-Three and Three-in-One,
   God our judge and God our saviour,
   God our heaven on earth begun!

6 Triumphant hosts on high
   give thanks eternally
   and 'Holy, holy, holy' cry,
   'great Trinity!'
   Hail Abraham's God and ours!
   one mighty hymn we raise,
   all power and majesty be yours
   and endless praise!

9
from a Hebrew doxology, T. Olivers
© in this version Jubilate Hymns†

1 The God of Abraham praise
   who reigns enthroned above;
   the ancient of eternal days
   and God of love!
   The Lord, the great I AM,
   by earth and heaven confessed –
   we bow before his holy name
   for ever blessed.

2 To him we lift our voice
   at whose supreme command
   from death we rise to gain the joys
   at his right hand:
   we all on earth forsake –
   its wisdom, fame, and power;
   the God of Israel we shall make
   our shield and tower.

3 Though nature's strength decay,
   and earth and hell withstand,
   at his command we fight our way
   to Canaan's land:
   the water's deep we pass
   with Jesus in our view,
   and through the howling wilderness
   our path pursue.

4 He by his name has sworn –
   on this we shall depend,
   and as on eagles' wings upborne
   to heaven ascend:
   there we shall see his face,
   his power we shall adore,
   and sing the wonders of his grace
   for evermore.

5 There rules the Lord our king,
   the Lord our righteousness,
   victorious over death and sin,
   the prince of peace:
   on Zion's sacred height
   his kingdom he maintains,
   and glorious with his saints in light
   for ever reigns.

10
© David Mowbray†

1 We believe in God Almighty,
   maker of the earth and sky;
   all we see and all that's hidden
   is his work unceasingly:
   God our Father's loving kindness
   with us till the day we die –
   evermore and evermore.

2 We believe in Christ the Saviour,
   Son of God and Son of Man;
   born of Mary, preaching, healing,
   crucified, yet risen again:
   he ascended to the Father
   there in glory long to reign –
   evermore and evermore.

3 We believe in God the Spirit,
   present in our lives today;
   speaking through the prophets' writings,
   guiding travellers on their way:
   to our hearts he brings forgiveness
   and the hope of endless joy –
   evermore and evermore.

11
I. Watts

1 We give immortal praise
   to God the Father's love
   for all our comforts here
   and better hopes above:
      he sent his own
      eternal Son,
      to die for sins
      that we had done.

2 To God the Son belongs
   immortal glory too,
   who bought us with his blood
   from everlasting woe:
      and now he lives,
      and now he reigns,
      and sees the fruit
      of all his pains.

3 To God the Spirit's name
immortal worship give,
whose new-creating power
makes the dead sinner live:
  his work completes
  the great design,
  and fills the soul
  with joy divine.

4 To God the Trinity
be endless honours done,
the undivided Three,
and the mysterious One:
  where reason fails
  with all her powers,
  there faith prevails,
  and love adores.

12 G. Rorison
© in this version Jubilate Hymns†

1 Three-in-One and One-in-Three,
ruler of the earth and sea:
hear our praise, O Trinity,
holy chant and psalm.

2 Light of lights, with morning shine,
bring to us your light divine;
make our lives your holy shrine –
set our hearts aflame.

3 Light of lights, when falls the even,
let it close on sins forgiven;
guard us in the peace of heaven –
spread your holy calm.

4 Three-in-One and One-in-Three,
faint our songs on earth may be;
yet in heaven's glory we
shall adore your name.

13 after Francis of Assisi, W. H. Draper
© in this version Jubilate Hymns†

1 All creatures of our God and king,
lift up your voice and with us sing
  Alleluia, alleluia!
Bright burning sun with golden beam,
soft shining moon with silver gleam,
  O praise him, O praise him,
  Alleluia, alleluia, alleluia!

2 Swift rushing wind so wild and strong,
white clouds that sail in heaven along,
  O praise him, alleluia!
New rising dawn in praise rejoice,
you lights of evening find a voice;
  O praise him . . .

3 Cool flowing water, pure and clear,
make music for your Lord to hear,
  Alleluia, alleluia!
Fierce fire so masterful and bright
giving to us both warmth and light,
  O praise him . . .

4 Earth ever fertile, day by day
bring forth your blessings on our way,
  O praise him, alleluia!
All fruit and crops that richly grow,
all trees and flowers God's glory show;
  O praise him . . .

5 People and nations, take your part,
love and forgive with all your heart;
  Alleluia, alleluia!
All who long pain and sorrow bear,
trust God and cast on him your care;
  O praise him . . .

6 Death, once the ancient enemy,
hear now our Easter melody,
  O praise him, alleluia!
You are the pathway home to God,
our door to life through Christ our Lord;
  O praise him . . .

7 Let all things their creator bless
and worship him in lowliness,
  Alleluia, alleluia!
Praise, praise the Father, praise the Son,
and praise the Spirit, Three-in-One,
  O praise him . . .

14 from Jubilate Deo (Psalm 100), W. Kethe
© in this version Jubilate Hymns†

1 All people that on earth do dwell,
sing to the Lord with cheerful voice:
serve him with joy, his praises tell,
come now before him and rejoice!

2 Know that the Lord is God indeed,
he formed us all without our aid;
we are the flock he loves to feed,
the sheep who by his hand are made.

3 O enter then his gates with praise,
and in his courts his love proclaim;
give thanks and bless him all your days:
let every tongue confess his name.

4 The Lord our mighty God is good,
his mercy is for ever sure;
his truth at all times firmly stood,
and shall from age to age endure.

5 Praise God the Father, God the Son,
and God the Spirit evermore;
all praise to God the Three-in-One,
let heaven rejoice and earth adore!

15 from *Jubilate Deo* (Psalm 100)
I. Watts and J. Wesley

1 Before Jehovah's awesome throne,
you nations, bow with sacred joy;
know that the Lord is God alone –
he can create, and he destroy.

2 His sovereign power, without our aid,
formed us and fashioned us of old;
and when like wandering sheep we strayed,
he brought us back into his fold.

3 We'll crowd your gates with thankful songs,
high as the heavens our voices raise;
and earth with her ten thousand tongues
shall fill your courts with sounding praise.

4 Wide as the world is your command,
vast as eternity your love;
firm as a rock your truth shall stand,
when rolling years shall cease to move.

16 from *Venite* (Psalm 95)
© Christopher Idle†

1 Come with all joy to sing to God
our saving rock, the living Lord:
in glad thanksgiving seek his face
with songs of victory and grace.

2 In holiness and light arrayed
above all gods that we have made,
he is the one almighty king
and his the glory that we sing.

3 The earth is his from east to west,
from ocean-floor to mountain-crest;
he made the seas and formed the lands,
he shaped the islands by his hands.

4 Come near to worship! come with faith,
bow down to him who gives us breath:
God is our shepherd, he alone;
we are his people, all his own.

5 But if you hear God's voice today
do not reject what he will say:
when Israel wandered from God's path
they suffered forty years of wrath.

6 That generation went astray;
they did not want to know his way:
they put their saviour to the test,
and saw his power, but lost their rest.

7 So to the God of earth and heaven,
the Father, Spirit, Son, be given
praise now, as praise has ever been
and ever shall be praise – Amen!

17 from *Jubilate Deo* (Psalm 100)
© Michael Baughen†

1 Come, rejoice before your maker
all you peoples of the earth;
serve the Lord your God with gladness,
come before him with a song!

2 Know for certain that Jehovah
is the true and only God:
we are his, for he has made us;
we are sheep within his fold.

3 Come with grateful hearts before him,
enter now his courts with praise;
show your thankfulness towards him,
give due honour to his name.

4 For the Lord our God is gracious –
everlasting in his love;
and to every generation
his great faithfulness endures.

18 from *Venite* (Psalm 95)
© Michael Perry†

1 Come, worship God who is worthy of honour,
enter his presence with thanks and a song!
he is the rock of his people's salvation,
to whom our jubilant praises belong.

2 Ruled by his might
are the heights of the mountains,
held in his hands are the depths of the earth;
his is the sea, his the land, for he made them,
king above all gods, who gave us our birth.

3 We are his people, the sheep of his pasture,
he is our maker and to him we pray;
gladly we kneel in obedience before him –
great is the God whom we worship this day!

4 Now let us listen, for God speaks among us,
open our hearts and receive what he says:
peace be to all who remember his goodness,
trust in his promises, walk in his ways!

19 after Cædmon
© Christopher Idle†

1 Now praise the protector of heaven,
the purpose and power of the Lord;
all praise for his work shall be given –
our guide and defender and God.

2 In God's wise and wonderful plan
was made every marvellous thing;
in him all our blessings began –
the Father of glory, the king.

3 He first made the sky's lofty dome,
  our holy creator and guard;
  then furnished the earth for our home –
  almighty, eternal, the Lord.

4 We worship before you, great Father of light,
  while angels adore you, all veiling their sight;
  our praises we render, O Father, to you
  whom only the splendour of light
    hides from view.

20 I. Watts
© in this version Jubilate Hymns†

1 I'll praise my maker while I've breath,
  and when my voice is lost in death,
  praise shall possess my noblest powers;
  my days of praise are never past
  while life and thought and being last
  or immortality endures.

2 Happy are those whose hopes rely
  on God the Lord, who made the sky,
  the earth, the sea, the night and day;
  his truth for ever stands secure,
  he keeps his promise to the poor,
  and none who seeks is turned away.

3 The Lord gives eyesight to the blind,
  he calms and heals the troubled mind,
  he sends the wounded conscience peace;
  he helps the stranger in distress,
  the widow and the fatherless,
  and grants the prisoner glad release.

4 I'll praise him while he lends me breath,
  and when my voice is lost in death
  praise shall employ my noblest powers;
  my days of praise are never past
  while life and thought and being last
  or immortality endures.

21 W. C. Smith
© in this version Jubilate Hymns†

1 Immortal, invisible, God only wise,
  in light inaccessible hid from our eyes;
  most holy, most glorious, the ancient of days,
  almighty, victorious,
    your great name we praise.

2 Unresting, unhasting, and silent as light,
  nor wanting nor wasting, you rule us in might;
  your justice like mountains
    high soaring above,
  your clouds which are fountains
    of goodness and love.

3 To all life you give, Lord,
    to both great and small,
  in all life you live, Lord, the true life of all:
  we blossom and flourish, uncertain and frail;
  we wither and perish, but you never fail.

22 © Michael Saward†

1 King of the universe, Lord of the ages,
  maker of all things, sustainer of life;
  source of authority, wise and just creator,
  hope of the nations: we praise and adore.

2 Powerful in majesty, throned in the heavens –
  sun, moon and stars by your word are upheld;
  time and eternity bow within your presence,
  Lord of the nations: we praise and adore.

3 Wisdom unsearchable, fathomless
      knowledge
  past understanding by our clever brain;
  ground of reality, basis of all order,
  guide to the nations: we praise and adore.

4 Justice and righteousness, holy, unswerving –
  all that is tainted shall burn in your flame;
  sword-bearing deity, punisher of evil,
  judge of the nations: we praise and adore.

5 Ruler and potentate, sage and lawgiver,
  humbled before you, unworthy we bow:
  in our extremity, show us your forgiveness,
  merciful Father: we praise and adore.

23 after J. Milton
© in this version Michael Saward†

1 Let us gladly with one mind
  praise the Lord, for he is kind:
    for his mercy shall endure,
    ever faithful, ever sure.

2 He has made the realms of space,
  all things have their ordered place:
    for his mercy . . .

3 He created sky and sea,
  field and mountain, flower and tree:
    for his mercy . . .

4 Every creature, great and small –
  God alone has made them all:
    for his mercy . . .

5 Then he fashioned humankind,
  crown of all that he designed:
    for his mercy . . .

6 He has shaped our destiny –
  heaven for all eternity:
    for his mercy . . .

7 Glory then to God on high,
  'Glory!' let creation cry:
    for his mercy . . .

24
after W. Kethe
R. Grant

1 O worship the King all glorious above,
  and gratefully sing his power and his love,
  our shield and defender, the Ancient of Days,
  pavilioned in splendour
    and girded with praise.

2 O tell of his might and sing of his grace,
  whose robe is the light, whose canopy space;
  his chariots of wrath
    the deep thunder-clouds form,
  and dark is his path on the wings of the storm.

3 The earth, with its store of wonders untold,
  Almighty, your power has founded of old,
  established it fast by a changeless decree,
  and round it has cast like a garment the sea.

4 Your bountiful care what tongue can recite?
  it breathes in the air, it shines in the light;
  it streams from the hills,
    it descends to the plain,
  and sweetly distils in the dew and the rain.

5 We children of dust are feeble and frail –
  in you we will trust, for you never fail;
  your mercies how tender,
    how firm to the end!
  our maker, defender, redeemer and friend.

6 O measureless Might, unchangeable Love,
  whom angels delight to worship above!
  your ransomed creation with glory ablaze,
  in true adoration shall sing to your praise!

25
from Psalm 148
© Michael Perry†

1 Praise him, praise him, praise him,
  powers and dominations;
  praise his name in glorious light,
    you creatures of the day:
  moon and stars, ring praises
    through the constellations –
  Lord God, whose word
    shall never pass away!

2 Praise him, praise him, praise him,
    ocean depths and waters;
  elements of earth and heaven,
    your several praises blend:
  birds and beasts and cattle,
    Adam's sons and daughters,
  worship the king
    whose reign shall never end!

3 Praise him, praise him, praise him,
    saints of God who fear him;
  to the highest name of all,
    concerted anthems raise,
  all you seed of Israel,
    holy people near him
  whom he exalts to power
    and crowns with praise!

26
from Ecclesiasticus 42–43
© Christopher Idle†

1 The works of the Lord are created in wisdom,
  we view the earth's wonders
    and call him to mind;
  we hear what he says
    in the world we discover,
  and God shows his glory in all that we find.

2 Not even the angels have ever been granted
  to tell the full story of nature and grace;
  but open to God is all human perception,
  the mysteries of time
    and the secrets of space.

3 The sun every morning lights up his creation,
  the moon marks the rhythm
    of months in their turn;
  the glittering stars are arrayed in his honour,
  adorning the years as they ceaselessly burn.

4 The wind is his breath
    and the clouds are his signal,
  the rain and the snow
    are the robes of his choice;
  the storm and the lightning,
    his watchmen and heralds,
  the crash of the thunder,
    the sound of his voice.

5 The song is unfinished;
    how shall we complete it,
  and where find the skill
    to perfect all his praise?
  At work in all places,
    he cares for all peoples –
  how great is the Lord to the end of all days!

27
from Ecclesiasticus 1
© Christopher Idle†

1 Who can measure heaven and earth?
  God was present at their birth;
  who can number seeds or sands?
  every grain is in his hands:
  through creation's countless days
  every dawn sings out his praise.

2 Who can tell what wisdom brings,
first of all created things?
One alone is truly wise,
hidden from our earthbound eyes:
knowledge lies in him alone –
God, the Lord upon his throne!

3 Wisdom in his plans he laid,
planted her in all he made;
granted her to humankind,
sowed her truth in every mind:
but with richest wisdom blessed
those who love him first and best.

4 Wisdom gives the surest wealth,
brings her children life and health;
teaches us to fear the Lord,
marks a universe restored:
heaven and earth she will outlast –
happy those who hold her fast!

28 J. Newton
© in this version Jubilate Hymns†

1 Amazing grace – how sweet the sound –
that saved a wretch like me!
I once was lost, but now am found;
was blind, but now I see.

2 God's grace first taught my heart to fear,
his grace my fears relieved;
how precious did that grace appear
the hour I first believed!

3 Through every danger, trial and snare
I have already come;
his grace has brought me safe thus far,
and grace will lead me home.

4 The Lord has promised good to me,
his word my hope secures;
my shield and stronghold he shall be
as long as life endures.

5 And when this earthly life is past,
and mortal cares shall cease,
I shall possess with Christ at last
eternal joy and peace.

29 T. B. Pollock
© in this version Jubilate Hymns†

1 Faithful Shepherd, feed me
in the pastures green;
faithful Shepherd, lead me
where your steps are seen:

2 Hold me fast, and guide me
in the narrow way;
so, with you beside me,
I need never stray:

3 Daily bring me nearer
to the heavenly shore;
make my faith grow clearer,
help me love you more:

4 Consecrate each pleasure,
every joy and pain;
you are all my treasure,
all I hope to gain:

5 Day by day prepare me
as you purpose best,
mercy shall pursue me
to your promised rest.

30 from Psalm 147
© Timothy Dudley-Smith

1 Fill your hearts with joy and gladness,
sing and praise your God and mine!
Great the Lord in love and wisdom,
might and majesty divine!
He who framed the starry heavens
knows and names them as they shine.

2 Praise the Lord, his people, praise him!
wounded souls his comfort know;
those who fear him find his mercies,
peace for pain and joy for woe;
humble hearts are high exalted,
human pride and power laid low.

3 Praise the Lord for times and seasons,
cloud and sunshine, wind and rain;
spring to melt the snows of winter
till the waters flow again;
grass upon the mountain pastures,
golden valleys thick with grain.

4 Fill your hearts with joy and gladness,
peace and plenty crown your days;
love his laws, declare his judgements,
walk in all his words and ways;
he the Lord and we his children –
praise the Lord, all people, praise!

31 I. Watts
© in this version Jubilate Hymns†

1 Give to our God immortal praise,
mercy and truth are all his ways;
wonders of grace to God belong:
repeat his mercies in your song.

2 Give to the Lord of lords renown,
the King of kings with glory crown:
his mercies ever shall endure
when lords and kings are known no more.

3 He built the earth, he spread the sky,
  and fixed the starry lights on high;
  wonders of grace to God belong:
  repeat his mercies in your song.

4 He fills the sun with morning light,
  he bids the moon direct the night;
  his mercies ever shall endure
  when suns and moons shall shine no more.

5 He sent his Son with power to save
  from guilt and darkness and the grave;
  wonders of grace to God belong:
  repeat his mercies in your song.

6 All through this world he guides our feet
  and leads us to his heavenly seat;
  his mercies ever shall endure
  when this our world shall be no more.

2 So may this generous God
  through all our life be near us;
  to fill our hearts with joy,
  and with his peace to cheer us:
  to keep us in his grace,
  and guide us when perplexed;
  to free us from all ills
  in this world and the next.

3 All praise and thanks to God
  who reigns in highest heaven,
  to Father and to Son
  and Spirit now be given:
  this one eternal God,
  whom heaven and earth adore,
  is he who was, is now,
  and shall be evermore.

32 © Michael Perry†

1 Like a mighty river flowing,
  like a flower in beauty growing,
  far beyond all human knowing
    is the perfect peace of God.

2 Like the hills serene and even,
  like the coursing clouds of heaven,
  like the heart that's been forgiven
    is the perfect peace of God.

3 Like the summer breezes playing,
  like the tall trees softly swaying,
  like the lips of silent praying
    is the perfect peace of God.

4 Like the morning sun ascended,
  like the scents of evening blended,
  like a friendship never ended
    is the perfect peace of God.

5 Like the azure ocean swelling,
  like the jewel all-excelling,
  far beyond our human telling
    is the perfect peace of God.

33 after M. Rinkart
       Catherine Winkworth

1 Now thank we all our God
  with hearts and hands and voices;
  such wonders he has done!
  in him the world rejoices.
  He, from our mothers' arms,
  has blessed us on our way
  with countless gifts of love,
  and still is ours today.

34 I. Watts

1 O bless the Lord, my soul!
  let all within me join
  and help my tongue to praise his name
  whose mercies are divine.

2 O bless the Lord, my soul!
  let not his mercies lie
  forgotten in unthankfulness,
  from lack of praise to die.

3 For God forgives our sins
  and God relieves our pain;
  the Lord who heals our sicknesses
  renews our strength again.

4 He crowns our life with love
  when ransomed from the grave;
  he who redeemed my soul from hell
  has sovereign power to save.

5 The Lord provides our food
  and gives the sufferers rest;
  the Lord has judgement for the proud
  and justice for the oppressed.

6 His mighty works and ways
  by Moses he made known,
  but gave the world his truth and grace
  by his belovèd Son.

35 P. Doddridge
       © in this version Jubilate Hymns†

1 O God of Jacob, by whose hand
  your children still are fed;
  who through this earthly pilgrimage
  your people safely led:

2 Our vows, our prayers, we now present
before your gracious throne;
as you have been their faithful God,
so always be our own!

3 Through each perplexing path of life
our wandering footsteps guide;
give us today our daily bread,
and for our needs provide.

4 O spread your covering wings around
till all our wanderings cease,
and at our heavenly Father's home
we shall arrive in peace.

4 A thousand ages in your sight
are like an evening gone;
short as the watch that ends the night,
before the rising sun.

5 Time, like an ever-rolling stream,
will bear us all away;
we pass forgotten, as a dream
dies with the dawning day.

6 O God, our help in ages past,
our hope for years to come:
be our defence while life shall last,
and our eternal home!

36 © Michael Perry†

1 O God beyond all praising,
        we worship you today
and sing the love amazing
        that songs cannot repay;
for we can only wonder
        at every gift you send,
at blessings without number
        and mercies without end:
we lift our hearts before you
        and wait upon your word,
we honour and adore you,
        our great and mighty Lord.

2 Then hear, O gracious Saviour,
        accept the love we bring,
that we who know your favour
        may serve you as our king;
and whether our tomorrows
        be filled with good or ill,
we'll triumph through our sorrows
        and rise to bless you still:
to marvel at your beauty
        and glory in your ways,
and make a joyful duty
        our sacrifice of praise.

37 I. Watts

1 O God, our help in ages past,
our hope for years to come,
our shelter from the stormy blast,
and our eternal home:

2 Beneath the shadow of your throne
your people lived secure;
sufficient is your arm alone,
and our defence is sure.

3 Before the hills in order stood,
or earth from darkness came,
from everlasting you are God,
to endless years the same.

38 H. F. Lyte

1 Praise, my soul, the king of heaven!
to his feet your tribute bring:
ransomed, healed, restored, forgiven,
who like me his praise should sing?
        Alleluia, alleluia!
praise the everlasting king!

2 Praise him for his grace and favour
to our fathers in distress;
praise him still the same as ever,
slow to blame and swift to bless:
        Alleluia, alleluia!
glorious in his faithfulness!

3 Father-like, he tends and spares us;
all our hopes and fears he knows,
in his hands he gently bears us,
rescues us from all our foes,
        Alleluia, alleluia!
widely as his mercy flows.

4 Angels, help us to adore him –
you behold him face to face;
sun and moon, bow down before him,
praise him, all in time and space:
        Alleluia, alleluia!
praise with us the God of grace!

39 J. Addison
© in this version Jubilate Hymns†

1 When all your mercies, O my God,
my thankful soul surveys,
uplifted by the view, I'm lost
in wonder, love and praise.

2 Unnumbered blessings to my soul
your tender care bestowed
before my infant heart perceived
from whom these blessings flowed.

3 Ten thousand thousand precious gifts
   my daily thanks employ;
   nor is the least a thankful heart
   that takes those gifts with joy.

4 In health and sickness, joy and pain,
   your goodness I'll pursue;
   and after death, in distant worlds,
   the glorious theme renew.

5 Throughout eternity, O Lord,
   a joyful song I'll raise;
   but all eternity's too short
   to utter all your praise!

40 after J. Neander
Catherine Winkworth and others

1 Praise to the Lord,
     the almighty, the king of creation!
   O my soul, praise him,
     for he is your health and salvation!
   Come, all who hear;
     brothers and sisters, draw near,
   praise him in glad adoration!

2 Praise to the Lord,
     above all things so mightily reigning;
   keeping us safe at his side,
     and so gently sustaining.
   Have you not seen
     all you have needed has been
   met by his gracious ordaining?

3 Praise to the Lord,
     who shall prosper our work
     and defend us;
   surely his goodness and mercy
     shall daily attend us.
   Ponder anew
     what the almighty can do,
   who with his love will befriend us.

4 Praise to the Lord –
     O let all that is in me adore him!
   All that has life and breath,
     come now with praises before him!
   Let the 'Amen!'
     sound from his people again –
   gladly with praise we adore him!

41 from Psalm 34
© Timothy Dudley-Smith

1 Tell his praise in song and story,
   bless the Lord with heart and voice;
   in my God is all my glory –
   come before him and rejoice:
   join to praise his name together,
   he who hears his people's cry;
   tell his praise, come wind or weather,
   shining faces lifted high.

2 To the Lord whose love has found them
   cry the poor in their distress;
   swift his angels camped around them
   prove him sure to save and bless.
   God it is who hears our crying
   though the spark of faith be dim:
   taste and see! beyond denying
   blessed are those who trust in him.

3 Taste and see! In faith draw near him,
   trust the Lord with all your powers;
   seek and serve him, love and fear him,
   life and all its joys are ours –
   true delight in holy living,
   peace and plenty, length of days:
   come, my children, with thanksgiving
   bless the Lord in songs of praise.

4 In our need he walks beside us,
   ears alert to every cry;
   watchful eyes to guard and guide us,
   love that whispers 'It is I'.
   Good shall triumph, wrong be righted,
   God has pledged his promised word;
   so with ransomed saints united
   join to praise our living Lord!

42 from *Magnificat* (Luke 1)
© Timothy Dudley-Smith

1 Tell out, my soul, the greatness of the Lord!
   unnumbered blessings, give my spirit voice;
   tender to me the promise of his word –
   in God my saviour shall my heart rejoice.

2 Tell out, my soul, the greatness of his name!
   make known his might,
     the deeds his arm has done;
   his mercy sure, from age to age the same –
   his holy name: the Lord, the mighty one.

3 Tell out, my soul, the greatness of his might!
   powers and dominions lay their glory by;
   proud hearts and stubborn wills
     are put to flight,
   the hungry fed, the humble lifted high.

4 Tell out, my soul, the glories of his word!
   firm is his promise, and his mercy sure:
   tell out, my soul, the greatness of the Lord
   to children's children and for evermore!

43

from *A General Thanksgiving* by E. Reynolds
J. E. Seddon, © Mrs M. Seddon†

1 Thank you, O Lord of earth and heaven,
   thank you for all your love has planned;
   thank you for food and daily blessings,
   gifts from your ever-gracious hand.

2 Thank you for such a great salvation,
   mercy as boundless as the sea;
   thank you for love which died to save us,
   love which gave all to set us free.

3 Thank you for means of grace and guidance,
   gifts of your Spirit, strength divine;
   thank you for word and prayer and symbol,
   food for our souls in bread and wine.

4 Thank you for that blessed hope of glory,
   great day when Christ shall come again,
   day when, in perfect love and justice
   he in his majesty shall reign.

5 Grant us, because of all your mercies,
   lips which proclaim our thanks and praise;
   lives which, in loving glad surrender,
   serve and adore you all their days.

6 Glory to God our heavenly Father,
   glory to Jesus, God the Son,
   glory to God the Holy Spirit,
   glory to God the Three-in-One.

44

H. W. Baker
© in this version Jubilate Hymns†

1 The king of love my shepherd is,
   whose goodness fails me never;
   I nothing lack if I am his
   and he is mine for ever.

2 Where streams of living water flow
   a ransomed soul, he leads me;
   and where the fertile pastures grow,
   with food from heaven feeds me.

3 Perverse and foolish I have strayed,
   but in his love he sought me;
   and on his shoulder gently laid,
   and home, rejoicing, brought me.

4 In death's dark vale I fear no ill
   with you, dear Lord, beside me;
   your rod and staff my comfort still,
   your cross before to guide me.

5 You spread a banquet in my sight
   of love beyond all knowing;
   and O the gladness and delight
   from your pure chalice flowing!

6 And so through all the length of days
   your goodness fails me never:
   Good Shepherd, may I sing your praise
   within your house for ever!

45

from Psalm 23 © in this version Christopher Idle†
(see also traditional version, 591)

1 The Lord my shepherd rules my life
   and gives me all I need;
   he leads me by refreshing streams,
   in pastures green I feed.

2 The Lord revives my failing strength,
   he makes my joy complete;
   and in right paths, for his name's sake,
   he guides my faltering feet.

3 Though in a valley dark as death,
   no evil makes me fear;
   your shepherd's staff protects my way,
   for you are with me there.

4 While all my enemies look on
   you spread a royal feast;
   you fill my cup, anoint my head,
   and treat me as your guest.

5 Your goodness and your gracious love
   pursue me all my days;
   your house, O Lord, shall be my home –
   your name, my endless praise.

6 To Father, Son, and Spirit, praise!
   to God whom we adore
   be worship, glory, power and love,
   both now and evermore.

46

from Psalm 34, N. Tate and N. Brady
© in this version Jubilate Hymns†

1 Through all the changing scenes of life,
   in trouble and in joy,
   the praises of my God shall still
   my heart and tongue employ.

2 O glorify the Lord with me,
   with me exalt his name!
   when in distress, to him I called –
   he to my rescue came.

3 The hosts of God encamp around
   the dwellings of the just;
   his saving help he gives to all
   who in his mercy trust.

4 O taste his goodness, prove his love!
   experience will decide
   how blessed they are, and only they,
   who in his truth confide.

5 Fear him, you saints, and you will then
   have nothing else to fear;
   his service shall be your delight,
   your needs shall be his care.

6 To Father, Son and Spirit, praise!
   to God whom we adore
   be worship, glory, power and love,
   both now and evermore!

47 from Psalm 89
© Timothy Dudley-Smith

1 Timeless love! We sing the story,
   praise his wonders, tell his worth;
   love more fair than heaven's glory,
   love more firm than ancient earth!
   Tell his faithfulness abroad –
   who is like him? Praise the Lord!

2 By his faithfulness surrounded,
   north and south his hand proclaim;
   earth and heaven formed and founded,
   skies and seas, declare his name!
   Wind and storm obey his word –
   who is like him? Praise the Lord!

3 Truth and righteousness enthrone him,
   just and equal are his ways;
   more than happy, those who own him,
   more than joy, their songs of praise!
   Sun and shield and great reward –
   who is like him? Praise the Lord!

48 from Psalm 121, J. D. S. Campbell
© in this version Jubilate Hymns†

1 Unto the hills around me
         I lift up my longing eyes;
   whence shall my hope and my salvation come
         and whence arise?
   From God the Lord shall come my certain aid,
   from God the Lord,
         who heaven and earth has made.

2 Your God will never let your footsteps stray,
         his grasp is sure;
   he will not sleep, but holds your life in his;
         you are secure:
   God never slumbers; he is always there,
   and keeps his people in his tender care.

3 God is the Lord, your stronghold
         and defence, your shield and shade;
   he will protect by his almighty power
         the life he made:
   no sun shall harm by day, nor moon by night;
   he is your guardian, you are his delight.

4 From every evil he shall keep your soul,
         from every sin;
   God shall preserve your life as you go out,
         as you come in:
   guarding above you, he whom we adore
   will keep you henceforth and for evermore.

49 after Germanus, J. M. Neale
© in this version Jubilate Hymns†

1 A great and mighty wonder:
   redemption drawing near!
   the virgin bears the infant,
   the prince of peace is here!
   Repeat the hymn again:
       'To God on high be glory,
       and peace on earth. Amen.'

2 The Word becomes incarnate
   and yet remains on high;
   the shepherds hear the anthem
   as glory fills the sky –
   repeat the hymn again:
       'To God on high . . .

3 The angels sing the story:
   rejoice, O distant lands!
   you valleys, forests, mountains,
   and oceans, clap your hands!
   Repeat the hymn again:
       'To God on high . . .

4 He comes to save all nations:
   let all now hear his word!
   approach and bring him worship,
   the saviour and the Lord!
   Repeat the hymn again:
       'To God on high . . .

50 T. Pestel
© in this version Jubilate Hymns†

1 Behold, the great Creator makes
   himself a house of clay;
   a robe of human form he takes
   for ever from this day.

2 Hear this! – the wise eternal Word
   as Mary's infant cries;
   a servant is our mighty Lord,
   and God in cradle lies.

3 Glad shepherds run to view this sight,
   a choir of angels sings;
   wise men from far with pure delight
   adore the King of kings.

4 These wonders all the world amaze
   and shake the starry frame;
   the host of heaven stand to gaze,
   and bless the Saviour's name.

5 Join then, all hearts that are not stone,
   and all our voices prove
   to celebrate the holy one,
   the God of peace and love.

51
after Mary MacDonald
L. Macbean

1 Child in the manger, infant of Mary,
outcast and stranger, Lord of all!
child who inherits all our transgressions,
all our demerits on him fall.

2 Once the most holy child of salvation
gentle and lowly lived below:
now as our glorious mighty redeemer,
see him victorious over each foe.

3 Prophets foretold him, infant of wonder;
angels behold him on his throne:
worthy our saviour of all their praises;
happy for ever are his own.

52
C. Wesley
© in this version Jubilate Hymns†

1 Come, O long-expected Jesus,
born to set your people free!
from our fears and sins release us,
Christ in whom our rest shall be.

2 Israel's strength and consolation,
born salvation to impart;
dear desire of every nation,
joy of every longing heart:

3 Born your people to deliver,
born a child and yet a king;
born to reign in us for ever,
now your gracious kingdom bring:

4 By your own eternal Spirit
rule in all our hearts alone;
by your all-sufficient merit
raise us to your glorious throne.

53
© Timothy Dudley-Smith

1 Child of the stable's secret birth,
the Lord by right of the lords of earth;
let angels sing of a king new-born –
the world is weaving a crown of thorn:
a crown of thorn for that infant head
cradled soft in the manger bed.

2 Eyes that shine in the lantern's ray;
a face so small in its nest of hay –
face of a child who is born to scan
the world he made, through the eyes of man:
and from that face in the final day
earth and heaven shall flee away.

3 Voice that rang through the courts on high
contracted now to a wordless cry,
a voice to master the wind and wave,
the human heart and the hungry grave:
the voice of God through the cedar trees
rolling forth as the sound of seas.

4 Infant hands in a mother's hand,
for none but Mary may understand
whose are the hands and the fingers curled
but his who fashioned and made our world;
and through these hands in the hour of death
nails shall strike to the wood beneath.

5 Child of the stable's secret birth,
the Father's gift to a wayward earth,
to drain the cup in a few short years
of all our sorrows, our sins and tears –
ours the prize for the road he trod:
risen with Christ; at peace with God.

54
W. C. Smith

1 Earth was waiting, spent and restless,
with a mingled hope and fear,
faithful men and women praying,
'Surely, Lord, the day is near:
the Desire of all the nations –
it is time he should appear!'

2 Then the Spirit of the Highest
to a virgin meek came down,
and he burdened her with blessing,
and he pained her with renown;
for she bore the Lord's anointed
for his cross and for his crown.

3 Earth has groaned and laboured for him
since the ages first began,
for in him was hid the secret
which through all the ages ran –
Son of Mary, Son of David,
Son of God, and Son of Man.

55
from *Nunc Dimittis* (Luke 2)
© Timothy Dudley-Smith

1 Faithful vigil ended,
watching, waiting cease:
Master, grant your servant
his discharge in peace.

2 All the Spirit promised,
all the Father willed,
now these eyes behold it
perfectly fulfilled.

3 This your great deliverance
sets your people free;
Christ their light uplifted
all the nations see.

4 Christ, your people's glory!
watching, doubting cease;
grant to us your servants
our discharge in peace.

56 after Prudentius, J. M. Neale and H. W. Baker
© in this version Jubilate Hymns†

1 God of God, the uncreated,
love before the world began;
he the source and he the ending,
Son of God and Son of Man,
Lord of all the things that have been,
master of the eternal plan,
    evermore and evermore.

2 He is here, whom generations
sought throughout the ages long;
promised by the ancient prophets,
justice for a world of wrong,
God's salvation for the faithful:
him we praise in endless song
    evermore and evermore.

3 Happy is that day for ever
when, by God the Spirit's grace,
lowly Mary, virgin mother,
bore the saviour of our race.
Man and child, the world's redeemer
now displays his sacred face
    evermore and evermore.

4 Praise him, heaven of the heavens,
praise him, angels in the height;
priests and prophets, bow before him,
saints who longed to see this sight.
Let no human voice be silent,
in his glory hearts unite
    evermore and evermore!

5 Christ be praised with God the Father,
and the Holy Spirit, praised!
hymns of worship, high thanksgiving
echo through a world amazed:
Honour, majesty, dominion!
songs of victory be raised
    evermore and evermore!

57 © Timothy Dudley-Smith

1 Had he not loved us
he had never come,
yet is he love
and love is all his way;
low to the mystery
of the virgin's womb
Christ bows his glory –
born on Christmas Day.

2 Had he not loved us
he had never come;
had he not come
he need have never died,
nor won the victory
of the vacant tomb,
the awful triumph
of the crucified.

3 Had he not loved us
he had never come;
still were we lost
in sorrow, sin and shame,
the doors fast shut
on our eternal home
which now stand open –
for he loved and came.

58 from *Nunc Dimittis* (Luke 2)
© Michael Perry†

1 Jesus, hope of every nation,
light of heaven upon our way;
promise of the world's salvation,
spring of life's eternal day!

2 Saints by faith on God depending
wait to see Messiah born;
sin's oppressive night is ending
in the glory of the dawn.

3 Look, he comes! – the long-awaited
Christ, redeemer, living Word;
hope and faith are vindicated
as with joy we greet the Lord.

4 Glory in the highest heaven
to the Father, Spirit, Son;
and on earth let praise be given
to our God, the Three-in-One!

59 C. Wesley and others

1 Hark! the herald angels sing
glory to the new-born King;
peace on earth and mercy mild,
God and sinners reconciled!
Joyful all you nations rise,
join the triumph of the skies;
with the angelic host proclaim,
'Christ is born in Bethlehem':
    Hark! the herald angels sing
    glory to the new-born King.

2 Christ, by highest heaven adored,
Christ, the everlasting Lord;
late in time behold him come,
offspring of a virgin's womb:
veiled in flesh the Godhead see,
hail the incarnate Deity!
pleased as man with us to dwell,
Jesus our Emmanuel:
    Hark! the herald . . .

3 Hail the heaven-born Prince of peace,
hail the Sun of righteousness;
light and life to all he brings,
risen with healing in his wings:
mild, he lays his glory by,
born that we no more may die;
born to raise us from the earth,
born to give us second birth:
    Hark! the herald . . .

60 © Timothy Dudley-Smith

1 Holy child, how still you lie!
safe the manger, soft the hay;
faint upon the eastern sky
breaks the dawn of Christmas Day.

2 Holy child, whose birthday brings
shepherds from their field and fold,
angel choirs and eastern kings,
myrrh and frankincense and gold:

3 Holy child – what gift of grace
from the Father freely willed!
In your infant form we trace
all God's promises fulfilled.

4 Holy child, whose human years
span like ours delight and pain;
one in human joys and tears,
one in all but sin and stain:

5 Holy child, so far from home,
all the lost to seek and save,
to what dreadful death you come,
to what dark and silent grave!

6 Holy child, before whose name
powers of darkness faint and fall;
conquered, death and sin and shame –
Jesus Christ is Lord of all!

7 Holy child, how still you lie!
safe the manger, soft the hay;
clear upon the eastern sky
breaks the dawn of Christmas Day.

61 after the *Liturgy of James*, G. Moultrie
© in this version Jubilate Hymns†

1 Let all mortal flesh keep silence,
and with fear and trembling stand;
set your minds on things eternal,
for with blessing in his hand
Christ our God to earth descending
comes our homage to command.

2 King of kings, yet born of Mary,
once upon the earth he stood;
Lord of lords we now perceive him
in his body and his blood –
he will give to all the faithful
his own self for heavenly food.

3 Rank on rank the host of heaven
stream before him on the way;
as the Light of light descending
from the realms of endless day
vanquishes the powers of evil,
clears the gloom of hell away.

4 At his feet the six-winged seraphs,
cherubim with sleepless eye,
veil their faces in his presence
as with ceaseless voice they cry:
Alleluia, alleluia,
alleluia, Lord most high!

62 Christina Rossetti
© in this version Jubilate Hymns†

1 Love came down at Christmas,
love all lovely, love divine;
love was born at Christmas –
star and angels gave the sign.

2 Worship we the Godhead,
love incarnate, love divine;
worship we our Jesus –
what shall be our sacred sign?

3 Love shall be our token,
love be yours and love be mine;
love to God and neighbour,
love for prayer and gift and sign.

63 F. Houghton, © Overseas Missionary Fellowship and in this version Jubilate Hymns†

1 Lord, you were rich beyond all splendour,
yet, for love's sake, became so poor;
leaving your throne in glad surrender,
sapphire-paved courts for stable floor:
Lord, you were rich beyond all splendour,
yet, for love's sake, became so poor.

2 You are our God beyond all praising,
yet, for love's sake, became a man;
stooping so low, but sinners raising
heavenwards, by your eternal plan:
you are our God, beyond all praising,
yet, for love's sake, became a man.

3 Lord, you are love beyond all telling,
Saviour and King, we worship you;
Emmanuel, within us dwelling,
make us and keep us pure and true:
Lord, you are love beyond all telling,
Saviour and King, we worship you.

2 God from God,
Light from light,
he who abhors not the virgin's womb;
very God, begotten, not created:
O come . . .

3 Sing, choirs of angels,
sing in exultation!
Sing, all you citizens of heaven above,
'Glory to God in the highest!'
O come . . .

4 Yes, Lord, we greet you,
born for our salvation;
Jesus, to you be glory given!
Word of the Father now in flesh appearing:
O come . . .

OR on Christmas morning:

4 Yes, Lord, we greet you,
born this happy morning;
Jesus, to you be glory given!
Word of the Father now in flesh appearing:
O come . . .

64 C. Wesley
© in this version Jubilate Hymns†

1 To us a child of royal birth,
heir of the promises, is given;
the Invisible appears on earth,
the Son of Man, the God of heaven.

2 A saviour born, in love supreme
he comes our fallen souls to raise;
he comes his people to redeem
with all the fulness of his grace.

3 The Christ foretold by prophecy
and filled with all the Spirit's power,
our prophet, priest and king is he,
the mighty Lord whom we adore.

4 The Lord of hosts, the God most high
who leaves his throne to live on earth,
with joy we welcome from the sky
and take into our hearts by faith.

65 after J. F. Wade, F. Oakeley and others
(see also traditional version, 597)

1 O come, all you faithful,
joyful and triumphant!
O come now, O come now, to Bethlehem!
Come and behold him,
born the king of angels:
O come, let us adore him,
O come, let us adore him,
O come, let us adore him, Christ the Lord!

66 from the Latin, J. M. Neale and others
© in this version Jubilate Hymns†

1 O come, O come, Emmanuel
and ransom captive Israel
who mourns in lonely exile here
until the Son of God draws near:
Rejoice, rejoice!
Emmanuel shall come to you, O Israel.

2 O come, true Branch of Jesse, free
your children from this tyranny;
from depths of hell your people save
to rise victorious from the grave:
Rejoice, rejoice . . .

3 O come, bright Daybreak, come and cheer
our spirits by your advent here;
dispel the long night's lingering gloom
and pierce the shadows of the tomb:
Rejoice, rejoice . . .

4 O come, strong Key of David, come
and open wide our heavenly home;
make safe the way that leads on high,
and close the path to misery:
Rejoice, rejoice . . .

5 O come, O come, great Lord of might
who long ago on Sinai's height
gave all your tribes the ancient law,
in cloud and majesty and awe:
Rejoice, rejoice . . .

67
Cecil F. Alexander

1 Once in royal David's city
 stood a lowly cattle shed,
 where a mother laid her baby
 in a manger for his bed:
 Mary was that mother mild,
 Jesus Christ, her little child.

2 He came down to earth from heaven
 who is God and Lord of all;
 and his shelter was a stable
 and his cradle was a stall:
 with the poor and meek and lowly
 lived on earth our saviour holy.

3 And through all his wondrous childhood
 he would honour and obey,
 love and watch the gentle mother
 in whose tender arms he lay:
 Christian children all should be
 kind, obedient, good as he.

4 For he is our childhood's pattern:
 day by day like us he grew;
 he was little, weak and helpless;
 tears and smiles like us he knew:
 and he feels for all our sadness,
 and he shares in all our gladness.

5 And our eyes at last shall see him,
 through his own redeeming love;
 for that child, so dear and gentle,
 is our Lord in heaven above:
 and he leads his children on
 to the place where he has gone.

6 Not in that poor lowly stable
 with the oxen standing by,
 we shall see him, but in heaven,
 set at God's right hand on high:
 there his children gather round
 bright like stars, with glory crowned.

68
© Timothy Dudley-Smith

1 The darkness turns to dawn,
 the dayspring shines from heaven;
 for unto us a child is born,
 to us a Son is given.

2 The Son of God most high,
 before all else began,
 a virgin's son behold him lie,
 the new-born Son of Man.

3 God's Word of truth and grace
 made flesh with us to dwell;
 the brightness of the Father's face,
 the child Emmanuel.

4 How rich his heavenly home!
 How poor his human birth!
 As mortal man he stoops to come,
 the light and life of earth.

5 A servant's form, a slave,
 the Lord consents to share;
 our sin and shame, our cross and grave,
 he bows himself to bear.

6 Obedient and alone
 upon that cross to die,
 and then to share the Father's throne
 in majesty on high.

7 And still God sheds abroad
 that love so strong to send
 a saviour, who is Christ the Lord,
 whose reign shall never end.

69
from John 1
© Michael Saward†

1 When things began to happen,
 before the birth of time,
 the Word was with the Father
 and shared his holy name:
 without him there was nothing –
 all life derives from him;
 his light shines in the darkness –
 an unextinguished beam.

2 He came to his creation,
 the work of his own hand;
 he entered his own country
 but they would not respond:
 yet some gave their allegiance
 of life and heart and mind;
 thus they became his subjects
 and he became their friend.

3 Conceived by heaven's mercy,
 this was no human birth;
 for they are God's own children
 redeemed from sin and death:
 and they beheld his glory,
 so full of grace and truth;
 in Christ, God's Son, our saviour,
 whom we adore by faith.

70
© Timothy Dudley-Smith

1 Within a crib my saviour lay,
 a wooden manger filled with hay,
 come down for love on Christmas Day:
 all glory be to Jesus!

2 Upon a cross my saviour died,
  to ransom sinners crucified,
  his loving arms still open wide:
      all glory be to Jesus!

3 A victor's crown my saviour won,
  his work of love and mercy done,
  the Father's high-ascended Son:
      all glory be to Jesus!

71 from Isaiah 9, J. Morison
‹ in this version Jubilate Hymns†

1 The people who in darkness walked
  have seen a glorious light:
  that light shines out on those who lived
  in shadows of the night.

2 To greet you, Sun of righteousness,
  the gathering nations come;
  rejoicing as when reapers bring
  their harvest treasures home.

3 For now to us a child is born,
  to us a son is given;
  and on his shoulder ever rests
  all power in earth and heaven.

4 His name shall be the prince of peace,
  eternally adored;
  most wonderful of counsellors,
  the great and mighty Lord.

5 His peace and righteous government
  shall over all extend;
  on judgement and on justice based,
  his reign shall never end.

72 verses 1, 2 unknown
verse 3 J. T. McFarland

1 Away in a manger, no crib for a bed,
  the little Lord Jesus laid down his sweet head;
  the stars in the bright sky
      looked down where he lay;
  the little Lord Jesus asleep on the hay.

2 The cattle are lowing, the baby awakes,
  but little Lord Jesus no crying he makes:
  I love you, Lord Jesus –
      look down from on high
  and stay by my side until morning is nigh.

3 Be near me, Lord Jesus; I ask you to stay
  close by me for ever and love me, I pray;
  bless all the dear children
      in your tender care,
  and fit us for heaven to live with you there.

73 ‹ Michael Walker

1 A messenger named Gabriel
  came to the land of Israel;
  and he proclaimed that Mary's son
  was God's messiah, holy One.
      O Jesus Christ, strong Son of God,
      once born for us at Bethlehem:
      we listen to the angels' song
      and worship you for ever.

2 Angelic hosts of God most high
  with radiant glory fill the sky;
  enraptured voices joyful sing
  to welcome Christ, the new-born king.
      O Jesus Christ . . .

3 In awesome fear and bitter cold
  the shepherds huddle in their fold;
  then since the message is for them
  they make their way to Bethlehem.
      O Jesus Christ . . .

4 Within the sacred stable-shrine
  they see the holy child divine;
  the manger stands amidst the straw
  and humble folk their God adore.
      O Jesus Christ . . .

5 Since then have passed two thousand years
  of human misery and tears;
  yet Christ alone can bring release:
  he loves us still – the prince of peace.
      O Jesus Christ . . .

74 from *Quem Pastores Laudavere*, G. B. Caird
revised by the author 1981, ‹ Mrs V. Caird

1 Shepherds came, their praises bringing,
  who had heard the angels singing:
  'Far from you be fear unruly,
  Christ is king of glory born.'

2 Wise men whom a star had guided
  incense, gold, and myrrh provided,
  made their sacrifices truly
  to the king of glory born.

3 Jesus born the king of heaven,
  Christ to us through Mary given,
  to your praise and honour duly
  be resounding glory done.

75 © Timothy Dudley-Smith

1 A song was heard at Christmas
to wake the midnight sky:
a saviour's birth, and peace on earth,
and praise to God on high.
The angels sang at Christmas
with all the hosts above,
and still we sing the newborn King,
his glory and his love.

2 A star was seen at Christmas,
a herald and a sign,
that all might know the way to go
to find the child divine.
The wise men watched at Christmas
in some far eastern land,
and still the wise in starry skies
discern their Maker's hand.

3 A tree was grown at Christmas,
a sapling green and young:
no tinsel bright with candlelight
upon its branches hung.
But he who came at Christmas
our sins and sorrow bore,
and still we name his tree of shame
our life for evermore.

4 A child was born at Christmas
when Christmas first began:
the Lord of all a baby small,
the Son of God made man.
For love is ours at Christmas,
and life and light restored,
and so we praise through endless days
the Saviour, Christ the Lord.

76 after P. Gerhardt, Catherine Winkworth
© in this version Jubilate Hymns†

1 All my heart this night rejoices,
as I hear,
far and near,
sweetest angel voices.
'Christ is born!' their choirs are singing,
till the air
everywhere
now with joy is ringing.

2 Listen! from a humble manger
comes the call,
'One and all,
run from sin and danger!
Christians come, let nothing grieve you:
you are freed!
All you need
I will surely **give** you.'

3 Gather, then, from every nation;
here let all,
great and small,
kneel in adoration;
love him who with love is yearning:
Hail the star
that from far
bright with hope is burning!

4 You, my Lord, with love I'll cherish,
live to you,
and with you
dying, shall not perish,
but shall dwell with you for ever
far on high,
in the joy
that can alter never.

77 J. Montgomery
© in this version Jubilate Hymns†

1 Angels from the realms of glory,
wing your flight through all the earth;
heralds of creation's story
now proclaim Messiah's birth!
Come and worship
Christ, the new-born king;
come and worship,
worship Christ the new-born king.

2 Shepherds in the fields abiding,
watching by your flocks at night,
God with us is now residing:
see, there shines the infant light!
Come and worship . . .

3 Wise men, leave your contemplations!
brighter visions shine afar;
seek in him the hope of nations,
you have seen his rising star:
Come and worship . . .

4 Though an infant now we view him,
he will share his Father's throne,
gather all the nations to him;
every knee shall then bow down:
Come and worship . . .

78 J. Byrom
© in this version Jubilate Hymns†

1 Christians, awake, salute the happy morn
on which the saviour of the world was born;
rise to adore the mystery of love
which hosts of angels chanted from above!
With them the joyful tidings first begun
of God incarnate and the virgin's Son.

2 First, to the watchful shepherds it was told,
who heard the herald angel's voice: 'Behold,
I bring good news of your Messiah's birth
to you and all the nations here on earth!
This day has God fulfilled his promised word;
this day is born a saviour, Christ the Lord!'

3 To Bethlehem these eager shepherds ran
to see the wonder of our God made man;
they found, with Joseph and the holy maid,
her son, the saviour, in a manger laid.
Amazed, with joy this story they proclaim,
the first apostles of his infant fame.

4 Let us, like those good shepherds,
    now employ
our grateful voices to declare the joy:
Christ, who was born on this most happy day,
round all the earth his glory shall display.
Saved by his love, unceasing we shall sing
eternal praise to heaven's almighty king.

79 © Michael Saward†

1 Christmas for God's holy people
is a time of joy and peace:
so, all Christian men and women,
hymns and carols let us raise
    to our God
come to earth,
Son of Man, by human birth.

2 Child of Mary, virgin mother,
peasant baby, yet our king,
cradled there among the oxen:
joyful carols now we sing
    to our God . . .

3 Angel armies sang in chorus
at our Christ's nativity –
he who came to share our nature:
so we sing with gaiety
    to our God . . .

4 Shepherds hurried to the manger,
saw the babe in Bethlehem,
glorified the God of heaven:
now we join to sing with them
    to our God . . .

5 Infant lowly, born in squalor,
prophet, king and great high priest,
Word of God, to us descending:
still we sing, both great and least,
    to our God . . .

80 from an old Dorset carol
© Michael Saward†

1 Come all you good people
    and burst into song!
be joyful and happy, your praises prolong;
remember the birthday of Jesus our king,
who brings us salvation: his glory we sing.

2 His mother, a virgin so gentle and pure,
was told of God's promise,
    unchanging and sure,
foretelling the birthday of Jesus our king,
who brings us salvation: his glory we sing.

3 To Bethlehem hurried the shepherds amazed,
with stories of angels
    and heavens that blazed,
proclaiming the birthday of Jesus our king,
who brings us salvation: his glory we sing.

4 So come let us honour the babe in the hay
and give him our homage and worship today,
recalling the birthday of Jesus our king,
who brings us salvation: his glory we sing.

81 © Michael Perry†

1 Come and sing the Christmas story
    this holy night!
Christ is born: the hope of glory
    dawns on our sight.
Alleluia! earth is ringing
with a thousand angels singing –
hear the message they are bringing
    this holy night.

2 Jesus, Saviour, child of Mary
    this holy night,
in a world confused and weary
    you are our light.
God is in a manger lying,
manhood taking, self denying,
life embracing, death defying
    this holy night.

3 Lord of all! Let us acclaim him
    this holy night;
king of our salvation name him,
    throned in the height.
Son of Man – let us adore him,
all the earth is waiting for him;
Son of God – we bow before him
    this holy night.

82
© Michael Perry†

1 Glad music fills the Christmas sky –
a hymn of praise, a song of love;
the angels worship high above
and Mary sings her lullaby.

2 Of tender love for God she sings,
the chosen mother of the Son;
she knows that wonders have begun,
and trusts for all the future brings.

3 The angel chorus of the skies
who come to tell us of God's grace
have yet to know his human face,
to watch him die, to see him rise.

4 Let praise be true and love sincere,
rejoice to greet the saviour's birth;
let peace and honour fill the earth
and mercy reign – for God is here!

5 Then lift your hearts and voices high,
sing once again the Christmas song:
for love and praise to Christ belong –
in shouts of joy, and lullaby.

83
after German authors
© Michael Perry†

1 Jesus Christ the Lord is born,
all the bells are ringing!
angels greet the holy One
    and shepherds hear them singing,
    and shepherds hear them singing:

2 'Go to Bethlehem today,
find your king and saviour:
glory be to God on high,
    to earth his peace and favour,
    to earth his peace and favour!'

3 Held within a cattle stall,
loved by love maternal,
see the master of us all,
    our Lord of lords eternal,
    our Lord of lords eternal!

4 Soon shall come the wise men three,
rousing Herod's anger;
mothers' hearts shall broken be
    and Mary's son in danger,
    and Mary's son in danger.

5 Death from life and life from death,
our salvation's story:
let all living things give breath
    to Christmas songs of glory,
    to Christmas songs of glory!

84
traditional
© in this version Jubilate Hymns†

1 God rest you merry, gentlemen,
let nothing you dismay!
for Jesus Christ our saviour
was born on Christmas Day,
to save us all from Satan's power
when we had gone astray:
    O tidings of comfort and joy,
    comfort and joy;
    O tidings of comfort and joy!

2 At Bethlehem in Judah
the holy babe was born;
they laid him in a manger
on this most happy morn,
at which his mother Mary
did neither fear nor scorn:
    O tidings of comfort and joy . . .

3 From God our heavenly Father
a holy angel came;
the shepherds saw the glory
and heard the voice proclaim
that Christ was born in Bethlehem –
and Jesus is his name:
    O tidings of comfort and joy . . .

4 Fear not, then said the angel,
let nothing cause you fright;
to you is born a saviour
in David's town tonight,
to free all those who trust in him
from Satan's power and might:
    O tidings of comfort and joy . . .

5 The shepherds at these tidings
rejoiced in heart and mind,
and on the darkened hillside
they left their flocks behind,
and went to Bethlehem straightway
this holy child to find:
    O tidings of comfort and joy . . .

6 And when to Bethlehem they came
where Christ the infant lay;
they found him in a manger
where oxen fed on hay,
and there beside her newborn child
his mother knelt to pray:
    O tidings of comfort and joy . . .

7 Now to the Lord sing praises,
all people in this place!
with Christian love and fellowship
each other now embrace,
and let this Christmas festival
all bitterness displace:
    O tidings of comfort and joy . . .

85 from *In Dulci Jubilo*
J. M. Neale

1 Good Christians all, rejoice
with heart and soul and voice!
listen now to what we say,
Jesus Christ is born today;
ox and ass before him bow
and he is in the manger now!
  Christ is born today;
  Christ is born today!

2 Good Christians all, rejoice
with heart and soul and voice!
hear the news of endless bliss,
Jesus Christ was born for this:
he has opened heaven's door
and we are blessed for evermore!
  Christ was born for this;
  Christ was born for this.

3 Good Christians all, rejoice
with heart and soul and voice!
now you need not fear the grave;
Jesus Christ was born to save:
come at his most gracious call
to find salvation, one and all!
  Christ was born to save;
  Christ was born to save!

86 from the Polish
Edith M. G. Reed

1 Infant holy, infant lowly,
for his bed a cattle stall;
oxen lowing, little knowing
Christ the babe is Lord of all.
Swift are winging angels singing,
nowells ringing, tidings bringing:
  Christ the babe is Lord of all;
  Christ the babe is Lord of all!

2 Flocks were sleeping, shepherds keeping
vigil till the morning new,
saw the glory, heard the story –
tidings of a gospel true.
Thus rejoicing, free from sorrow,
praises voicing greet tomorrow:
  Christ the babe was born for you;
  Christ the babe was born for you!

87 E. H. Sears
Ⓒ in this version Jubilate Hymns†

1 It came upon the midnight clear,
that glorious song of old,
from angels bending near the earth
to touch their harps of gold:
'Through all the earth, goodwill and peace
from heaven's all-gracious king!'
The world in solemn stillness lay
to hear the angels sing.

2 With sorrow brought by sin and strife
the world has suffered long
and, since the angels sang, have passed
two thousand years of wrong:
the nations, still at war, hear not
the love-song which they bring:
O hush the noise and cease the strife,
to hear the angels sing!

3 And those whose journey now is hard,
whose hope is burning low,
who tread the rocky path of life
with painful steps and slow:
O listen to the news of love
which makes the heavens ring!
O rest beside the weary road
and hear the angels sing!

4 And still the days are hastening on –
by prophets seen of old –
towards the fulness of the time
when comes the age foretold:
then earth and heaven renewed shall see
the prince of peace, their king;
and all the world repeat the song
which now the angels sing.

88 P. Brooks

1 O little town of Bethlehem,
how still we see you lie!
Above your deep and dreamless sleep
the silent stars go by:
yet in your dark streets shining
is everlasting light;
the hopes and fears of all the years
are met in you tonight.

2 For Christ is born of Mary
and, gathered all above
while mortals sleep, the angels keep
their watch of wondering love:
O morning stars, together
proclaim the holy birth,
and praises sing to God the king,
and peace to all the earth.

3 How silently, how silently
the wondrous gift is given!
So God imparts to human hearts
the blessings of his heaven:
no ear may hear his coming,
but in this world of sin,
where meek souls will receive him – still
the dear Christ enters in.

4 O holy child of Bethlehem,
descend to us, we pray;
cast out our sin and enter in,
be born in us today!
We hear the Christmas angels
the great glad tidings tell –
O come to us, abide with us,
our Lord Emmanuel.

89 © Timothy Dudley-Smith

1 O Prince of peace whose promised birth
the angels sang with 'Peace on earth,'
peace be to us and all beside,
    peace to us all –
peace to the world this Christmastide.

2 O Child who found to lay your head
no place but in a manger bed,
come where our doors stand open wide,
    peace to us all –
    peace to the world –
peace in our homes this Christmastide.

3 O Christ whom shepherds came to find,
their joy be ours in heart and mind;
let grief and care be laid aside,
    peace to us all –
    peace to the world –
    peace in our homes –
peace in our hearts this Christmastide.

4 O Saviour Christ, ascended Lord,
our risen prince of life restored,
our love who once for sinners died,
    peace to us all –
    peace to the world –
    peace in our homes –
    peace in our hearts –
peace with our God this Christmastide!

90 E. Caswall
© in this version Jubilate Hymns†

1 See, amid the winter snow,
born for us on earth below;
see, the gentle Lamb appears,
promised from eternal years:
    Hail, O ever-blessèd morn;
    hail, redemption's happy dawn;
    sing through all Jerusalem:
    'Christ is born in Bethlehem!'

2 Low within a manger lies
he who built the starry skies;
he who, throned in height sublime,
reigns above the cherubim:
    Hail, O ever-blessèd morn . . .

3 Say, you humble shepherds, say
what's your joyful news today?
tell us why you left your sheep
on the lonely mountain steep:
    Hail, O ever-blessèd morn . . .

4 'As we watched at dead of night,
all around us shone a light;
angels singing Peace on earth
told us of a Saviour's birth.'
    Hail, O ever-blessèd morn . . .

5 Sacred infant, king most dear,
what a tender love was here,
thus to come from highest bliss
down to such a world as this!
    Hail, O ever-blessèd morn . . .

6 Holy saviour, born on earth,
teach us by your lowly birth;
grant that we may ever be
taught by such humility.
    Hail, O ever-blessèd morn . . .

91 © Michael Perry†

1 See him lying on a bed of straw:
a draughty stable with an open door;
Mary cradling the babe she bore –
the prince of glory is his name.
    O now carry me to Bethlehem
    to see the Lord appear to men –
    just as poor as was the stable then,
    the prince of glory when he came.

2 Star of silver, sweep across the skies,
show where Jesus in the manger lies;
shepherds, swiftly from your stupor rise
to see the saviour of the world!
    O now carry . . .

3 Angels, sing again the song you sang,
bring God's glory to the heart of man;
sing that Bethl'em's little baby can
be salvation to the soul.
    O now carry . . .

4 Mine are riches, from your poverty;
from your innocence, eternity;
mine, forgiveness by your death for me,
child of sorrow for my joy.
    O now carry . . .

92 S. Baring-Gould

1   Sing lullaby!
lullaby baby, now reclining:
    sing lullaby!
Hush, do not wake the infant king;
angels are watching, stars are shining
over the place where he is lying:
    sing lullaby.

2   Sing lullaby!
lullaby baby, sweetly sleeping:
    sing lullaby!
Hush, do not wake the infant king;
soon will come sorrow with the morning,
soon will come bitter grief and weeping:
    sing lullaby!

3   Sing lullaby!
lullaby baby, gently dozing:
    sing lullaby!
Hush, do not wake the infant king;
soon comes the cross, the nails, the piercing,
then in the grave at last reposing:
    sing lullaby!

4   Sing lullaby!
lullaby! Is the baby waking?
    sing lullaby!
Hush, do not stir the infant king,
dreaming of Easter, joyful morning,
conquering death, its bondage breaking:
    sing lullaby!

93 unknown
© in this version Word & Music†

1 The first nowell the angel did say
was to Bethlehem's shepherds
        in fields as they lay;
in fields where they lay keeping their sheep
on a cold winter's night that was so deep:
    Nowell, nowell, nowell, nowell,
    born is the king of Israel!

2 Then wise men from a country far
looked up and saw a guiding star;
they travelled on by night and day
to reach the place where Jesus lay:
    Nowell, nowell . . .

3 At Bethlehem they entered in,
on bended knee they worshipped him;
they offered there in his presence
their gold and myrrh and frankincense:
    Nowell, nowell . . .

4 Then let us all with one accord
sing praises to our heavenly Lord;
for Christ has our salvation wrought
and with his blood our life has bought:
    Nowell, nowell . . .

94 N. Tate

1 While shepherds watched their flocks
        by night
all seated on the ground,
the angel of the Lord came down
and glory shone around.

2 'Fear not,' said he – for mighty dread
had seized their troubled mind –
'Good news of greatest joy I bring
to you and all mankind.

3 'To you in Bethlehem this day
is born of David's line
a saviour, who is Christ the Lord.
And this shall be the sign:

4 'The heavenly babe you there shall find
to human view displayed,
in simple clothing tightly wrapped
and in a manger laid.'

5 Thus spoke the seraph, and forthwith
appeared a shining throng
of angels praising God, who thus
addressed their joyful song:

6 'All glory be to God on high,
and to the earth be peace!
To those on whom his favour rests
goodwill shall never cease.'

95 after J. Mohr
J. F. Young

1 Silent night! holy night!
all is calm, all is bright
round the virgin and her child:
holy infant, so gentle and mild,
    sleep in heavenly peace;
    sleep in heavenly peace!

2 Silent night! holy night!
shepherds quail at the sight,
glory streams from heaven afar:
heavenly hosts sing, 'Alleluia,
  Christ the saviour is born,
  Christ the saviour is born.'

3 Silent night! holy night!
Son of God, love's pure light:
radiant beams your holy face
with the dawn of saving grace,
  Jesus, Lord, at your birth,
  Jesus, Lord, at your birth.

96 from the Latin
J. M. Neale verses 1 and 2, P. Dearmer verses 3 and 4

1 Jesus, good above all other,
gentle child of gentle mother;
in a stable born our brother,
whom the angel hosts adore:

2 Jesus, cradled in a manger,
keep us free from sin and danger;
and to all, both friend and stranger,
give your blessing evermore.

3 Jesus, for your people dying,
risen master, death defying;
Lord of heaven, your grace supplying,
come to us – be present here!

4 Lord, in all our doings guide us:
pride and hate shall not divide us;
we'll go on with you beside us,
and with joy we'll persevere.

97 © Timothy Dudley-Smith

1 Lord, who left the highest heaven
for a homeless human birth
and, a child within a stable,
came to share the life of earth –
with your grace and mercy bless
all who suffer homelessness.

2 Lord, who sought by cloak of darkness
refuge under foreign skies
from the swords of Herod's soldiers,
ravaged homes, and parents' cries –
may your grace and mercy rest
on the homeless and oppressed.

3 Lord, who lived secure and settled,
safe within the Father's plan,
and in wisdom, stature, favour
growing up from boy to man –
with your grace and mercy bless
all who strive for holiness.

4 Lord, who leaving home and kindred,
followed still as duty led,
sky the roof and earth the pillow
for the prince of glory's head –
with your grace and mercy bless
sacrifice for righteousness.

5 Lord, who in your cross and passion
hung beneath a darkened sky,
yet whose thoughts were for your mother,
and a thief condemned to die –
may your grace and mercy rest
on the helpless and distressed.

6 Lord, who rose to life triumphant
with our whole salvation won,
risen, glorified, ascended,
all the Father's purpose done –
may your grace, all conflict past,
bring your children home at last.

98 C. Wordsworth
© in this version Jubilee Hymns†

1 Songs of thankfulness and praise,
Jesus, Lord, to you we raise;
once revealed, when heaven's star
brought the wise men from afar;
branch of royal David's stem
in your birth at Bethlehem,
  Word before the world began,
  God revealed to us in man.

2 God revealed at Jordan's stream,
prophet, priest and king supreme;
once revealed in power divine
changing water into wine;
Cana's holy wedding guest
keeping to the last the best;
  Word before . . .

3 God revealed in valiant fight,
conquering the devil's might;
sins forgiven, sickness healed,
life restored and God revealed:
once revealed in gracious will
ever bringing good from ill,
  Word before . . .

4 Stars shall fall and heavens fade,
sun and moon shall dark be made;
Christ will then like lightning shine,
all will see the glorious sign;
all will then the trumpet hear,
all will see the Son appear,
  Word before . . .

1 As with gladness men of old
  did the guiding star behold,
  as with joy they hailed its light,
  leading onward, gleaming bright:
  so, most gracious Lord, may we
  evermore your splendour see.

2 As with joyful steps they sped
  to that lowly manger bed,
  there to bend the knee before
  Christ whom heaven and earth adore:
  so with ever-quickening pace
  may we seek your throne of grace.

3 As they offered gifts most rare
  at your cradle plain and bare,
  so may we with holy joy
  pure and free from sin's alloy,
  all our costliest treasures bring,
  Christ, to you, our heavenly king.

4 Holy Jesus, every day
  keep us in the narrow way,
  and when earthly things are past,
  bring our ransomed souls at last:
  where they need no star to guide,
  where no clouds your glory hide.

5 In the heavenly city bright
  none shall need created light –
  you, its light, its joy, its crown,
  you its sun which goes not down;
  there for ever may we sing
  alleluias to our king.

100 © Christopher Idle†

1 Wise men, they came to look for wisdom,
  finding one wiser than they knew;
  rich men, they met with one yet richer –
  King of the kings, they knelt to you:
      Jesus, our wisdom from above,
      wealth and redemption, life and love.

2 Pilgrims they were, from unknown countries,
  searching for one who knows the world;
  lost are their names,
      and strange their journeys,
  famed is their zeal to find the child:
      Jesus, in you the lost are claimed,
      aliens are found, and known, and named.

3 Magi, they stooped to see your splendour,
  led by a star to light supreme;
  promised Messiah, Lord eternal,
  glory and peace are in your name.
      Joy of each day, our Song by night,
      shine on our path your holy light.

4 Guests of their God, they opened treasures,
  incense and gold and solemn myrrh;
  welcoming one too young to question
  how came these gifts, and what they were.
      Gift beyond price of gold or gem,
      make among us your Bethlehem.

101 Jan Struther
© Oxford University Press

1 Lord of all hopefulness, Lord of all joy,
  whose trust, ever childlike,
      no cares could destroy:
  be there at our waking, and give us, we pray,
  your bliss in our hearts, Lord,
      at the break of the day.

2 Lord of all eagerness, Lord of all faith,
  whose strong hands were skilled
      at the plane and the lathe:
  be there at our labours, and give us, we pray,
  your strength in our hearts, Lord,
      at the noon of the day.

3 Lord of all kindliness, Lord of all grace,
  your hands swift to welcome,
      your arms to embrace:
  be there at our homing, and give us, we pray,
  your love in our hearts, Lord,
      at the eve of the day.

4 Lord of all gentleness, Lord of all calm,
  whose voice is contentment,
      whose presence is balm:
  be there at our sleeping,
      and give us, we pray,
  your peace in our hearts, Lord,
      at the end of the day!

102 S. T. C. Lowry

1 Son of God, eternal saviour,
  source of life and truth and grace;
  Son of Man whose birth among us
  hallows all our human race:
  Christ our head, for all your people
  you have never ceased to plead;
  fill us with your love and pity,
  heal our wrongs, and help our need.

2 Lord, as you have lived for others,
  so may we for others live;
  freely have your gifts been granted,
  freely may your servants give:
  yours the gold and yours the silver,
  all the wealth of sea and land;
  we but stewards of your riches
  held in trust at your command.

3 Come, O Christ, and reign among us,
   king of love, and prince of peace;
   hush the storm of strife and passion,
   bid its cruel discords cease:
   by your patient years of toiling,
   by your silent hours of pain,
   quench our fevered thirst for pleasure,
   shame our selfish greed for gain.

4 Son of God, eternal saviour,
   source of life and truth and grace;
   Son of Man, whose birth among us
   hallows all our human race:
   you have prayed and you have purposed
   that your people shall be one;
   grant to us our hope's fulfilment –
   here on earth your will be done!

103
G. H. Smyttan
© in this version Jubilate Hymns†

1 Forty days and forty nights
   you were fasting in the wild;
   forty days and forty nights
   tempted and yet undefiled.

2 Burning heat throughout the day,
   bitter cold when light had fled;
   prowling beasts around your way,
   stones your pillow, earth your bed.

3 Shall not we your trials share,
   learn your discipline of will;
   and with you by fast and prayer
   wrestle with the powers of hell?

4 So if Satan, pressing hard,
   soul and body would destroy:
   Christ who conquered, be our guard;
   give to us the victor's joy.

5 Saviour, may we hear your voice –
   keep us constant at your side;
   and with you we shall rejoice
   at the eternal Eastertide.

104
Cecil F. Alexander

1 Jesus calls us! – in the tumult
   of our life's wild restless sea;
   day by day his voice re-echoes
   saying, 'Christian, follow me!'

2 As of old, apostles heard it
   by the Galilean lake,
   turned from home and toil and kindred,
   leaving all for his dear sake.

3 Jesus calls us – from the worship
   of the vain world's golden store,
   from each rival that would claim us,
   saying, 'Christian, love me more!'

4 In our joys and in our sorrows,
   days of toil and hours of ease,
   still he calls, in cares and pleasures,
   'Christian, love me more than these!'

5 Jesus calls us! – by your mercies,
   Saviour, make us hear your call,
   give to you our heart's obedience,
   serve and love you best of all.

105
J. G. Whittier
© in this version Jubilate Hymns†

1 Immortal love for ever full,
   for ever flowing free,
   for ever shared, for ever whole,
   a never-ebbing sea!

2 Upon our lips we bear the name
   all other names above;
   yet love alone knows whence it came,
   that all-embracing love.

3 We may not climb the heavenly steeps
   to bring the Lord Christ down;
   in vain we search the lowest deeps,
   for him no depths can drown.

4 But warm, sweet, tender, even yet
   a present help is he;
   and faith has still its Olivet,
   and love its Galilee.

5 The margin of his robe we feel
   through sorrow and through pain;
   we touch the Lord whose love can heal,
   and we are whole again.

6 Through him the earliest prayers are said
   that children's lips can frame;
   the last low whispers of our dead
   are burdened with his name.

7 Alone, O Love no words can tell,
   your saving name is given;
   to turn aside from you is hell,
   to walk with you is heaven!

106
© Randle Manwaring

1 With loving hands,
   at work among the suffering
   and broken hearts, he ministers,
     who is their king.

2 With wounded hands,
  outstretched upon a cruel tree,
  he lies and then is lifted up
    in agony.

3 With pleading hands,
  towards the world he longs to bless,
  he waits, with heaven's life to fill
    our emptiness.

107 J. Conder

1 My Lord, I did not choose you
  for that could never be;
  my heart would still refuse you
  had you not chosen me:
  you took the sin that stained me,
  you cleansed me, made me new,
  for you, Lord, had ordained me
  that I should live in you.

2 Unless your grace had called me
  and taught my opening mind
  the world would have enthralled me,
  to heavenly glories blind:
  my heart knows none above you;
  for you I long, I thirst,
  and know that, if I love you,
  Lord, you have loved me first.

108 © Timothy Dudley-Smith

1 O changeless Christ, for ever new,
  who walked our earthly ways,
  still draw our hearts as once you drew
  the hearts of other days.

2 As once you spoke by plain and hill
  or taught by shore and sea,
  so be today our teacher still,
  O Christ of Galilee.

3 As wind and storm their master heard
  and his command fulfilled,
  may troubled hearts receive your word,
  the tempest-tossed be stilled.

4 And as of old to all who prayed
  your healing hand was shown,
  so be your touch upon us laid,
  unseen but not unknown.

5 In broken bread, in wine outpoured,
  your new and living way
  proclaim to us, O risen Lord,
  O Christ of this our day.

6 O changeless Christ, till life is past
  your blessing still be given;
  then bring us home, to taste at last
  the timeless joys of heaven.

109 from John 2
© Christopher Idle†

1 Jesus, come! for we invite you,
  guest and master, friend and Lord;
  now, as once at Cana's wedding,
  speak, and let us hear your word:
  lead us through our need or doubting,
  hope be born and joy restored.

2 Jesus, come! transform our pleasures,
  guide us into paths unknown;
  bring your gifts, command your servants,
  let us trust in you alone:
  though your hand may work in secret,
  all shall see what you have done.

3 Jesus, come in new creation,
  heaven brought near in power divine;
  give your unexpected glory
  changing water into wine:
  rouse the faith of your disciples –
  come, our first and greatest Sign!

4 Jesus, come! surprise our dullness,
  make us willing to receive
  more than we can yet imagine,
  all the best you have to give:
  let us find your hidden riches,
  taste your love, believe, and live!

110 J. Keble and W. J. Hall

1 Blessed are the pure in heart,
  for they shall see our God;
  the secret of the Lord is theirs,
  their soul is Christ's abode.

2 The Lord, who left the heavens
  our life and peace to bring;
  to dwell in lowliness with us,
  our pattern and our king:

3 Still to the lowly soul
  himself he will impart;
  and for his dwelling and his throne
  chooses the pure in heart.

4 Lord, we your presence seek:
  our inner life renew;
  give us a pure and lowly heart,
  a temple fit for you.

111
Rosamond Herklots
© Oxford University Press

1 'Forgive our sins as we forgive,'
you taught us, Lord, to pray;
but you alone can grant us grace
to live the words we say.

2 How can your pardon reach and bless
the unforgiving heart
that broods on wrongs, and will not let
old bitterness depart?

3 In blazing light your cross reveals
the truth we dimly knew:
what trivial debts are owed to us,
how great our debt to you!

4 Lord, cleanse the depths within our souls
and bid resentment cease;
then, bound to all in bonds of love,
our lives will spread your peace.

112
H. C. A. Gaunt
© Oxford University Press

1 Lord Jesus, once you spoke to men,
upon the mountain, in the plain:
O help us listen now, as then,
and wonder at your words again.

2 We all have secret fears to face,
our minds and motives to amend;
we seek your truth, we need your grace,
our living Lord and present friend.

3 The gospel speaks – and we receive
your light, your love, your own command:
O help us live what we believe
in daily work of heart and hand.

113
G. Doane

1 You are the way, to you alone
from sin and death we run:
and those who would the Father seek
must seek him through the Son.

2 You are the truth, your word alone
true wisdom can impart:
you only can inform the mind
and purify the heart.

3 You are the life, the empty tomb
proclaims your conquering arm:
and those who put their trust in you,
nor death nor hell shall harm.

4 You are the way, the truth, the life:
grant us that way to see,
that truth to keep, that life to know
through all eternity.

114
C. W. Everest

1 'Take up your cross,' the Saviour said,
'if you would my disciple be;
deny yourself, forsake the world,
and humbly follow after me.'

2 Take up your cross – let not its weight
fill your weak soul with vain alarm;
his strength shall bear your spirit up,
and brace your heart, and nerve your arm.

3 Take up your cross, nor heed the shame
nor let your foolish pride rebel;
the Lord for you the cross endured
to save your soul from death and hell.

4 Take up your cross, then, in his strength,
and calmly every danger brave;
he guides us to a better home,
and leads to conquest of the grave.

5 Take up your cross and follow Christ,
nor think till death to lay it down;
for only they who bear the cross
may hope to win the glorious crown.

115
Brian Wren
© Oxford University Press

1 Christ upon the mountain peak
stands alone in glory blazing;
let us, if we dare to speak,
with the saints and angels praise him –
    Alleluia!

2 Trembling at his feet we saw
Moses and Elijah speaking:
all the prophets and the law
shout through them their joyful greeting –
    Alleluia!

3 Swift the cloud of glory came,
God proclaiming in its thunder
Jesus as his Son by name!
nations, cry aloud in wonder –
    Alleluia!

4 This is God's belovèd Son!
law and prophets fade before him,
First and Last, and only One:
let creation now adore him –
    Alleluia!

116 © Timothy Dudley-Smith

1 Our Saviour Christ once knelt in prayer
with none but three disciples there,
upon a lonely mountain high
beneath a blue expanse of sky –
below them, far as eye could see,
the little hills of Galilee.

2 There as he prays a radiance bright
transfigures all his form to light;
his robe in dazzling splendour shows
a purer white than sunlit snows,
while on his countenance divine
transcendent glories burn and shine.

3 So for a moment stands revealed
what human form and flesh concealed;
while Moses and Elijah share
in earth and heaven mingled there,
with him whom prophecy foresaw,
the true fulfiller of the law.

4 The shadowed summit, wrapped in cloud,
sounds to a voice that echoes loud:
'This is my true belovèd Son,
listen to him, my chosen one.'
The glory fades; with all its pains
the road to Calvary remains.

5 Give to us, Lord, the eyes to see
as saw those first disciples three:
a teacher true, a friend indeed,
the risen saviour sinners need,
the Son whose praise eternal rings,
the Lord of lords and King of kings!

117 © Christopher Idle†

1 When Jesus led his chosen three
to lift the shadow from their sight,
and on the mountain let them see
his face transfigured, crowned with light:
what grace that day to them was given!
to men on earth, a glimpse of heaven.

2 There Moses and Elijah stood
and spoke about his exodus,
their freedom purchased by his blood,
a passover most marvellous!
The law and prophets meet their Lord,
see God revealed, and man restored.

3 Then from the cloud there came a voice,
'This is my own belovèd Son;'
the scriptures' theme, the Father's choice,
their master stood supreme, alone:
they saw his glory, and they heard
the one eternal, living Word.

4 So may we see and know this grace –
the truth which like a burning light
illuminates the darkest place
till Christ himself shall end the night:
when to his people's longing eyes
God's day shall dawn, his sun shall rise.

118 © Christopher Idle†

1 My Lord, you wore no royal crown;
you did not wield the powers of state,
nor did you need a scholar's gown
or priestly robe, to make you great.

2 You never used a killer's sword
to end an unjust tyranny;
your only weapon was your word,
for truth alone could set us free.

3 You did not live a world away
in hermit's cell or desert cave,
but felt our pain and shared each day
with those you came to seek and save.

4 You made no mean or cunning move,
chose no unworthy compromise,
but carved a track of burning love
through tangles of deceit and lies.

5 You came unequalled, undeserved,
to be what I was meant to be;
you came to serve, not to be served,
a light for all the world to see.

6 So when I stumble, set me right;
command my life as you require;
let all your gifts be my delight
and you, my Lord, my one desire.

119 H. Milman
© in this version Jubilate Hymns†

1 Ride on, ride on in majesty
as all the crowds 'Hosanna!' cry:
through waving branches slowly ride,
O Saviour, to be crucified.

2 Ride on, ride on in majesty,
in lowly pomp ride on to die:
O Christ, your triumph now begin
with captured death, and conquered sin!

3 Ride on, ride on in majesty –
the angel armies of the sky
look down with sad and wondering eyes
to see the approaching sacrifice.

4 Ride on, ride on in majesty,
the last and fiercest foe defy:
the Father on his sapphire throne
awaits his own anointed Son.

5 Ride on, ride on in majesty,
in lowly pomp ride on to die:
bow your meek head to mortal pain,
then take, O God, your power and reign!

120
after Theodulph, J. M. Neale
© in this version Jubilate Hymns†

All glory, praise and honour,
to you, redeemer, king,
to whom the lips of children
made sweet hosannas ring.

1 You are the king of Israel,
great David's greater son;
you ride in lowly triumph,
the Lord's anointed one!
All glory, praise . . .

2 The company of angels
are praising you on high,
and we with all creation
together make reply:
All glory, praise . . .

3 The people of the Hebrews
with palms before you went;
our praise and prayer and anthems
before you we present.
All glory, praise . . .

4 To you before your passion
they sang their hymns of praise;
to you, now high exalted,
our melody we raise:
All glory, praise . . .

5 As you received their praises,
accept the prayers we bring,
for you delight in goodness
O good and gracious king!
All glory, praise . . .

121
Ann Richter and others
© in this version Jubilate Hymns†

1 We were not there to see you come
to this poor world of sin and death,
nor did we see your humble home,
your childhood spent in Nazareth:
but we believe your footsteps trod
its streets and paths, O Son of God.

2 We did not see you lifted high
or feel the taunts they flung at you,
nor were we there to hear your cry,
'Forgive, they know not what they do!'
Yet we believe the deed was done
which shook the earth and veiled the sun.

3 We did not stand beside the tomb
upon that resurrection day,
nor met you in the upper room,
nor walked with you along the way:
but we believe the angel said,
'Why seek the living with the dead?'

4 We were not with the chosen few
who saw you vanish from their sight,
nor could we fall and worship you,
the risen, ascended, Lord of might:
yet we believe that mortal eyes
from that far mountain saw you rise.

5 And now you reign enthroned on high
and bless your waiting people here;
we still may look up to the sky
yet cannot see your glory there:
but we believe your faithful word –
O come to us, exalted Lord!

122
© Timothy Dudley-Smith

1 A purple robe, a crown of thorn,
a reed in his right hand;
before the soldiers' spite and scorn
I see my saviour stand.

2 He bears between the Roman guard
the weight of all our woe;
a stumbling figure bowed and scarred
I see my saviour go.

3 Fast to the cross's spreading span,
high in the sunlit air,
all the unnumbered sins of man
I see my saviour bear.

4 He hangs, by whom the world was made,
beneath the darkened sky;
the everlasting ransom paid,
I see my saviour die.

5 He shares on high his Father's throne
who once in mercy came;
for all his love to sinners shown
I sing my saviour's name.

123
after J. Heerman, R. Bridges
© in this version Jubilate Hymns†

1 Ah, holy Jesus, how have you offended
that man to judge you has in hate pretended?
By foes derided, by your own rejected,
O most afflicted!

2 Who was the guilty?
  who brought this upon you?
It is my treason, Lord, that has undone you;
and I, O Jesus, it was I denied you,
  I crucified you.

3 See how the Shepherd
  for the sheep is offered,
the slave has sinned
  and yet the Son has suffered;
for our atonement hangs the saviour bleeding,
  God interceding.

4 For me, kind Jesus, was your incarnation,
your dying sorrow and your life's oblation;
your bitter passion and your desolation,
  for my salvation.

5 O mighty Saviour, I cannot repay you,
I do adore you and will here obey you:
recall your mercy and your love unswerving,
  not my deserving.

124 I. Watts

1 Alas! and did my saviour bleed,
and did my sovereign die?
Did he devote that sacred head
for such a one as I?

2 Was it for sins that I had done
he suffered on the tree?
amazing pity, grace unknown
and love beyond degree!

3 Well might the sun in darkness hide
and shut his glories in
when Christ, the mighty maker, died
to bear the creature's sin.

4 Dear Saviour, how can I repay
the debt of love I owe?
Lord, take my very self I pray
your work, your will to do.

125 © Christopher Idle†

1 Downtrodden Christ, to you we pray
who at the third hour of the day
were led away and nailed up high
in naked shame beneath the sky:
  Show through the pain
    that scars your face
  the love of God, and our disgrace.

2 Uplifted Christ, to you we pray
who at the sixth hour of the day
took all our guilt upon that tree
in darkness, blood, and agony:
  Look on our pride and unbelief,
  grant us repentance and relief.

3 Outstretching Christ, to you we pray
who at the ninth hour of the day
alone dismissed your final breath
and opened heaven by your death:
  Come to our dying world and reign,
  that we with you may live again.

126 from the Italian c.1815
E. Caswall

1 Glory be to Jesus,
who, in bitter pains,
poured for me the life-blood
from his sacred veins.

2 Grace and life eternal
in that blood I find:
blessed be his compassion
wonderfully kind!

3 Abel's blood for vengeance
pleaded to the skies,
but the blood of Jesus
for our pardon cries.

4 When that blood is sprinkled
on our guilty hearts,
Satan in confusion
terror-struck departs.

5 When this earth exulting
lifts its praise on high,
angel hosts rejoicing
make their glad reply.

6 Raise your thankful voices,
swell the mighty flood;
louder still and louder
praise the Lamb of God!

127 from The Song of Christ's Glory (Philippians 2)
© Gavin Reid

1 Empty he came
as a man to our race,
equal with God
yet forsaking his place –
  humbly he served in our world,
  humbly he served in our world.

2 Lowlier still,
  he was willing to die
  nailed to a cross
  as the people passed by –
      bravely he died in our world,
      bravely he died in our world.

3 Raised by our God
  for us all to revere,
  given a name
  that shall stand without peer –
      honoured as Lord in our world,
      honoured as Lord in our world.

4 Give us that mind
  that refuses to claim
  even our rights,
  make our outlook the same –
      humbly to serve in our world,
      humbly to serve in our world.

128 J. Evans
in this version Jubilate Hymns†

1 Hark! the voice of love and mercy
  sounds aloud from Calvary;
  see, it tears the temple curtain,
  shakes the earth and veils the sky:
      'It is finished, it is finished!' –
  hear the dying Saviour cry.

2 Finished – all the types and shadows
  of the ceremonial law;
  God fulfils what he has promised –
  death and hell shall reign no more:
      'It is finished, it is finished!' –
  Christ has opened heaven's door.

3 Saints and angels shout his praises,
  his great finished work proclaim;
  all on earth and all in heaven
  join to bless Emmanuel's name:
      'Alleluia, alleluia,
  endless glory to the Lamb!'

129 Christopher Idle†

1 He stood before the court
  on trial instead of us;
  he met its power to hurt,
  condemned to face the cross:
  our king, accused
  of treachery;
  our God, abused
  for blasphemy!

2 These are the crimes that tell
  the tale of human guilt;
  our sins, our death, our hell –
  on these the case is built:
  to this world's powers
  their Lord stays dumb;
  the guilt is ours,
  no answers come.

3 The sentence must be passed,
  the unknown prisoner killed;
  the price is paid at last,
  the law of God fulfilled:
  he takes our blame,
  and from that day
  the accuser's claim
  is wiped away.

4 Shall we be judged and tried?
  in Christ our trial is done;
  we live, for he has died,
  our condemnation gone:
  in Christ are we
  both dead and raised,
  alive and free –
  his name be praised!

130 P. P. Bliss

1 Man of sorrows! what a name
  for the Son of God, who came
  ruined sinners to reclaim:
      Alleluia! what a saviour!

2 Mocked by insults harsh and crude,
  in my place condemned he stood;
  sealed my pardon with his blood:
      Alleluia! what a saviour!

3 Guilty, helpless, lost were we:
  blameless Lamb of God was he,
  sacrificed to set us free:
      Alleluia! what a saviour!

4 He was lifted up to die:
  'It is finished!' was his cry;
  now in heaven exalted high:
      Alleluia! what a saviour!

5 When he comes, our glorious king,
  all his ransomed home to bring;
  then again this song we'll sing:
      'Alleluia! what a saviour!'

131
W. W. How
‹ in this version Jubilate Hymns†

1 It is a thing most wonderful –
 almost too wonderful to be –
 that God's own Son should come from heaven
 and die to save a child like me.

2 And yet I know that it is true:
 he came to this poor world below,
 and wept and toiled, and mourned and died,
 only because he loved us so.

3 I cannot tell how he could love
 a child so weak and full of sin;
 his love must be most wonderful
 if he could die my love to win.

4 I sometimes think about the cross,
 and shut my eyes, and try to see
 the cruel nails, and crown of thorns,
 and Jesus crucified for me.

5 But, even could I see him die,
 I could but see a little part
 of that great love which, like a fire,
 is always burning in his heart.

6 How wonderful it is to know
 his love for me so free and sure;
 but yet more wonderful to see
 my love for him so faint and poor.

7 And yet I want to love you, Lord:
 O teach me how to grow in grace,
 that I may love you more and more
 until I see you face to face.

4 So, living Lord, prepare us now
 your willing helplessness to share;
 to give ourselves in sacrifice
 to overcome the world's despair;
 in love to give our lives away
 and claim your victory today.

133
○ Michael Perry†

1 Lord Jesus, for my sake you come,
 the Son of Man, and God most high;
 you leave behind your Father's home
 to live and serve, to love and die.

2 Your eyes seek out our world's distress
 through insult, grief and agony;
 they meet our tears with tenderness
 yet blaze upon our blasphemy.

3 Are these the robes that make men proud,
 is this the crown that you must wear?
 your face is set, your head is bowed,
 and silently you persevere.

4 You never grasped at selfish gain,
 and yet your hands are marked with blood;
 transfixed by nails, they cling in pain
 to sorrow on a cross of wood.

5 Lord Jesus, come to me anew;
 your hands, your eyes, your thoughts be mine,
 until I learn to love like you
 and live on earth the life divine.

132
○ Alan Gaunt

1 Lord Christ, we praise your sacrifice,
 your life in love so freely given:
 for those who took your life away
 you prayed, that they might be forgiven;
 and there, in helplessness arrayed,
 God's power was perfectly displayed.

2 Once helpless in your mother's arms,
 dependent on her mercy then,
 you made yourself again, by choice,
 as helpless in the hands of men;
 and at their mercy crucified,
 you claimed your victory and died.

3 Though helpless and rejected then
 you're now as risen Lord acclaimed;
 for ever, by your victory,
 is God's eternal love proclaimed –
 the love which goes through death to find
 new life and hope for humankind.

134
from *Poems of Father Andrew*
‹ A. R. Mowbray and Company,
after H. E. Hardy, in this version Jubilate Hymns†

1 O dearest Lord, your sacred head
 with thorns was pierced for me:
 pour out your blessing on my head,
 that yours my thoughts may be.

2 O dearest Lord, your sacred hands
 with nails were pierced for me:
 pour out your blessing on my hands
 that yours my work may be.

3 O dearest Lord, your sacred feet
 with nails were pierced for me:
 pour out your blessing on my feet
 that yours my path may be.

4 O dearest Lord, your sacred heart
 with spear was pierced for me:
 pour out your Spirit in my heart
 that yours my life may be.

135
after H. Pink
© David Mowbray†

1 O Christ, the Master Carpenter,
  high on a cross you died;
  a wooden cross, with iron nails,
  a spear thrust in your side.

2 O Christ, upon that Friday cross
  your work on earth was done;
  yet, truly, in my life today
  your work has just begun.

3 O Christ, take up your workman's tools
  and shape my life anew,
  that I who now appear rough-hewn
  may be restored by you.

4 O Christ, the Master Carpenter,
  let beauty gently shine
  within the workshop of my life –
  the praise be yours, not mine.

136
S. Crossman
© in this version Jubilate Hymns†

1 My song is love unknown,
  my saviour's love for me;
  love to the loveless shown
  that they might lovely be:
  but who am I, that for my sake
  my Lord should take frail flesh and die?

2 He came from heaven's throne
  salvation to bestow;
  but they refused, and none
  the longed-for Christ would know:
  this is my friend, my friend indeed,
  who at my need his life did spend.

3 Sometimes they crowd his way
  and his sweet praises sing,
  resounding all the day
  hosannas to their king:
  then 'crucify' is all their breath,
  and for his death they thirst and cry.

4 Why, what has my Lord done
  to cause this rage and spite?
  he made the lame to run,
  and gave the blind their sight:
  what injuries! yet these are why
  the Lord most high so cruelly dies.

5 With angry shouts, they have
  my dear Lord done away;
  a murderer they save,
  the prince of life they slay!
  yet willingly he bears the shame
  that through his name all might be free.

6 Here might I stay and sing
  of him my soul adores;
  never was love, dear King,
  never was grief like yours! –
  this is my friend in whose sweet praise
  I all my days could gladly spend.

137
from Isaiah 53, Brian Foley
© Faber Music Ltd

1 See, Christ was wounded for our sake,
  and bruised and beaten for our sin,
  so by his sufferings we are healed,
  for God has laid our guilt on him.

2 Look on his face, come close to him –
  see, you will find no beauty there:
  despised, rejected, who can tell
  the grief and sorrow he must bear?

3 Like sheep that stray we leave God's path,
  to choose our own and not his will;
  like sheep to slaughter he has gone,
  obedient to his Father's will.

4 Cast out to die by those he loved,
  reviled by those he died to save,
  see how sin's pride has sought his death,
  see how sin's hate has made his grave.

5 For on his shoulders God has laid
  the weight of sin that we should bear;
  so by his passion we have peace,
  through his obedience and his prayer.

138
© Timothy Dudley-Smith

1 No weight of gold or silver
  can measure human worth;
  no soul secures its ransom
  with all the wealth of earth:
  no sinners find their freedom
  but by the gift unpriced,
  the Lamb of God unblemished,
  the precious blood of Christ.

2 Our sins, our griefs and troubles
  he bore and made his own;
  we hid our faces from him,
  rejected and alone;
  his wounds are for our healing,
  our peace is by his pain –
  behold, the Man of sorrows,
  the Lamb for sinners slain!

3 In Christ the past is over,
a new world now begins;
with him we rise to freedom
who saves us from our sins:
we live by faith in Jesus
to make his glory known –
behold, the Man of sorrows,
the Lamb upon his throne!

after Bernard of Clairvaux and P. Gerhardt
J. W. Alexander and H. W. Baker
© in this version Jubilate Hymns†

139

1 O sacred head surrounded
by crown of piercing thorn;
O royal head so wounded,
reviled and put to scorn:
death's shadows rise before you,
the glow of life decays,
yet angel hosts adore you
and tremble as they gaze!

2 Your youthfulness and vigour
are spent, your strength is gone,
and in your tortured figure
I see death drawing on:
what agony of dying,
what love, to sinners free!
My Lord, all grace supplying,
O turn your face on me!

3 Your sinless soul's oppression
was all for sinners' gain;
mine, mine was the transgression,
but yours the deadly pain:
I bow my head, my Saviour,
for I deserve your place;
O grant to me your favour,
and heal me by your grace.

4 What language shall I borrow
to thank you, dearest Friend,
for this your dying sorrow,
your mercy without end?
Lord, make me yours for ever:
your servant let me be;
and may I never, never
betray your love for me.

140 J. H. Newman

1 Praise to the Holiest in the height,
and in the depth be praise;
in all his words most wonderful,
most sure in all his ways!

2 O loving wisdom of our God!
when all was sin and shame,
a second Adam to the fight
and to the rescue came.

3 O wisest love! that flesh and blood,
which did in Adam fail,
should strive afresh against the foe,
should strive and should prevail;

4 And that the highest gift of grace
should flesh and blood refine:
God's presence and his very self,
and essence all-divine.

5 O generous love! that he who came
as man to smite our foe,
the double agony for us
as man should undergo:

6 And in the garden secretly,
and on the cross on high,
should teach his brethren, and inspire
to suffer and to die.

7 Praise to the Holiest in the height,
and in the depth be praise;
in all his words most wonderful,
most sure in all his ways!

141 © Michael Perry†

1 The hands of Christ, the caring hands,
they nailed them to a cross of wood;
the feet that climbed the desert road
and brought the news of peace with God,
they pierced them through.

2 The kingly Christ, the saviour-king,
they ringed his head with briars woven;
the lips that freely spoke of heaven,
that told the world of sins forgiven,
they mocked with wine.

3 Too late for life, in death too late
they tried to maim him with a spear;
for sacrilege they could not bear –
the sabbath comes, so they must tear
the heart from God.

4 To him be praise, all praise to him
who died upon the cross of pain;
whose agonies were not in vain –
for Christ the Lord is risen again
and brings us joy!

142 after the Latin by Venantius Fortunatus
J. M. Neale, © in this version Jubilate Hymns†

1 Sing, my tongue, the glorious battle,
sing the final, fierce affray!
how the cross became a triumph
where our sin was borne away;
how, the pains of death enduring,
earth's Redeemer won the day.

2 When at last the appointed fulness
of the sacred time had come,
he was sent, the world's Creator,
from the Father's heavenly home;
and he came in truest manhood
from a humble virgin's womb.

3 Now the thirty years are ended
which on earth he willed to see;
willingly he goes to suffer,
born to set his people free;
on the cross the Lamb is lifted,
there the sacrifice to be.

4 Gall and vinegar they offer,
mocking him with thorns and reed;
nails and spear, the Saviour piercing,
make his sacred body bleed:
by that blood the whole creation
from the stain of sin is freed.

5 Praise and honour to the Father,
praise and honour to the Son,
praise and honour to the Spirit,
ever Three and ever One:
one in triumph, one in glory
while eternal ages run!   (Amen)

143 © Timothy Dudley-Smith

1 The Lord made man, the scriptures tell,
to bear his image and his sign;
yet we by nature share as well
the ancient mark of Adam's line.

2 In Adam's fall falls every man,
with every gift the Father gave:
the crown of all creation's plan
becomes a rebel and a slave.

3 Herein all woes are brought to birth,
all aching hearts and sunless skies:
brightness is gone from all the earth,
the innocence of nature dies.

4 Yet Adam's children, born to pain,
by self enslaved, by sin enticed,
still may by grace be born again,
children of God, beloved in Christ.

5 In Christ is Adam's ransom met,
earth, by his cross, is holy ground;
Eden indeed is with us yet –
in Christ are life and freedom found!

144 W. Cowper
© in this version Jubilate Hymns†

1 There is a fountain opened wide
where life and hope begin;
for Christ the Lord was crucified
to cleanse us from our sin.

2 The dying thief rejoiced to see
that fountain in his day;
and there have I, as vile as he,
washed all my sins away.

3 O Lamb of God, your precious blood
shall never lose its power,
till all the ransomed church of God
be saved to sin no more.

4 And since, by faith, I saw the stream
your flowing wounds supply,
redeeming love has been my theme,
and shall be till I die.

5 When this poor, lisping, stammering tongue
lies silent in the grave,
then in a nobler, sweeter song
I'll sing your power to save.

145 © Michael Saward†

1 Through all our days we'll sing the praise
of Christ, the resurrected;
who, though divine, did not decline
to be by men afflicted:
pain, pain and suffering –
he knew its taste, he bore its sting;
peace, peace has come to earth
through Christ our king and saviour.

2 His birth obscure, his family poor,
he owned no crown, no kingdom;
yet those who grope in darkness, hope
since he brought light and freedom:
shame, shame and agony –
though guiltless he of felony;
shout, shout his sinless name,
our Jesus, king and saviour.

3 At fearful cost his life he lost
that death might be defeated;
the Man of Love, now risen above,
in majesty is seated:
low, low was his descent
to those by sin and sorrow bent;
life, life to all who trust
the Lord, our king and saviour.

4　And all who trust will find they must
　　obey the will of heaven;
　　for grief intense can make some sense
　　to those who are forgiven:
　　hard, hard the road he trod –
　　the Son of Man, the Son of God;
　　hope, hope in Christ alone,
　　our reigning king and saviour.

146　T. Kelly

1　We sing the praise of him who died,
　　of him who died upon the cross;
　　the sinner's hope let none deride –
　　for this we count the world but loss.

2　Inscribed upon the cross we see
　　in shining letters, 'God is Love';
　　he bears our sins upon the tree,
　　he brings us mercy from above.

3　The cross – it takes our guilt away,
　　it holds the fainting spirit up;
　　it cheers with hope the gloomy day
　　and sweetens every bitter cup:

4　It makes the coward spirit brave
　　and nerves the feeble arm for fight;
　　it takes the terror from the grave
　　and gilds the bed of death with light:

5　The balm of life, the cure of woe,
　　the measure and the pledge of love;
　　the sinner's refuge here below,
　　the angels' theme in heaven above.

147　I. Watts

1　When I survey the wondrous cross
　　on which the prince of glory died,
　　my richest gain I count as loss,
　　and pour contempt on all my pride.

2　Forbid it, Lord, that I should boast
　　save in the cross of Christ my God;
　　the very things that charm me most –
　　I sacrifice them to his blood.

3　See from his head, his hands, his feet,
　　sorrow and love flow mingled down:
　　when did such love and sorrow meet,
　　or thorns compose so rich a crown?

4　Were the whole realm of nature mine,
　　that were an offering far too small;
　　love so amazing, so divine,
　　demands my soul, my life, my all!

148　Cecil F. Alexander

1　There is a green hill far away
　　outside a city wall,
　　where our dear Lord was crucified,
　　who died to save us all.

2　We may not know, we cannot tell
　　what pains he had to bear,
　　but we believe it was for us
　　he hung and suffered there.

3　He died that we might be forgiven,
　　he died to make us good;
　　that we might go at last to heaven,
　　saved by his precious blood.

4　There was no other good enough
　　to pay the price of sin;
　　he, only, could unlock the gate
　　of heaven – and let us in.

5　Lord Jesus, dearly you have loved;
　　and we must love you too,
　　and trust in your redeeming blood
　　and learn to follow you.

149　© Timothy Dudley-Smith

1　All shall be well!
　　for on our Easter skies
　　see Christ the sun
　　　　of righteousness arise.

2　All shall be well!
　　the sacrifice is made;
　　the sinner freed,
　　　　the price of pardon paid.

3　All shall be well!
　　the cross and passion past;
　　dark night is done,
　　　　bright morning come at last.

4　All shall be well!
　　within our Father's plan
　　death has no more
　　　　dominion over man.

5　Jesus alive!
　　rejoice and sing again,
　　'All shall be well
　　　　for evermore, Amen!'

150
C. Wesley
© in this version Jubilate Hymns†

1 All creation join to say:
　Christ the Lord is risen today!
　raise your joys and triumphs high;
　sing, you heavens, and earth reply:
　　Alleluia!

2 Love's redeeming work is done;
　fought the fight, the battle won:
　see, our Sun's eclipse has passed;
　see, the dawn has come at last!
　　Alleluia!

3 Vain the stone, the watch, the seal:
　Christ has burst the gates of hell;
　death in vain forbids his rise –
　Christ has opened paradise:
　　Alleluia!

4 Now he lives, our glorious king;
　now, O death, where is your sting?
　Once he died, our souls to save –
　where's your victory, boasting grave?
　　Alleluia!

5 So we rise where Christ has led,
　following our exalted head;
　made like him, like him we rise –
　ours the cross, the grave, the skies:
　　Alleluia!

6 Hail the Lord of earth and heaven!
　praise to you by both be given;
　every knee to you shall bow,
　risen Christ, triumphant now:
　　Alleluia!

151
after C. Wordsworth
verses 2 and 3 © Jubilate Hymns†

1 Alleluia, alleluia!
　　hearts to heaven and voices raise:
　sing to God a hymn of gladness,
　　sing to God a hymn of praise;
　he who on the cross a victim
　　for the world's salvation bled –
　Jesus Christ, the king of glory,
　　now is risen from the dead.

2 Alleluia, Christ is risen!
　　death at last has met defeat:
　see the ancient powers of evil
　　in confusion and retreat;
　once he died, and once was buried:
　　now he lives for evermore,
　Jesus Christ, the world's redeemer,
　　whom we worship and adore.

3 Christ is risen, we are risen!
　　set your hearts on things above:
　there in all the Father's glory
　　lives and reigns our king of love;
　hear the word of peace he brings us,
　　see his wounded hands and side!
　now let every wrong be ended,
　　every sin be crucified.

4 Alleluia, alleluia!
　　glory be to God on high:
　alleluia to the Saviour
　　who has gained the victory;
　alleluia to the Spirit,
　　fount of love and sanctity:
　alleluia, alleluia
　　to the Triune Majesty!

152
from John 20
© Michael Perry†

1 Comes Mary to the grave:
　no singing bird has spoken,
　nor has the world awoken,
　and in her grief all love lies lost
　　and broken.

2 Says Jesus at her side,
　no longer Jesus dying,
　'Why, Mary, are you crying?'
　She turns, with joy, 'My Lord! my love!'
　　replying.

3 With Mary on this day
　we join our voices praising
　the God of Jesus' raising,
　and sing the triumph of his love
　　amazing.

153
after M. Weisse
Catherine Winkworth

1 Christ the Lord is risen again,
　Christ has broken every chain;
　hear the angel voices cry,
　singing evermore on high:
　　Alleluia!

2 He who gave for us his life,
　who for us endured the strife,
　is our paschal lamb today;
　we too sing for joy and say:
　　Alleluia!

3 He who bore all pain and loss
　comfortless upon the cross
　lives in glory now on high,
　pleads for us and hears our cry:
　　Alleluia!

4 He who slumbered in the grave
   is exalted now to save;
   through the universe it rings
   that the lamb is King of kings:
       Alleluia!

5 Now he bids us tell abroad
   how the lost may be restored,
   how the penitent forgiven,
   how we too may enter heaven:
       Alleluia!

6 Christ, our paschal lamb indeed,
   all your ransomed people feed!
   take our sins and guilt away;
   let us sing by night and day:
       Alleluia!

154

C. A. Alington
© Hymns Ancient & Modern Ltd

1 Good Christians all, rejoice and sing!
   now is the triumph of our king;
   to all the world glad news we bring:
       Alleluia, alleluia, alleluia!

2 The Lord of life is risen today;
   death's mighty stone is rolled away:
   let every tongue rejoice and say,
       'Alleluia, alleluia, alleluia!'

3 We praise in songs of victory
   that love, that life, which cannot die,
   and sing with hearts uplifted high,
       'Alleluia, alleluia, alleluia!'

4 Your name we bless, O risen Lord,
   and sing today with one accord
   the life laid down, the life restored:
       Alleluia, alleluia, alleluia!

155

after a fourteenth century author
unknown (eighteenth century)

1 Jesus Christ is risen today,   Alleluia,
   our triumphant holy day;   alleluia,
   who did once upon the cross   alleluia,
   suffer to redeem our loss.   alleluia!

2 Hymns of joy then let us sing   Alleluia,
   praising Christ our heavenly king; alleluia,
   who endured the cross and grave   alleluia,
   sinners to redeem and save!   alleluia!

3 But the pains which he endured   Alleluia,
   our salvation have procured;   alleluia,
   now above the sky he's king   alleluia,
   where the angels ever sing.   alleluia!

156

after C. F. Gellert, Frances E. Cox
© in this version Jubilate Hymns†

1 Jesus lives! Your terrors now
   can, O death, no more appal us:
   Jesus lives! – by this we know
   you, O grave, cannot enthral us:
       Alleluia!

2 Jesus lives! – henceforth is death
   but the gate of life immortal;
   this shall calm our trembling breath
   when we pass its gloomy portal:
       Alleluia!

3 Jesus lives! – for us he died:
   then, alone to Jesus living,
   pure in heart may we abide,
   glory to our saviour giving:
       Alleluia!

4 Jesus lives! – this bond of love
   neither life nor death shall sever,
   powers in hell or heaven above
   tear us from his keeping never:
       Alleluia!

5 Jesus lives! – to him the throne
   over all the world is given;
   may we go where he is gone,
   rest and reign with him in heaven:
       Alleluia!

157

from the Latin, J. M. Neale
© in this version Jubilate Hymns†

1 Light's glittering morning fills the sky,
   heaven thunders out its victor cry;
       Alleluia, alleluia!
   earth shouts her Easter triumph high,
   and groaning hell makes wild reply.
       Alleluia, alleluia,
       alleluia, alleluia, alleluia!

2 For Christ the Lord, the mighty king,
   closes with death and draws its sting;
       Alleluia, alleluia!
   he tramples down the powers of night,
   brings out his ransomed saints to light.
       Alleluia . . .

3 His rocky tomb the threefold guard
   of watch and stone and seal had barred,
       Alleluia, alleluia!
   but now in royal triumph high
   he comes from death to victory!
       Alleluia . . .

4 Hell's gates are broken down at last,
   our days of mourning now are past;
      Alleluia, alleluia!
   'Weep not,' an angel voice has said,
   'Jesus is risen from the dead!'
      Alleluia, alleluia,
      alleluia, alleluia, alleluia!

5 All praise be yours, O risen Lord,
   from death to endless life restored;
      Alleluia, alleluia!
   to Father, Son and Spirit be
   all power and praise eternally!
      Alleluia . . .

158 R. Lowry

1 Low in the grave he lay,
   Jesus my saviour,
   waiting the coming day,
   Jesus my Lord!
      Up from the grave he arose
      as the victor over all his foes;
      he arose in triumph from the dark domain,
      and he lives for ever
      with his saints to reign –
      he arose, he arose,
      Alleluia – Christ arose!

2 Vainly they guard his bed,
   Jesus my saviour;
   vainly they seal the dead,
   Jesus my Lord!
      Up from the grave he arose . . .

3 Death cannot keep his prey,
   Jesus my saviour;
   he tore the bars away,
   Jesus my Lord!
      Up from the grave he arose . . .

159 from *The Easter Anthems*
© David Mowbray†

1 Now lives the Lamb of God,
   our Passover, the Christ,
   who once with nails and wood
   for us was sacrificed:
      Come, keep the feast, the anthem sing
      that Christ indeed is Lord and king!

2 Now risen from the dead
   Christ never dies again;
   in us, with Christ as head,
   sin nevermore shall reign:
      Come, keep the feast . . .

3 In Adam all must die,
   forlorn and unforgiven;
   in Christ all come alive,
   the second Man from heaven.
      Come, keep the feast . . .

4 Give praise to God alone
   who life from death can bring;
   whose mighty power can turn
   the winter into spring:
      Come, keep the feast . . .

160 after John of Damascus
J. M. Neale

1 Spring has come for us today!
   Christ has burst his prison,
   and from three days' sleep in death
   like the sun has risen.
   All the winter of our sins,
   long and dark, is dying:
   welcome now the light of Christ,
   life and joy supplying!

2 Alleluia! let us sing
   to our king immortal
   who in triumph broke the bars
   of the tomb's dark portal.
   Alleluia! to our God,
   Father, Son, and Spirit:
   to your holy name be praise,
   honour, power, and merit.

161 after John of Damascus
J. M. Neale

1 The day of resurrection!
   come, spread the news abroad;
   the passover of gladness,
   the passover of God:
   from death to life eternal,
   from earth up to the sky,
   our Christ has brought us over
   with hymns of victory.

2 Now let the skies be joyful
   and earth sing back her praise;
   let all the nations worship
   the God of endless days:
   let all things seen and unseen
   their joyful music blend,
   for Christ the Lord has risen –
   our triumph knows no end!

162
from 1 Corinthians 15 etc.
© Michael Saward†

1 These are the facts
   as we have received them,
   these are the truths
   that the Christian believes,
   this is the basis of all of our preaching:
   Christ died for sinners
   and rose from the tomb.

2 These are the facts
   as we have received them:
   Christ has fulfilled
   what the scriptures foretold,
   Adam's whole family
   in death had been sleeping,
   Christ through his rising restores us to life.

3 These are the facts
   as we have received them:
   we, with our saviour, have died on the cross;
   now, having risen, our Jesus lives in us,
   gives us his Spirit and makes us his home.

4 These are the facts
   as we have received them:
   we shall be changed in the blink of an eye,
   trumpets shall sound as we face life immortal,
   this is the victory through Jesus our Lord.

5 These are the facts
   as we have received them,
   these are the truths
   that the Christian believes,
   this is the basis of all of our preaching:
   Christ died for sinners
   and rose from the tomb.

163
from the Latin, F. Pott
© in this version Jubilate Hymns†

1 The strife is past, the battle done;
   now is the victor's triumph won –
   O let the song of praise be sung,
   Alleluia!

2 Death's mightiest powers have done their
      worst;
   and Jesus has his foes dispersed –
   let shouts of praise and joy outburst,
   Alleluia!

3 On the third day he rose again,
   glorious in majesty to reign –
   sing out with joy the glad refrain,
   Alleluia!

4 Lord over death, our wounded king,
   save us from Satan's deadly sting
   that we may live for you and sing,
   Alleluia!

164
© Timothy Dudley-Smith

1 This day above all days
   glad hymns of triumph bring;
   lift every heart to love and praise
   and every voice to sing:
      for Jesus is risen,
   our glorious Lord and king!

2 Christ keeps his Eastertide!
   The Father's power descends;
   the shuttered tomb he opens wide,
   the rock-hewn grave he rends:
      for Jesus is risen,
   and death's dominion ends!

3 What sovereign grace is found
   in Christ for all our need!
   The powers of sin and death are bound,
   the ransomed captives freed:
      for Jesus is risen,
   the prince of life indeed!

4 So lift your joyful songs
   with all the hosts on high,
   where angel and archangel throngs
   his ceaseless praises cry:
      for Jesus is risen,
   and lives no more to die!

165
after G. R. Woodward
© in this version Jubilate Hymns†

1 This joyful Eastertide
   away with sin and sadness!
   our Lord, the crucified,
   has filled our hearts with gladness:
      Had Christ, who once was slain,
      not burst his three-day prison
      our faith would be in vain –
      but now has Christ arisen,
      arisen, arisen, arisen!

2 My being shall rejoice
   secure within God's keeping,
   until the trumpet voice
   shall wake us from our sleeping:
      Had Christ . . .

3 Death's waters lost their chill
   when Jesus crossed the river;
   his love shall reach me still,
   his mercy is for ever:
      Had Christ . . .

166
after Venantius Fortunatus, J. Ellerton
© in this version Jubilate Hymns†

1 Welcome, happy morning!
   age to age shall say;
   hell today is conquered,
   heaven is won today:
   come then, True and Faithful,
   now fulfil your word;
   this is your third morning:
   rise, O buried Lord!

2 Earth with joyful welcome
   clothes herself for spring;
   greets with life reviving
   her returning king:
   flowers in every pasture,
   leaves on every bough,
   speak of sorrows ended;
   Jesus triumphs now!

3 Author and sustainer,
   source of life and breath;
   you for our salvation
   trod the path of death:
   Jesus Christ is living,
   God for evermore!
   Now let all creation
   hail him and adore.

4 Loose our souls imprisoned
   bound with Satan's chain;
   all that now is fallen,
   raise to life again!
   show your face in brightness,
   shine the whole world through;
   hope returns with daybreak,
   life returns with you.

167
after E. L. Budry, R. B. Hoyle
© World Student Christian Federation,
and in this version Jubilate Hymns†

1 Yours be the glory! risen, conquering Son;
   endless is the victory over death you won;
   angels robed in splendour
      rolled the stone away,
   kept the folded grave clothes
      where your body lay:
      Yours be the glory! risen, conquering Son:
      endless is the victory over death you won.

2 See! Jesus meets us, risen from the tomb,
   lovingly he greets us, scatters fear and gloom;
   let the church with gladness
      hymns of triumph sing!
   for her Lord is living, death has lost its sting:
      Yours be the glory . . .

3 No more we doubt you, glorious prince of life:
   what is life without you? aid us in our strife;
   make us more than conquerors
      through your deathless love,
   bring us safe through Jordan
      to your home above:
      Yours be the glory . . .

168
after Fulbert of Chartres
R. Campbell

1 You choirs of new Jerusalem,
   your sweetest notes employ
   the paschal victory to hymn
   in songs of holy joy!

2 For Judah's Lion burst his chains
   and crushed the serpent's head;
   he cries aloud through death's domains
   to wake the imprisoned dead.

3 Devouring depths of hell their prey
   at his command restore;
   his ransomed hosts pursue their way
   where Jesus goes before.

4 Triumphant in his glory now –
   to him all power is given;
   to him in one communion bow
   all saints in earth and heaven.

5 All glory to the Father be,
   the Spirit and the Son:
   all glory to the One-in-Three
   while endless ages run.

169 S. Medley

1 I know that my redeemer lives –
   what comfort this assurance gives!
   he lives, he lives, who once was dead,
   he lives, my everlasting Head.

2 He lives, triumphant from the grave,
   he lives, eternally to save;
   he lives, to bless me with his love,
   and intercedes for me above.

3 He lives to help in time of need,
   he lives, my hungry soul to feed;
   he lives, and grants me daily breath,
   he lives, and I shall conquer death.

4 He lives, my kind, wise, constant friend,
   who still will guard me to the end;
   he lives, and while he lives I'll sing,
   Jesus, my prophet, priest, and king.

5 He lives, my saviour, to prepare
  a place in heaven, and lead me there;
  he lives, all glory to his name,
  Jesus, unchangeably the same.

170 W. C. Dix

1 Alleluia, sing to Jesus!
  his the sceptre, his the throne:
  Alleluia! – his the triumph,
  his the victory alone.
  Hear the songs of holy Zion
  thunder like a mighty flood:
  'Jesus out of every nation
  has redeemed us by his blood!'

2 Alleluia! – not as orphans
  are we left in sorrow now:
  Alleluia! – he is near us;
  faith believes, nor questions how.
  Though the cloud from sight received him
  whom the angels now adore,
  shall our hearts forget his promise,
  'I am with you evermore'?

3 Alleluia! – bread of heaven,
  here on earth our food, our stay:
  Alleluia! – here the sinful
  come to you from day to day.
  Intercessor, friend of sinners,
  earth's redeemer, plead for me,
  where the songs of all the sinless
  sweep across the crystal sea.

4 Alleluia, sing to Jesus!
  his the sceptre, his the throne:
  Alleluia! his the triumph,
  his the victory alone.
  Hear the songs of holy Zion
  thunder like a mighty flood:
  'Jesus out of every nation
  has redeemed us by his blood!'

171 © Christopher Idle†

1 Ascended Christ, who gained
  the glory that we sing,
  anointed and ordained,
  our prophet, priest, and king:
      by many tongues
      the church displays
      your power and praise
      in all her songs.

2 No titles, thrones, or powers
  can ever rival yours;
  no passing mood of ours
  can turn aside your laws:
      you reign above
      each other name
      of worth or fame,
      the Lord of love.

3 Now from the Father's side
  you make your people new;
  since for our sins you died
  our lives belong to you:
      from our distress
      you set us free
      for purity
      and holiness.

4 You call us to belong
  within one body here;
  in weakness we are strong
  and all your gifts we share:
      in you alone
      we are complete
      and at your feet
      with joy bow down.

5 All strength is in your hand,
  all power to you is given;
  all wisdom to command
  in earth and hell and heaven:
      beyond all words
      creation sings
      the King of kings
      and Lord of lords.

172 Caroline M. Noel
© in this version Jubilate Hymns†

1 At the name of Jesus every knee shall bow,
  every tongue confess him king of glory now;
  this the Father's pleasure,
      that we call him Lord,
  who from the beginning was the mighty word.

2 At his voice creation sprang at once to sight,
  all the angel faces, all the hosts of light;
  thrones and dominations,
      stars upon their way,
  all the heavenly orders, in their great array.

3 Humbled for a season, to receive a name
  from the lips of sinners unto whom he came;
  faithfully he bore it spotless to the last,
  brought it back victorious
      when from death he passed.

4 Bore it up triumphant with its human light,
  through all ranks of creatures
      to the central height;
  to the eternal Godhead, to the Father's throne,
  filled it with the glory of his triumph won.

5 Name him, Christians, name him,
    with love strong as death,
but with awe and wonder,
    and with bated breath;
he is God the saviour, he is Christ the Lord,
ever to be worshipped, trusted and adored.

6 In your hearts enthrone him;
    there let him subdue
all that is not holy, all that is not true;
crown him as your captain
    in temptation's hour,
let his will enfold you in its light and power.

7 With his Father's glory Jesus comes again,
angel hosts attend him
    and announce his reign;
for all wreaths of empire meet upon his brow,
and our hearts confess him king of glory now.

173 © Michael Saward†

1 Christ triumphant, ever reigning,
Saviour, Master, King!
Lord of heaven, our lives sustaining,
hear us as we sing:
    Yours the glory and the crown,
    the high renown, the eternal name.

2 Word incarnate, truth revealing,
Son of Man on earth!
power and majesty concealing
by your humble birth:
    Yours the glory . . .

3 Suffering servant, scorned, ill-treated,
victim crucified!
death is through the cross defeated,
sinners justified:
    Yours the glory . . .

4 Priestly king, enthroned for ever
high in heaven above!
sin and death and hell shall never
stifle hymns of love:
    Yours the glory . . .

5 So, our hearts and voices raising
through the ages long,
ceaselessly upon you gazing,
this shall be our song:
    Yours the glory . . .

174 M. Bridges and G. Thring
© in this version Jubilate Hymns†

1 Crown him with many crowns,
the Lamb upon his throne,
while heaven's eternal anthem drowns
all music but its own!
Awake, my soul, and sing
of him who died to be
your saviour and your matchless king
through all eternity.

2 Crown him the Lord of life
triumphant from the grave,
who rose victorious from the strife
for those he came to save:
his glories now we sing
who died and reigns on high;
he died eternal life to bring
and lives that death may die.

3 Crown him the Lord of love,
who shows his hands and side –
those wounds yet visible above
in beauty glorified.
No angel in the sky
can fully bear that sight,
but downward bends his burning eye
at mysteries so bright.

4 Crown him the Lord of peace –
his kingdom is at hand;
from pole to pole let warfare cease
and Christ rule every land!
A city stands on high,
his glory it displays,
and there the nations 'Holy' cry
in joyful hymns of praise.

5 Crown him the Lord of years,
the potentate of time,
creator of the rolling spheres
in majesty sublime:
all hail, Redeemer, hail,
for you have died for me;
your praise shall never, never fail
through all eternity!

175 J. Bakewell and others
© in this version Jubilate Hymns†

1 Hail, our once-rejected Jesus!
Hail, our Galilean king!
You have suffered to release us,
hope and joy and peace to bring.
Patient friend and holy saviour,
bearer of our sin and shame;
by your merits we find favour,
life is given through your name.

2 Paschal Lamb, by God appointed,
all our sins on you were laid;
by almighty love anointed,
full atonement you have made.
All your people are forgiven
through the virtue of your blood;
opened is the gate of heaven,
we are reconciled with God.

3 Jesus! Heavenly hosts adore you,
seated at your Father's side;
crucified, this world once saw you,
now in glory you abide.
There for sinners you are pleading,
and our place you now prepare;
always for us interceding,
till in glory we appear.

4 Worship, honour, power and blessing
you are worthy to receive;
loudest praises, without ceasing,
right it is for us to give.
Help us, bright angelic spirits –
joined with ours, your voices raise;
help to show our saviour's merits,
help to sing Emmanuel's praise.

176 C. Wesley and T. Cotterill

1 Hail the day that sees him rise   Alleluia,
to his throne beyond the skies,   alleluia,
Christ, the Lamb for sinners given,   alleluia,
enters now the highest heaven: alleluia!

2 There for him high triumph waits: Alleluia,
Lift your heads, eternal gates,   alleluia,
he has conquered death and sin,   alleluia,
take the King of glory in: alleluia!

3 See! the heaven its Lord receives,   Alleluia,
yet he loves the earth he leaves;   alleluia,
though returning to his throne,   alleluia,
still he calls mankind his own.   alleluia!

4 Still for us he intercedes,   Alleluia,
his prevailing death he pleads,   alleluia,
near himself prepares our place,   alleluia,
he the first-fruits of our race.   alleluia!

5 Lord, though parted from our sight   Alleluia,
far beyond the starry height,   alleluia,
lift our hearts that we may rise   alleluia,
one with you beyond the skies: alleluia!

6 There with you we shall remain,   Alleluia,
share the glory of your reign,   alleluia,
there your face unclouded view,   alleluia,
find our heaven of heavens in you.   alleluia!

177 from Revelation 1
© Timothy Dudley-Smith

1 He walks among the golden lamps
on feet like burnished bronze:
his hair as snows of winter white,
his eyes with fire aflame, and bright
his glorious robe of seamless light
surpassing Solomon's.

2 And in his hand the seven stars,
and from his mouth a sword:
his voice the thunder of the seas;
all creatures bow to his decrees
who holds the everlasting keys
and reigns as sovereign Lord.

3 More radiant than the sun at noon,
who was, and is to be:
who was, from everlasting days;
who lives, the Lord of all our ways –
to him be majesty and praise
for all eternity.

178 from the Latin
J. Chandler

1 Jesus our hope, our heart's desire,
your work of grace we sing:
you are the saviour of the world,
its maker and its king.

2 How vast the mercy and the grace,
how great the love must be,
which led you to a cruel death
to set your people free!

3 But now the chains of death are burst,
the ransom has been paid,
and you are at your Father's side
in glorious robes arrayed

4 All praise to you, triumphant Lord
ascended high in heaven –
to God, the Father, Spirit, Son,
be praise and glory given!

179 T. Kelly
© in this version Jubilate Hymns†

1 Look, you saints, the sight is glorious!
see the man of sorrows now
from the fight returned victorious –
every knee to him shall bow:
Crown him, crown him,
crown him, crown him –
crowns befit the victor's brow.

2 Crown the saviour, angels, crown him!
rich the trophies Jesus brings;
in the seat of power enthrone him
while the vault of heaven rings:
    Crown him, crown him,
    crown him, crown him,
    crown the saviour King of kings.

3 Sinners in derision crowned him,
mocked the dying saviour's claim;
saints and angels crowd around him,
sing his triumph, praise his name:
    Crown him, crown him,
    crown him, crown him;
    spread abroad the victor's fame.

4 Hear the shout as he is greeted,
hear those loud triumphant chords!
Jesus Christ in glory seated –
O what joy the sight affords!
    Crown him, crown him,
    crown him, crown him;
    King of kings, and Lord of lords!

180 C. Wesley

1 Rejoice, the Lord is king!
your Lord and king adore:
mortals, give thanks and sing,
and triumph evermore:
    Lift up your heart, lift up your voice:
    rejoice! – again I say, rejoice!

2 Jesus, the saviour, reigns,
the God of truth and love;
when he had purged our stains
he took his seat above:
    Lift up your heart . . .

3 His kingdom cannot fail,
he rules both earth and heaven;
the keys of death and hell
to Jesus now are given:
    Lift up your heart . . .

4 He sits at God's right hand,
till all his foes submit
and bow to his command
and fall beneath his feet:
    Lift up your heart . . .

5 Rejoice in glorious hope!
Jesus the judge shall come
and take his servants up
to their eternal home:
    We soon shall hear the archangel's voice:
    the trumpet sounds – rejoice, rejoice!

181 C. Wordsworth

1 See, the conqueror mounts in triumph,
see the king in royal state,
riding on the clouds, his chariot,
to his heavenly palace gate!
    hear the choirs of angel voices
    joyful alleluias sing!
    and the gates on high are opened
    to receive their mighty king.

2 He who on the cross has suffered,
he who from the grave arose –
he has conquered sin and Satan,
he has overcome his foes:
    while he lifts his hands in blessing,
    he is parted from his friends;
    while their eager eyes behold him,
    in the clouds the Lord ascends.

3 You have raised our human nature
on the clouds to God's right hand;
there we sit in heavenly places,
there with you in glory stand:
    mighty Lord, in your ascension
    we by faith can see our own:
    Jesus reigns, adored by angels;
    God with us is on the throne!

182 T. Kelly

1 The head that once was crowned with thorns
is crowned with glory now;
a royal diadem adorns
the mighty victor's brow.

2 The highest place that heaven affords
is his, is his by right;
the King of kings and Lord of lords
and heaven's eternal light.

3 The joy of all who dwell above,
the joy of all below;
to whom he demonstrates his love
and grants his name to know.

4 To them the cross with all its shame,
with all its grace is given;
their name, an everlasting name,
their joy, the joy of heaven.

5 They suffer with their Lord below,
they reign with him above;
their profit and their joy to know
the mystery of his love.

6 The cross he bore is life and health,
though shame and death to him;
his people's hope, his people's wealth,
their everlasting theme.

183 J. Conder

1 The Lord is king! Lift up your voice,
   O earth, and all you heavens, rejoice;
   from world to world the song shall ring:
   'The Lord omnipotent is king!'

2 The Lord is king! Who then shall dare
   resist his will, distrust his care
   or quarrel with his wise decrees,
   or doubt his royal promises?

3 The Lord is king! Child of the dust,
   the judge of all the earth is just;
   holy and true are all his ways –
   let every creature sing his praise!

4 God reigns! He reigns with glory crowned:
   let Christians make a joyful sound!
   And Christ is seated at his side:
   the man of love, the crucified.

5 Come, make your needs, your burdens
         known:
   he will present them at the throne;
   and angel hosts are waiting there
   his messages of love to bear.

6 One Lord one kingdom all secures:
   he reigns, and life and death are yours;
   through earth and heaven one song shall ring:
   'The Lord omnipotent is king!'

184 M. Bruce
© in this version Jubilate Hymns†

1 Where high the heavenly temple stands,
   the house of God not made with hands,
   a great high priest our nature wears,
   the guardian of our race appears.

2 He who for us as surety stood
   and poured on earth his precious blood,
   pursues in heaven his mighty will,
   our saviour and our helper still.

3 Though now ascended up on high,
   he sees us with a brother's eye;
   he shares with us the human name
   and knows the frailty of our frame.

4 Our fellow-sufferer yet retains
   a fellow-feeling of our pains;
   he still remembers in the skies
   his tears, his agonies and cries.

5 With boldness therefore at his throne
   let us make all our sorrows known:
   to help us in the darkest hour,
   we ask for Christ the saviour's power.

185 after D. T. Niles
in © Christian Conference of Asia Hymnal,
© in this version Jubilate Hymns†

1 Won, the victor's crown;
   run, the saviour's race;
   done, the Father's will –
   all the work of grace:
   praise adorns his brow,
   fire is in his eyes;
   honoured is his name;
   glory is his prize.

2 Gone, the devil's power;
   pierced, the gloomy night;
   torn, the temple veil –
   faith has turned to sight:
   death has been destroyed,
   gates of hell cast down;
   Jesus on his throne
   wears the victor's crown!

186 from Psalm 98, Joel 2 etc.
© Michael Perry†

1 Blow upon the trumpet!
   clap your hands together,
   sound aloud the praises of the Lord your king.
   He has kept his promise,
   granting us salvation:
   let his people jubilantly shout and sing!

2 Blow upon the trumpet!
   let the nations tremble;
   see his power obliterate the sun and moon.
   This is God's own army
   bringing all to judgement,
   for the day of Jesus Christ is coming soon.

3 Blow upon the trumpet!
   arrows in the lightning
   fly the storm of battle where he marches on.
   Glory to our shepherd
   keeping us through danger,
   setting us like jewels in his royal crown.

4 Blow upon the trumpet!
   Christ is surely coming,
   heaven's forces mobilizing at his word.
   We shall rise to meet him:
   death at last is conquered,
   God gives us the victory
         through Christ our Lord!

187 from Baruch 4–5
‹ Christopher Idle†

1 City of God, Jerusalem,
    where he has set his love;
church of Christ that is one on earth
    with Jerusalem above:
here as we walk this changing world
    our joys are mixed with tears,
but the day will be soon
    when the Saviour returns
and his voice will banish our fears.

2 Sing and be glad, Jerusalem,
    for God does not forget;
he who said he would come to save
    never failed his people yet.
Though we are tempted by despair
    and daunted by defeat,
our invincible Lord
    will be seen in his strength,
and his triumph will be complete.

3 Sorrow no more, Jerusalem,
    discard your rags of shame!
take your crown as a gift from God
    who has called you by his name.
Put off your sin, and wear the robe
    of glory in its place;
you will shine in his light,
    you will share in his joy,
you will praise his wonderful grace.

4 Look all around, Jerusalem,
    survey from west to east;
sons and daughters of God the king
    are invited to his feast.
Out of their exile far away
    his scattered family come,
and the streets will resound
    with the songs of the saints
when the Saviour welcomes us home.

188 from Revelation 4–5 etc.
‹ Christopher Idle†

1 Come and see the shining hope
    that Christ's apostle saw;
on the earth, confusion,
    but in heaven an open door,
where the living creatures
    praise the Lamb for evermore:
Love has the victory for ever!
    Amen, he comes!
to bring his own reward!
    Amen, praise God!
for justice now restored;
    kingdoms of the world
become the kingdoms of the Lord:
Love has the victory for ever!

2 All the gifts you send us, Lord,
    are faithful, good, and true;
holiness and righteousness
    are shown in all you do:
who can see your greatest Gift
    and fail to worship you?
Love has the victory for ever!
    Amen, he comes! . . .

3 Power and salvation
    all belong to God on high!
So the mighty multitudes of heaven
    make their cry,
singing Alleluia!
    where the echoes never die:
Love has the victory for ever!
    Amen, he comes! . . .

189 W. B. Collyer and others
© in this version Jubilate Hymns†

1 Great God, what do I see and hear:
the end of things created!
the Judge of all the earth comes near
on clouds of glory seated:
the trumpet sounds, the graves restore
the dead which they contained before –
prepare, my soul, to meet him.

2 The dead in Christ shall first arise
at that last trumpet's sounding,
caught up to meet him in the skies,
with joy their Lord surrounding:
no gloomy fears their souls dismay;
his presence brings eternal day
for those prepared to meet him.

3 But sinners filled with guilty fears
shall see his wrath prevailing;
for they shall rise, and find their tears
and sighs are unavailing:
the day of grace is past and gone;
they trembling stand before the throne
all unprepared to meet him.

4 Great God, what do I see and hear:
the end of things created!
the Judge of all the earth comes near
on clouds of glory seated:
low at his cross I view the day
when heaven and earth shall pass away,
and thus prepare to meet him.

190
J. Montgomery

1 Hail to the Lord's anointed,
  great David's greater son!
  Hail, in the time appointed
  his reign on earth begun!
  He comes to break oppression,
  to set the captive free,
  to take away transgression
  and rule in equity.

2 He comes with comfort speedy
  to those who suffer wrong;
  to save the poor and needy
  and help the weak be strong:
  to give them songs for sighing,
  their darkness turn to light,
  whose souls, condemned and dying,
  are precious in his sight.

3 He shall come down like showers
  upon the fruitful earth;
  and love, joy, hope, like flowers
  spring in his path to birth:
  before him on the mountains
  shall peace, the herald, go;
  and righteousness in fountains
  from hill to valley flow.

4 Kings shall bow down before him
  and gold and incense bring;
  all nations shall adore him,
  his praise all people sing:
  to him shall prayer unceasing
  and daily vows ascend;
  his kingdom still increasing,
  a kingdom without end.

5 In all the world victorious,
  he on his throne shall rest;
  from age to age more glorious,
  all-blessing and all-blessed:
  the tide of time shall never
  his covenant remove;
  his name shall stand for ever,
  his changeless name of love.

191
A. Ainger
© in this version Jubilate Hymns†

1 God is working his purpose out,
  as year succeeds to year:
  God is working his purpose out,
  and the time is drawing near:
  nearer and nearer draws the time,
  the time that shall surely be,
    when the earth shall be filled
    with the glory of God,
    as the waters cover the sea.

2 From utmost east to utmost west,
  wherever foot has trod,
  by the mouth of many messengers
  rings out the voice of God:
  Listen to me you continents,
  you islands look to me,
    that the earth may be filled . . .

3 We shall march in the strength of God,
  with the banner of Christ unfurled,
  that the light of the glorious gospel of truth
  may shine throughout the world;
  we shall fight with sorrow and sin
  to set their captives free,
    that the earth may be filled . . .

4 All we can do is nothing worth
  unless God blesses the deed;
  vainly we hope for the harvest-tide
  till God gives life to the seed:
  nearer and nearer draws the time,
  the time that shall surely be,
    when the earth shall be filled . . .

192
from the Latin
E. Caswall

1 Hark! a trumpet call is sounding,
  'Christ is near,' it seems to say:
  'Cast away the dreams of darkness,
  children of the dawning day!'

2 Wakened by the solemn warning,
  let our earth-bound souls arise;
  Christ, our sun, all harm dispelling,
  shines upon the morning skies.

3 See! the Lamb, so long expected,
  comes with pardon down from heaven;
  let us haste, with tears of sorrow,
  one and all to be forgiven:

4 That, when next he comes in glory
  and the world is wrapped in fear
  with his mercy he may shield us,
  and with words of love draw near.

5 Honour, glory, might and blessing
  to the Father, and the Son,
  with the everlasting Spirit,
  while eternal ages run!

193 P. Doddridge

1 Hark the glad sound! – the Saviour comes,
   the Saviour promised long;
   let every heart prepare a throne
   and every voice a song.

2 He comes the prisoners to release
   in Satan's bondage held;
   the gates of brass before him burst,
   the iron fetters yield.

3 He comes the broken heart to bind,
   the wounded soul to cure;
   and with the treasures of his grace
   to enrich the humble poor.

4 Our glad hosannas, Prince of peace,
   your welcome shall proclaim;
   and heaven's eternal arches ring
   with your beloved name.

194 W. Y. Fullerton

1 I cannot tell why he whom angels worship
   should set his love upon the sons of men,
   or why as shepherd
      he should seek the wanderers,
   to bring them back,
      they know not how nor when.
   But this I know, that he was born of Mary
   when Bethlehem's manger was his only home,
   and that he lived at Nazareth and laboured;
   and so the saviour, saviour of the world,
      has come.

2 I cannot tell how silently he suffered
   as with his peace he graced
      this place of tears,
   nor how his heart upon the cross was broken,
   the crown of pain to three and thirty years.
   But this I know, he heals the broken-hearted
   and stays our sin and calms our lurking fear,
   and lifts the burden from the heavy-laden;
   for still the saviour, saviour of the world,
      is here.

3 I cannot tell how he will win the nations,
   how he will claim his earthly heritage,
   how satisfy the needs and aspirations
   of east and west, of sinner and of sage.
   But this I know, all flesh shall see his glory,
   and he shall reap the harvest he has sown,
   and some glad day
      his sun will shine in splendour
   when he the saviour, saviour of the world,
      is known.

4 I cannot tell how all the lands shall worship,
   when at his bidding every storm is stilled,
   or who can say how great the jubilation
   when all our hearts
      with love for him are filled.
   But this I know,
      the skies will sound his praises,
   ten thousand thousand human voices sing,
   and earth to heaven, and heaven to earth,
      will answer,
   'At last the saviour, saviour of the world,
      is king!'

195 G. Thring
© in this version Jubilate Hymns†

1 Jesus came – the heavens adoring –
   came with peace from realms on high;
   Jesus came for our redemption,
   humbly came on earth to die,
      Alleluia, alleluia!
   came in deep humility.

2 Jesus comes to us in mercy
   when our hearts are bowed with care;
   Jesus comes in power, to answer
   every earnest heartfelt prayer:
      Alleluia, alleluia!
   comes to save us from despair.

3 Jesus comes to hearts rejoicing –
   all the past he now forgives;
   Jesus comes to share his kingdom
   with the sinners he receives:
      Alleluia, alleluia!
   Death is conquered: Jesus lives!

4 Jesus comes on clouds triumphant
   when the heavens shall pass away;
   Jesus comes again in glory –
   let us then our homage pay,
      Alleluia! ever singing
   till the dawn of endless day.

196 after J. Cennick, C. Wesley and M. Madan
© in this version Jubilate Hymns†

1 Jesus comes with clouds descending –
   see the Lamb for sinners slain!
   thousand thousand saints attending
   join to sing the glad refrain:
      Alleluia, alleluia, alleluia!
   God appears on earth to reign.

2 Every eye shall then behold him
   robed in awesome majesty;
   those who jeered at him and sold him,
   pierced and nailed him to the tree,
      shamed and grieving . . .
   shall their true Messiah see.

3 All the wounds of cross and passion
   still his glorious body bears;
   cause of endless exultation
   to his ransomed worshippers.
      With what gladness . . .
      we shall see the Saviour's scars!

4 Yes, Amen! let all adore you
   high on your eternal throne;
   crowns and empires fall before you –
   claim the kingdom for your own.
      Come, Lord Jesus . . .
      everlasting God, come down!

197 I. Watts
         © in this version Jubilate Hymns†

1 Joy to the world – the Lord has come!
   let earth receive her king,
   let every heart prepare him room
      and heaven and nature sing,
      and heaven and nature sing,
      and heaven, and heaven and nature sing!

2 Joy to the earth – the saviour reigns!
   let songs be heard on high,
   while fields and streams and hills and plains
      repeat the sounding joy,
      repeat the sounding joy,
      repeat, repeat the sounding joy.

3 No more let sins and sorrows grow
   nor thorns infest the ground:
   he comes to make his blessings flow
      wherever guilt is found,
      wherever guilt is found,
      wherever, ever, guilt is found.

4 He rules the world with truth and grace,
   and makes the nations prove
   the glories of his righteousness,
      the wonders of his love,
      the wonders of his love,
      the wonders, wonders of his love.

198 from Isaiah 35
         © Michael Perry†

1 Let the desert sing
      and the wasteland flower,
   for the glory of God
      in its light and power
   shall be seen on the hills
      where he comes to save!

2 Then the blind shall see
      and the deaf shall hear
   and the lame shall leap
      like the fallow deer
   and the voice of the dumb
      shall shout aloud.

3 When the ransomed walk
      with their Lord that day
   on the perfect road
      called the Sacred Way,
   every tear shall give place
      to a song of joy!

199 after P. Nicolai
         © Christopher Idle†

1 Wake, O wake, and sleep no longer,
   for he who calls you is no stranger:
   awake, God's own Jerusalem!
   Hear, the midnight bells are chiming
   the signal for his royal coming:
   let voice to voice announce his name!
      We feel his footstep near,
      the Bridegroom at the door –
      Alleluia!
      The lamps will shine
      with light divine
   as Christ the saviour comes to reign.

2 Zion hears the sound of singing;
   her heart is thrilled with sudden longing:
   she stirs, and wakes, and stands prepared.
   Christ her friend, and lord, and lover,
   her star and sun and strong redeemer –
   at last his mighty voice is heard.
      The Son of God has come
      to make with us his home:
      sing Hosanna!
      The fight is won,
      the feast begun;
   we fix our eyes on Christ alone.

3 Glory, glory, sing the angels,
   while music sounds from strings and cymbals;
   all humankind, with songs arise!
   Twelve the gates into the city,
   each one a pearl of shining beauty;
   the streets of gold ring out with praise.
      All creatures round the throne
      adore the holy One
      with rejoicing:
      Amen be sung
      by every tongue
   to crown their welcome to the King.

200 from Isaiah 35
         © Christopher Idle†

1 When the King shall come again
   all his power revealing,
   splendour shall announce his reign,
   life and joy and healing:
   earth no longer in decay,
   hope no more frustrated;
   this is God's redemption day
   longingly awaited.

2 In the desert trees take root
fresh from his creation;
plants and flowers and sweetest fruit
join the celebration:
rivers spring up from the earth,
barren lands adorning;
valleys, this is your new birth,
mountains, greet the morning!

3 Strengthen feeble hands and knees,
fainting hearts, be cheerful!
God who comes for such as these
seeks and saves the fearful:
now the deaf can hear the dumb
sing away their weeping;
blind eyes see the injured come
walking, running, leaping.

4 There God's highway shall be seen
where no roaring lion,
nothing evil or unclean
walks the road to Zion:
ransomed people homeward bound
all your praises voicing,
see your Lord with glory crowned,
share in his rejoicing!

201 © Timothy Dudley-Smith

1 When the Lord in glory comes,
not the trumpets, not the drums,
not the anthem, not the psalm,
not the thunder, not the calm,
not the shout the heavens raise,
not the chorus, not the praise,
not the silences sublime,
not the sounds of space and time,
but his voice when he appears
shall be music to my ears;
    but his voice when he appears
    shall be music to my ears.

2 When the Lord is seen again,
not the glories of his reign,
not the lightnings through the storm,
not the radiance of his form,
not his pomp and power alone,
not the splendours of his throne,
not his robe and diadems,
not the gold and not the gems,
but his face upon my sight
shall be darkness into light;
    but his face upon my sight
    shall be darkness into light.

3 When the Lord to human eyes
shall bestride our narrow skies,
not the child of humble birth,
not the carpenter of earth,
not the man by all denied,
not the victim crucified,
but the God who died to save,
but the victor of the grave,
he it is to whom I fall,
Jesus Christ, my all in all;
    he it is to whom I fall,
    Jesus Christ, my all in all.

202 Frances R. Havergal
© in this version Jubilate Hymns†

1 You are coming, O my Saviour,
you are coming, O my King,
in your beauty all-resplendent,
in your glory all-transcendent –
well may we rejoice and sing:
coming! – in the opening east
brighter shines your heavenly light;
coming! – O my glorious Priest:
come in all your power and might!

2 You are coming, great Redeemer,
we shall meet you on your way;
we shall see you, we shall know you,
we shall bless you, we shall show you
all our hearts could never say:
there, enraptured by the view,
hearts and voices we will raise,
pouring out our love to you
in thanksgiving, worship, praise.

3 You are coming – at your table
we are witnesses for this;
with your love and grace you greet us,
in communion, Lord, you meet us –
foretaste of our coming bliss:
showing not your death alone,
and your love so rich and great,
but your coming and your throne,
all for which we long and wait.

4 O the joy to see you reigning,
you, my own belovèd Lord;
every tongue your name confessing –
worship, honour, glory, blessing
brought to you with one accord:
you, my Master and my Friend,
vindicated and renowned;
to the earth's remotest end
glorified, adored and crowned!

203 after E. Perronet and J. Rippon, © Jubilee Hymns†
(see also traditional version, 587)

1 All hail the power of Jesus' name!
let kings before him fall,
his power and majesty proclaim
and crown him Lord of all.

2 Come, crown him, moon and stars of night;
he made you, great and small:
bright sun, praise him who gave you light
and crown him Lord of all.

3 Crown him, you martyrs spurning pain,
who witnessed to his call;
now sing your victory-song again
and crown him Lord of all.

4 Let all who trust in Christ exclaim
in wonder, to recall
the one who bore our sin and shame,
and crown him Lord of all.

5 Then in that final judgement hour
when all rebellions fall,
we'll rise in his triumphant power
and crown him Lord of all.

204 from *The Song of Christ's Glory* (Philippians 2)
F. Bland Tucker and Jubilee Hymns
© The Church Pension Fund.

1 All praise to Christ, our Lord and king divine,
yielding your glory in your love's design,
that in our darkened hearts
    your grace might shine:
Alleluia!

2 You came to us in lowliness of thought;
by you the outcast and the poor were sought,
and by your death was our redemption
    bought:
Alleluia!

3 The mind of Christ is as our mind should be –
he was a servant, that we might be free;
humbling himself to death on Calvary:
Alleluia!

4 And so we see in God's great purpose, now
Christ has been raised above all creatures
    now;
and at his name shall every nation bow:
Alleluia!

5 Let every tongue confess with one accord,
in heaven and earth, that Jesus Christ is Lord,
and God the Father be by all adored:
Alleluia! (Amen.)

205 J. Hupton and J. M. Neale
© in this version Jubilee Hymns†

1 Alleluia! raise the anthem,
let the skies resound with praise;
sing to Christ who brought salvation,
wonderful his works and ways:
God eternal, Word incarnate,
whom the heaven of heavens obeys.

2 Long before he formed the mountains,
spread the seas or made the sky,
love eternal, free and boundless,
moved the Lord of life to die;
fore-ordained the Prince of princes
for the throne of Calvary.

3 There for us and our redemption
see him all his life-blood pour:
there he wins our full salvation,
dies that we may die no more –
then arising lives for ever,
King of kings, whom we adore.

4 Praise and honour to the Father,
praise and honour to the Son,
praise and honour to the Spirit,
ever Three and ever One:
one in grace and one in glory
while eternal ages run!

206 I. Watts

1 Come let us join our cheerful songs
with angels round the throne;
ten thousand thousand are their tongues,
but all their joys are one.

2 Worthy the Lamb who died, they cry,
to be exalted thus!
Worthy the Lamb, our lips reply,
for he was slain for us!

3 Jesus is worthy to receive
all praise and power divine;
and all the blessings we can give
with songs of heaven combine

4 Let all who live beyond the sky,
the air and earth and seas
unite to lift his glory high
and sing his endless praise!

5 Let all creation join in one
to bless the sacred name
of him who reigns upon the throne,
and to adore the Lamb!

207 © Frank Allred
and Michael Saward†

1 Come, let us worship the Christ of creation!
he set the numberless stars in their flight,
guiding the planets in accurate orbit:
King of the universe, rule us in might!

2 He is the image, the clear revelation;
in him there glows all the glory divine,
radiant in splendour, dispersing the shadows:
Light of the world, in our hearts ever shine!

3 He is our brother, the true incarnation;
unknown to many, disowned by his race;
he was forsaken, despised and rejected:
suffering Servant, we share your disgrace.

4 He is our saviour, our hope of redemption;
he won our freedom, the victim who died;
spotless and perfect,
        his life-blood he yielded:
Lamb of atonement, dispel all our pride!

5 He is our victor in whose resurrection
death is defeated, that we may receive
life for eternity, hope and forgiveness:
Lord of the grave, help us now to believe!

6 He is the giver who, since his ascension,
comes by his Spirit with gifts from above;
fills and renews us and gives us his kingdom:
Jesus, we long for the fruits of your love.

7 He is our monarch, enthroned in the heavens,
coming in triumph; yes, coming again!
Sin will be banished and we shall be with him:
come, then, in majesty! –
        come, Lord, and reign!

208 J. C. Winslow
© Mrs. J. Tyrrell

1 Come sing the praise of Jesus,
sing his love with hearts aflame,
sing his wondrous birth of Mary,
when to save the world he came;
tell the life he lived for others,
and his mighty deeds proclaim,
for Jesus Christ is king.
    Praise and glory be to Jesus,
    praise and glory be to Jesus,
    praise and glory be to Jesus,
    for Jesus Christ is king!

2 When foes arose and slew him,
he was victor in the fight;
over death and hell he triumphed
in his resurrection-might;
he has raised our fallen manhood
and enthroned it in the height,
for Jesus Christ is king.
    Praise and glory be to Jesus . . .

3 There's joy for all who serve him,
more than human tongue can say;
there is pardon for the sinner,
and the night is turned to day;
there is healing for our sorrows,
there is music all the way,
for Jesus Christ is king.
    Praise and glory be to Jesus . . .

4 We witness to his beauty,
and we spread his love abroad;
and we cleave the hosts of darkness,
with the Spirit's piercing sword;
we will lead the souls in prison
to the freedom of the Lord,
for Jesus Christ is king.
    Praise and glory be to Jesus . . .

5 To Jesus be the glory,
the dominion, and the praise;
he is Lord of all creation,
he is guide of all our ways;
and the world shall be his empire
in the fulness of the days,
for Jesus Christ is king.
    Praise and glory be to Jesus . . .

209 from the German, Lilian Stevenson
© Oxford University Press
and in this version Jubilate Hymns

1 Fairest Lord Jesus,
Lord of all creation,
Jesus, of God and man the Son;
you will I cherish,
you will I honour,
you are my soul's delight and crown.

2 Fair are the rivers,
meadows and forests
clothed in the fresh green robes of spring;
Jesus is fairer,
Jesus is purer,
he makes the saddest heart to sing.

3 Fair is the sunrise,
starlight and moonlight
spreading their glory across the sky;
Jesus shines brighter,
Jesus shines clearer,
than all the heavenly host on high.

4 All fairest beauty,
heavenly and earthly,
Jesus, my Lord, in you I see;
none can be nearer,
fairer or dearer,
than you, my Saviour, are to me.

210
P. Brennan
© Search Press

1 Hail Redeemer! king divine,
priest and Lamb, by God's design;
king whose reign shall never cease,
prince of everlasting peace:
  Angels, saints and nations sing,
  'Praise to Jesus Christ our king,
  Lord of earth and sky and sea,
  king of love on Calvary!'

2 King whose name creation thrills,
rule our minds, our hearts and wills,
till in peace each nation rings
with your praises, King of kings:
  Angels, saints and nations . . .

3 King most holy, king of truth,
guide the lowly, guide the youth;
Christ, the king of glory bright,
be to us eternal light:
  Angels, saints and nations . . .

211
J. Newton

1 How sweet the name of Jesus sounds
in a believer's ear!
it soothes our sorrows, heals our wounds
and drives away our fear.

2 It makes the wounded spirit whole,
and calms the troubled breast;
it satisfies the hungry soul,
and gives the weary rest.

3 Dear name, the rock on which I build,
my shield and hiding-place;
my never-failing treasury, filled
with boundless stores of grace!

4 Jesus, my shepherd, brother, friend,
my prophet, priest and king;
my Lord, my life, my way, my end –
accept the praise I bring.

5 Weak is the effort of my heart,
and cold my warmest thought;
but when I see you as you are,
I'll praise you as I ought.

6 Till then I would your love proclaim
with every fleeting breath;
and may the music of your name
refresh my soul in death.

212
F. H. Rowley
© Marshall, Morgan and Scott Ltd

1 I will sing the wondrous story
of the Christ who died for me;
how he left the realms of glory
for the cross of Calvary:
  Yes, I'll sing the wondrous story
  of the Christ who died for me,
  sing it with his saints in glory
  gathered by the crystal sea.

2 I was lost, but Jesus found me,
found the sheep that went astray;
raised me up and gently led me
back into the narrow way:
  Yes, I'll sing . . .

3 I was faint and fears possessed me,
I was bruised from many a fall;
hope was gone, and shame distressed me,
but his love has pardoned all:
  Yes, I'll sing . . .

4 Days of darkness still may meet me,
sorrow's path I often tread;
but his presence still is with me,
by his guiding hand I'm led:
  Yes, I'll sing . . .

5 He will keep me till the river
rolls its waters at my feet;
then at last he'll bring me over
saved by grace and made complete.
  Yes, I'll sing . . .

213
C. Wesley

1 Jesus! the name high over all
in hell or earth or sky;
angels again before it fall
  and devils fear and fly,
  and devils fear and fly.

2 Jesus! the name to sinners dear,
the name to sinners given;
it scatters all their guilty fear,
  it turns their hell to heaven,
  it turns their hell to heaven.

3 Jesus the prisoner's fetters breaks
and bruises Satan's head;
power into strengthless souls he speaks
  and life into the dead,
  and life into the dead.

4 O that the world might taste and see
the riches of his grace!
the arms of love that welcome me
  would all mankind embrace,
  would all mankind embrace.

5 His righteousness alone I show,
   his saving grace proclaim;
   this is my work on earth below,
      to cry 'Behold the Lamb!'
      to cry 'Behold the Lamb!'

6 Happy if with my final breath
   I may but gasp his name,
   preach him to all, and cry in death,
      'Christ Jesus is the Lamb!'
      'Christ Jesus is the Lamb!'

214 I. Watts

1 Join all the glorious names
   of wisdom, love and power,
   that ever mortals knew,
   that angels ever bore;
   all are too poor to speak his worth,
   too poor to set my Saviour forth!

2 Great Prophet of my God,
   my tongue shall bless your name:
   by you the joyful news
   of our salvation came;
   the joyful news of sins forgiven,
   of hell subdued and peace with heaven.

3 Jesus, my great High Priest,
   the Lamb of God who died!
   my guilty conscience seeks
   no sacrifice beside;
   the power of your atoning blood
   has won acceptance with my God.

4 Divine almighty Lord,
   my Conqueror and my King:
   your sceptre and your sword,
   your reigning grace I sing;
   yours is the power – and so I sit
   in willing service at your feet.

5 Now let my soul arise,
   and tread the tempter down;
   my Captain leads me on
   to conquest and a crown;
   the child of God shall win the day,
   though death and hell obstruct the way.

215 J. Newton

1 Let us love and sing and wonder;
   let us praise the saviour's name!
   he has hushed the law's loud thunder;
   he has quenched Mount Sinai's flame:
   he has freed us by his blood;
   he has brought us near to God.

2 Let us love the Lord who bought us,
   dying for our rebel race;
   called us by his word and taught us
   by the Spirit of his grace:
   he has freed us by his blood;
   he presents our souls to God.

3 Let us sing, though fierce temptation
   threatens hard to drag us down;
   for the Lord, our strong salvation,
   holds in view the conqueror's crown:
   he who freed us by his blood,
   soon will bring us home to God.

4 Let us praise, and join the chorus
   of the saints enthroned on high;
   here they trusted him before us –
   now their praises fill the sky:
   'You have freed us by your blood,
   you are worthy, Lamb of God!'

216 © Timothy Dudley-Smith

1 Saviour Christ,
   in praise we name him;
   all his deeds
   proclaim him:

2 Lamb of God
   for sinners dying;
   all our need
   supplying:

3 Risen Lord
   in glory seated;
   all his work
   completed:

4 King of kings
   ascended, reigning;
   all the world
   sustaining:

5 Christ is all!
   Rejoice before him:
   evermore
   adore him!

   Evermore . . .

217 C. Wesley

1 Love divine, all loves excelling,
   joy of heaven, to earth come down:
   fix in us your humble dwelling,
   all your faithful mercies crown.

2 Jesus, you are all compassion,
   boundless love that makes us whole:
   visit us with your salvation,
   enter every trembling soul.

3 Come, almighty to deliver,
  let us all your grace receive;
  suddenly return, and never,
  never more your temple leave.

4 You we would be always blessing,
  serve you as your hosts above,
  pray, and praise you without ceasing,
  glory in your perfect love.

5 Finish then your new creation:
  pure and sinless let us be;
  let us see your great salvation,
  perfect in eternity:

6 Changed from glory into glory
  till in heaven we take our place,
  there to cast our crowns before you,
  lost in wonder, love and praise!

218 © Timothy Dudley-Smith

1 Name of all majesty,
  fathomless mystery,
  king of the ages
  by angels adored;
      power and authority,
      splendour and dignity,
      bow to his mastery –
  Jesus is Lord!

2 Child of our destiny,
  God from eternity,
  love of the Father
  on sinners outpoured;
      see now what God has done
      sending his only Son,
      Christ the beloved One –
  Jesus is Lord!

3 Saviour of Calvary,
  costliest victory,
  darkness defeated
  and Eden restored;
      born as a man to die,
      nailed to a cross on high,
      cold in the grave to lie
  Jesus is Lord!

4 Source of all sovereignty,
  light, immortality,
  life everlasting
  and heaven assured;
      so with the ransomed, we
      praise him eternally,
      Christ in his majesty –
  Jesus is Lord!

219 C. Wesley

1 O for a thousand tongues to sing
  my great redeemer's praise,
  the glories of my God and king,
  the triumphs of his grace!

2 Jesus, the name that charms our fears
  and bids our sorrows cease;
  this music in the sinner's ears
  is life and health and peace.

3 He breaks the power of cancelled sin,
  he sets the prisoner free;
  his blood can make the foulest clean,
  his blood availed for me.

4 He speaks – and, listening to his voice,
  new life the dead receive,
  the mournful broken hearts rejoice,
  the humble poor believe.

5 Hear him, you deaf! his praise, you dumb,
  your loosened tongues employ;
  you blind, now see your saviour come,
  and leap, you lame, for joy!

6 My gracious Master and my God,
  assist me to proclaim
  and spread through all the earth abroad
  the honours of your name.

220 from Colossians 1
© Timothy Dudley-Smith

1 Praise be to Christ in whom we see
  the image of the Father shown,
  the first-born Son revealed and known,
  the truth and grace of deity;
  through whom creation came to birth,
  whose fingers set the stars in place,
  the unseen powers, and this small earth,
  the furthest bounds of time and space.

2 Praise be to him whose sovereign sway
  and will upholds creation's plan;
  who is, before all worlds began
  and when our world has passed away:
  Lord of the church, its life and head,
  redemption's price and source and theme,
  alive, the first-born from the dead,
  to reign as all-in-all supreme.

3 Praise be to him who, Lord most high,
  the fulness of the Godhead shares;
  and yet our human nature bears,
  who came as man to bleed and die:
  and from his cross there flows our peace
  who chose for us the path he trod,
  that so might sins and sorrows cease
  and all be reconciled to God.

221 from Hebrews 1
© Michael Perry†

1 The brightness of God's glory
    and the image of his being,
the heir of richest majesty,
    the arm of regal might;
creator of the universe
    all-knowing and all-seeing
is Christ who brings forgiveness
    and the lifting of our night.

2 Far greater than the angels
    is the author of salvation,
begotten of his Father's love
    before all time began;
our offering of righteousness,
    our refuge from temptation,
one hope in all our sufferings
    is Christ, the Son of Man.

3 How awesome is his perfect life
    unending and unbroken,
how faultless are his judgements
    and how faithful is his word!
Then hear, repent and worship him,
    obey, for God has spoken,
receive his Holy Spirit
    and acknowledge him as Lord!

222 from the Latin, J. M. Neale
© in this version Jubilate Hymns†

1 To the name of our salvation
honour, worship, let us pay;
which for many a generation
deep in God's foreknowledge lay:
saints of every race and nation
sing aloud that name today.

2 Jesus is the name we treasure
more than words can ever tell;
name of grace beyond all measure,
ear and heart delighting well:
this our refuge and our treasure
conquering sin and death and hell.

3 Highest name for adoration,
strongest name of victory,
sweetest name for meditation
in our pain and misery:
name for greatest veneration
by the citizens on high.

4 Name of love, whoever preaches
speaks like music to the ear;
who in prayer this name beseeches
finds its comfort ever near:
who its perfect wisdom reaches
heavenly joy possesses here.

5 Jesus! – name of all our praising
in this world to which you came;
here we sing of love amazing,
and your saving power proclaim;
hearts and voices heavenward raising,
all our hope is in your name!

223 from the German, E. Caswall
© in this version Jubilate Hymns†

1 When morning gilds the skies,
my heart awakening cries:
    May Jesus Christ be praised;
alike at work and prayer
I know my Lord is there:
    may Jesus Christ be praised!

2 When sadness fills my mind
my strength in him I find:
    may Jesus Christ be praised;
when earthly hopes grow dim
my comfort is in him:
    may Jesus Christ be praised!

3 The night becomes as day
when from the heart we say:
    May Jesus Christ be praised;
the powers of darkness fear
when this glad song they hear:
    May Jesus Christ be praised!

4 Be this, while life is mine,
my canticle divine:
    May Jesus Christ be praised;
be this the eternal song
through all the ages long:
    May Jesus Christ be praised!

224 C. Wesley

1 Away with our fears,
our troubles and tears:
the Spirit is come,
the witness of Jesus returned to his home.

2 Our advocate there
by his death and his prayer
the gift has obtained,
for us he has prayed,
    and the Comforter gained.

3 Our glorified Lord
has given his word
that his Spirit will stay,
and never again will be taken away.

4 Our heavenly guide
with us shall abide,
his comforts impart,
and set up his kingdom of love in our heart.

5 The heart that believes
his kingdom receives,
his power and his peace,
his life, and his joy's everlasting increase.

225
from Romans 8
© Timothy Dudley-Smith

1 Born by the Holy Spirit's breath,
loosed from the law of sin and death,
now cleared in Christ from every claim
no judgement stands against our name.

2 In us the Spirit makes his home
that we in him may overcome;
Christ's risen life, in all its powers,
its all-prevailing strength, is ours.

3 Children and heirs of God most high,
we by his Spirit 'Father' cry;
that Spirit with our spirit shares
to frame and breathe our wordless prayers.

4 One is his love, his purpose one:
to form the likeness of his Son
in all who, called and justified,
shall reign in glory at his side.

5 Nor death nor life, nor powers unseen,
nor height nor depth can come between;
we know through peril, pain and sword,
the love of God in Christ our Lord.

226
E. Hatch
© in this version Jubilate Hymns†

1 Breathe on me, breath of God:
fill me with life anew,
that as you love, so I may love,
and do what you would do.

2 Breathe on me, breath of God,
until my heart is pure,
until my will is one with yours
to do and to endure.

3 Breathe on me, breath of God;
fulfil my heart's desire,
until this earthly part of me
glows with your heavenly fire.

4 Breathe on me, breath of God;
so shall I never die,
but live with you the perfect life
of your eternity.

227
after S. Langton and E. Caswall
© in this version Jubilate Hymns†

1 Come, most Holy Spirit, come!
and from your celestial home
shed a ray of light divine;
come, O Father of the poor,
faithful advocate and sure,
let your radiance in us shine.

2 Heal our wounds, our strength renew;
on our dryness send your dew,
wash the stains of guilt away;
bend the stubborn heart and will,
melt the frozen, warm the chill,
guide the steps that go astray.

3 Send upon us from above
fruits of joy and peace and love,
gentleness, humility:
faithfulness and self-control,
goodness, kindness fill the soul –
give us true nobility.

4 On the faithful, who adore
and confess you, evermore
in your grace and power descend;
grant your kingdom's sure reward,
grant us your salvation, Lord,
grant us joys that never end.

228
© David Mowbray†

1 Christ on whom the Spirit rested
lived as one who cared for all;
by the watching crowds attested:
'This man has done all things well!'
God's own grace
on his face
blessing us with heavenly peace.

2 Swift the promised Spirit filled them:
rushing wind and tongues of flame;
now the master's presence thrilled them,
made them bold to preach his name,
bringing light,
day and night,
helping them to judge aright.

3 True and living God, your Spirit
brought creation to its birth;
with your help the meek inherit
all the treasures of the earth:
all things new
flow from you,
pure and beautiful and true.

4 Spirit of the Son and Father,
come to us with power today!
every life in fulness enter,
all your gifts in us set free:
all our days
let us raise
songs of gratitude and praise!

229 © John Bowers

Christians, lift up your hearts,
and make this a day of rejoicing;
God is our strength and song –
glory and praise to his name!

1 Praise for the Spirit of God,
who came to the waiting disciples;
there in the wind and the fire
God gave new life to his own:
Christians, lift up your hearts . . .

2 God's mighty power was revealed
when those who once were so fearful
now could be seen by the world
witnessing bravely for Christ:
Christians, lift up your hearts . . .

3 Praise that his love overflowed
in the hearts of all who received him,
joining together in peace
those once divided by sin:
Christians, lift up your hearts . . .

4 Strengthened by God's mighty power
the disciples went out to all nations,
preaching the gospel of Christ,
laughing at danger and death:
Christians, lift up your hearts . . .

5 Come, Holy Spirit, to us,
who live by your presence within us,
come to direct our course,
give us your life and your power:
Christians, lift up your hearts . . .

6 Spirit of God, send us out
to live to your praise and your glory;
yours is the power and the might,
ours be the courage and faith:
Christians, lift up your hearts . . .

230 F. Pratt Green
© Stainer & Bell Ltd

1 Let every Christian pray,
this day, and every day:
Come, Holy Spirit, come!
Was not the Church we love
commissioned from above?
Come, Holy Spirit, come!

2 The Spirit brought to birth
the church of Christ on earth
to seek and save the lost:
never has he withdrawn,
since that tremendous dawn,
his gifts at Pentecost.

3 Age after age, he strove
to teach her how to love:
Come, Holy Spirit, come;
age after age, anew
she proved the gospel true:
Come, Holy Spirit, come!

4 Only the Spirit's power
can fit us for this hour:
Come, Holy Spirit, come;
instruct, inspire, unite,
and make us see the light:
Come, Holy Spirit, come!

231 after Bianco da Siena, R. F. Littledale
© in this version Jubilate Hymns†

1 Come down, O Love divine!
seek out this soul of mine
and visit it with your own ardour glowing;
O Comforter, draw near,
within my heart appear,
and kindle it, your holy flame bestowing.

2 O let it freely burn
till earthly passions turn
to dust and ashes in its heat consuming;
and let your glorious light
shine ever on my sight,
and make my pathway clear,
by your illuming.

3 Let holy charity
my outward vesture be,
and lowliness become my inner clothing;
true lowliness of heart
which takes the humbler part,
and for its own shortcomings
weeps with loathing.

4 And so the yearning strong
with which the soul will long
shall far surpass the power of human telling;
for none can guess its grace
till we become the place
in which the Holy Spirit makes his dwelling.

232
after R. Maurus and J. Cosin
© in this version Jubilate Hymns†
(see also traditional version, 589)

1 Creator Spirit, come, inspire
  our lives with light and heavenly fire;
  now make us willing to receive
  the sevenfold gifts you freely give.

2 Your pure anointing from above
  is comfort, life, and fire of love:
  so heal with your eternal light
  the blindness of our human sight.

3 Anoint and cheer our saddened face
  with all the fulness of your grace;
  remove our fears, give peace at home –
  where you are guide, no harm can come.

4 Teach us to know the Father, Son,
  and you with them the Three-in-One;
  that through the ages all along
  this shall be our endless song:
      Praise to your eternal merit,
      Father, Son, and Holy Spirit. Amen.

233 J. R. Peacey
© Mrs. M. E. Peacey

1 Filled with the Spirit's power, with one accord
  the infant church confessed its risen Lord:
  O Holy Spirit, in the church today
  no less your power of fellowship display.

2 Now with the mind of Christ set us on fire,
  that unity may be our great desire;
  give joy and peace,
      give faith to hear your call,
  and readiness in each to work for all.

3 Widen our love, good Spirit, to embrace
  the people of all lands and every race;
  like wind and fire with life among us move,
  till we are known as Christ's,
      and Christians prove.

234 © Michael Saward†

1 Fire of God, titanic Spirit,
  burn within our hearts today;
  cleanse our sin – may we exhibit
  holiness in every way:
  purge the squalidness that shames us,
  soils the body, taints the soul;
  and through Jesus Christ who claims us,
  purify us, make us whole.

2 Wind of God, dynamic Spirit,
  breathe upon our hearts today;
  that we may your power inherit
  hear us, Spirit, as we pray:
  fill the vacuum that enslaves us –
  emptiness of heart and soul;
  and, through Jesus Christ who saves us,
  give us life and make us whole.

3 Voice of God, prophetic Spirit,
  speak to every heart today
  to encourage or prohibit,
  urging action or delay:
  clear the vagueness which impedes us –
  come, enlighten mind and soul;
  and, through Jesus Christ who leads us,
  teach the truth that makes us whole.

235 S. Longfellow

1 Holy Spirit, truth divine,
  dawn upon this soul of mine:
  voice of God, and inward light,
  wake my spirit, clear my sight.

2 Holy Spirit, love divine,
  glow within this heart of mine:
  kindle every high desire,
  purify me with your fire.

3 Holy Spirit, power divine,
  fill and nerve this will of mine:
  boldly may I always live,
  bravely serve and gladly give.

4 Holy Spirit, law divine,
  reign within this soul of mine:
  be my law, and I shall be
  firmly bound, for ever free.

5 Holy Spirit, peace divine,
  still this restless heart of mine:
  speak to calm this tossing sea,
  grant me your tranquillity.

6 Holy Spirit, joy divine,
  gladden now this heart of mine:
  in the desert ways I sing –
  spring, O living water, spring!

236 © Paul Wigmore†

1 May we, O Holy Spirit, bear your fruit –
  your joy and peace
      pervade each word we say;
  may love become of life the very root,
  and grow more deep and strong
      with every day.

2 May patience stem the harmful word
    and deed,
and kindness seek the good
    among the wrong;
may goodness far beyond our lips proceed,
as manifest in action as in song.

3 May faithfulness endure, yet as we grow
may gentleness lend courage to the weak;
and in our self-restraint help us to know
    the grace
        that made the King of Heaven meek.

237   Elizabeth A. P. Head

1 O Breath of life, come sweeping through us,
revive your church with life and power;
O Breath of life, come, cleanse, renew us
and fit your church to meet this hour.

2 O Breath of love, come breathe within us,
renewing thought and will and heart;
come, love of Christ, afresh to win us,
revive your church in every part!

3 O Wind of God, come bend us, break us
till humbly we confess our need;
then, in your tenderness remake us,
revive, restore – for this we plead.

238   H. W. Baker
       © in this version Jubilate Hymns†

1 O Holy Spirit, come to bless
your waiting church, we pray:
we long to grow in holiness
as children of the day.

2 Great Gift of our ascended king,
his saving truth reveal,
our tongues inspire his praise to sing,
our hearts his love to feel.

3 O come, creator Spirit, move
as on the formless deep;
give life and order, light and love,
where now is death or sleep.

4 We offer up to you, O Lord,
ourselves to be your throne,
our every thought and deed and word
to make your glory known.

5 O Holy Spirit, Lord of might,
through you all grace is given:
grant us to know and serve aright
one God in earth and heaven.

239   © Michael Saward†

1 O Holy Spirit, giver of life,
you bring our souls immortality;
yet in our hearts are struggle and strife –
we need your inward vitality:
    work out within us the Father's design,
    give to us life, O Spirit divine.

2 O Holy Spirit, giver of light
to minds where all is obscurity;
exchange for blindness, spiritual sight,
that we may grow to maturity:
    work out . . .

3 O Holy Spirit, giver of love,
and joy and peace and fidelity,
the fruitfulness which comes from above –
that self-control and humility:
    work out . . .

240   A. Reed
       © in this version Jubilate Hymns†

1 Spirit divine, inspire our prayers,
and make our hearts your home;
descend with all your gracious powers –
O come, great Spirit, come!

2 Come as the light – reveal our need,
our hidden failings show,
and lead us in those paths of life
in which the righteous go.

3 Come as the fire, and cleanse our hearts
with purifying flame;
let our whole life an offering be
to our redeemer's name.

4 Come as the dew, and gently bless
this consecrated hour;
may barren souls rejoice to know
your life-creating power.

5 Come as the dove, and spread your wings,
the wings of peaceful love,
and let your church on earth become
blessed as the church above.

6 Come as the wind, with rushing sound
and pentecostal grace,
that all the world with joy may see
the glory of your face.

241
Henriette Auber
© in this version Jubilate Hymns†

1 Our great Redeemer, as he breathed
his tender last farewell,
a guide, a comforter, bequeathed
with us to dwell.

2 He came in tongues of living flame
to teach, convince, subdue;
unseen as rushing wind he came –
as powerful too.

3 He comes sweet influence to impart –
a gracious, willing guest;
when he can find one humble heart
where he may rest.

4 And every virtue we possess,
and every victory won,
and every thought of holiness
are his alone.

5 Spirit of purity and grace,
our failing strength renew;
and make our hearts a worthier place
to welcome you.

242
© David Mowbray†

1 Spirit of God most high,
Lord of all power and might;
source of our Easter joy,
well-spring of life and light:
strip from the church its cloak of pride,
a stumbling-block to those outside.

2 Wind of God's Spirit, blow!
into the valley sweep,
bringing dry bones to life,
wakening each from sleep:
speak to the church your firm command,
and bid a scattered army stand.

3 Fire of God's Spirit, melt
every unbending heart;
your people's love renew
as at their journey's start;
your reconciling grace release
to bring the Christian family peace.

4 Spirit of Christ our Lord,
send us to do your will;
nothing need hold us back
for you are with us still:
forgetful of ourselves, may we
receive your gift of unity!

243
© Timothy Dudley-Smith

1 Spirit of God within me,
possess my human frame;
fan the dull embers of my heart,
stir up the living flame:
strive till that image Adam lost,
new minted and restored,
in shining splendour brightly bears
the likeness of the Lord.

2 Spirit of truth within me,
possess my thought and mind;
lighten anew the inward eye
by Satan rendered blind:
shine on the words that wisdom speaks
and grant me power to see
the truth made known to all in Christ,
and in that truth be free.

3 Spirit of love within me,
possess my hands and heart;
break through the bonds of self-concern
that seeks to stand apart:
grant me the love that suffers long,
that hopes, believes and bears;
the love fulfilled in sacrifice,
that cares as Jesus cares.

4 Spirit of life within me,
possess this life of mine;
come as the wind of heaven's breath,
come as the fire divine!
Spirit of Christ, the living Lord,
reign in this house of clay,
till from its dust with Christ I rise
to everlasting day.

244
J. E. Seddon
© Mrs. M. Seddon†

1 The Spirit came, as promised,
in God's appointed hour;
and now to each believer
he comes in love and power:
and by his Holy Spirit,
God seals us as his own;
and through the Son and Spirit
makes access to his throne.

2 The Spirit makes our bodies
the temple of the Lord;
he binds us all together
in faith and true accord:
the Spirit in his greatness,
brings power from God above;
and with the Son and Father
dwells in our hearts in love.

3 He bids us live together
   in unity and peace,
   employ his gifts in blessing,
   and let base passions cease:
   we should not grieve the Spirit
   by open sin or shame;
   nor let our words and actions
   deny his holy name.

4 The word, the Spirit's weapon,
   will bring all sin to light;
   and prayer, by his directing,
   will add new joy and might:
   be filled then with his Spirit,
   live out God's will and word;
   rejoice with hymns and singing,
   make music to the Lord!

245 Brian Wren
© Oxford University Press

1 There's a spirit in the air,
   telling Christians everywhere:
   praise the love that Christ revealed,
   living, working, in our world.

2 Lose your shyness, find your tongue,
   tell the world what God has done:
   God in Christ has come to stay;
   we can see his power today.

3 When believers break the bread,
   when a hungry child is fed,
   praise the love that Christ revealed,
   living, working, in our world.

4 Still his Spirit leads the fight,
   seeing wrong and setting right:
   God in Christ has come to stay;
   we can see his power today.

5 When a stranger's not alone,
   where the homeless find a home,
   praise the love that Christ revealed,
   living, working, in our world.

6 May his Spirit fill our praise,
   guide our thoughts and change our ways:
   God in Christ has come to stay;
   we can see his power today.

7 There's a Spirit in the air,
   calling people everywhere:
   praise the love that Christ revealed,
   living, working, in our world.

246 © Christopher Idle†

Spirit of holiness,
wisdom and faithfulness,
wind of the Lord,
blowing strongly and free:
strength of our serving
and joy of our worshipping –
Spirit of God, bring your fulness to me!

1 You came to interpret and teach us effectively
   all that the Saviour has spoken and done;
   to glorify Jesus is all your activity –
   promise and gift of the Father and Son:
   Spirit of holiness . . .

2 You came with your gifts
        to supply all our poverty,
   pouring your love on the church in her need;
   you came with your fruit
        for our growth to maturity,
   richly refreshing the souls that you feed:
   Spirit of holiness . . .

247 Anne Steele

1 Father of mercies, in your word
   what endless glory shines!
   For ever be your name adored
   for these celestial lines.

2 Here may the blind and hungry come
   and light and food receive;
   here shall the humble guest find room
   and taste and see and live.

3 Here the redeemer's welcome voice
   spreads heavenly peace around,
   and life and everlasting joys
   attend the glorious sound.

4 Here springs of consolation rise
   to cheer the fainting mind,
   and thirsty souls receive supplies
   and sweet refreshment find.

5 Divine instructor, gracious Lord,
   be now and always near:
   teach us to love your sacred word
   and view our saviour here.

248
G. W. Briggs, © 1953
by The Hymn Society of America/
Hope Publishing Company

1 God has spoken – by his prophets,
spoken his unchanging word;
each from age to age proclaiming
God the one, the righteous Lord;
in the world's despair and turmoil
one firm anchor still holds fast:
God is king, his throne eternal,
God the first and God the last.

2 God has spoken – by Christ Jesus,
Christ, the everlasting Son;
brightness of the Father's glory,
with the Father ever one:
spoken by the Word incarnate,
Life, before all time began,
light of light, to earth descending,
God, revealed as Son of Man.

3 God is speaking – by his Spirit
speaking to our hearts again;
in the age-long word expounding
God's own message, now as then.
Through the rise and fall of nations
one sure faith is standing fast:
God abides, his word unchanging,
God the first and God the last.

249 © Christopher Idle†

1 How sure the Scriptures are!
God's vital, urgent word,
as true as steel, and far
more sharp than any sword:
    So deep and fine,
    at his control
    they pierce where soul
    and spirit join.

2 They test each human thought,
refining like a fire;
they measure what we ought
to do and to desire:
    For God knows all –
    exposed it lies
    before his eyes
    to whom we call.

3 Let those who hear his voice
confronting them today,
reject the tempting choice
of doubting or delay:
    For God speaks still –
    his word is clear,
    so let us hear
    and do his will!

250 C. Wordsworth

1 Lord, make your word my rule,
in it may I rejoice;
your glory be my aim,
your holy will, my choice:

2 Your promises my hope,
your providence my guard;
your arm my strong support,
yourself my great reward.

251
H. W. Baker
© in this version Jubilate Hymns†

1 Lord your word shall guide us
and with truth provide us:
teach us to receive it
and with joy believe it.

2 When our foes are near us,
then your word shall cheer us –
word of consolation,
message of salvation.

3 When the storms distress us
and dark clouds oppress us,
then your word protects us
and its light directs us.

4 Who can tell the pleasure,
who recount the treasure
by your word imparted
to the simple-hearted?

5 Word of mercy, giving
courage to the living;
word of life, supplying
comfort to the dying.

6 O that we discerning
its most holy learning,
Lord, may love and fear you –
evermore be near you!

252 © Christopher Idle†

1 Powerful in making us wise to salvation,
witness to faith in Christ Jesus the Word;
breathed out for all by the life-giving Father –
these are the scriptures,
    and thus speaks the Lord.

2 Tool for employment and compass for travel,
map in the desert and lamp in the dark;
teaching, rebuking, correcting and training –
these are the scriptures,
    and this is their work.

3 History, prophecy, song and commandment,
gospel and letter and dream from on high;
written by men borne along by the Spirit –
these are the scriptures; on them we rely.

4 Gift for God's servants to fit them completely,
fully equipping to walk in his ways;
guide to good work and effective believing –
these are the scriptures,
for these we give praise!

253
Emily M. Crawford
© in this version Jubilate Hymns†

1 Speak, Lord, in the stillness,
speak your word to me;
help me now to listen
in expectancy.

2 Speak, O gracious Master,
in this quiet hour;
let me see your face, Lord,
feel your touch of power.

3 For the words you give me,
they are life indeed;
living Bread from heaven,
now my spirit feed.

4 Speak, your servant listens –
I await your word;
let me know your presence,
let your voice be heard!

5 Fill me with the knowledge
of your glorious will;
all your own good pleasure
in my life fulfil.

254 I. Watts

1 The heavens declare your glory, Lord!
in every star your wisdom shines;
but when our eyes behold your word,
we read your name in clearer lines.

2 Sun, moon, and stars convey your praise
to all the earth, and never stand;
so when your truth began its race,
it touched and glanced on every land.

3 Nor shall your spreading gospel rest
till through the world your truth has run;
till Christ has all the nations blessed
who see the light or feel the sun.

4 Great Sun of righteousness, arise
and bless the world with heavenly light!
your gospel makes the simple wise,
your laws are pure, your judgements right.

5 Your noblest wonders here we view
in souls renewed and sins forgiven:
Lord, cleanse my sins, my soul renew,
and make your word my guide to heaven.

255
R. T. Brooks
© 1954 by Agape, Carol Stream, IL 60187.

1 Thanks to God whose word was spoken
in the deed that made the earth;
his the voice that called a nation,
his the fires that tried its worth.
God has spoken:
praise him for his open word!

2 Thanks to God whose Word incarnate
heights and depths of life did share;
deeds and words and death and rising
grace in human form declare.
God has spoken:
praise him for his open word!

3 Thanks to God whose word was written
in the Bible's sacred page,
record of the revelation
showing God to every age.
God has spoken:
praise him for his open word!

4 Thanks to God whose word is published
in the tongues of every race;
see its glory undiminished
by the change of time or place.
God has spoken:
praise him for his open word!

5 Thanks to God whose word is answered
by the Spirit's voice within;
here we drink of joy unmeasured,
life redeemed from death and sin.
God is speaking:
praise him for his open word!

256 © Timothy Dudley-Smith

1 Christ be the Lord of all our days,
the swiftly-passing years:
Lord of our unremembered birth,
heirs to the brightness of the earth;
Lord of our griefs and fears.

2 Christ be the source of all our deeds,
the life our living shares;
the fount which flows from worlds above
to never-failing springs of love;
the ground of all our prayers.

3 Christ be the goal of all our hopes,
the end to whom we come;
guide of each pilgrim Christian soul
which seeks, as compass seeks the pole,
our many-mansioned home.

4 Christ be the vision of our lives,
of all we think and are;
to shine upon our spirits' sight
as light of everlasting light –
the bright and morning star.

257
<small>L. Tuttiett</small>
<small>© in this version Jubilate Hymns†</small>

1 Father, let us dedicate
all this year to you,
for the service small or great
you would have us do;
not from any painful thing
freedom can we claim,
but in all, that we may bring
glory to your name.

2 Can a child presume to choose
where or how to live?
can a Father's love refuse
all the best to give?
More you give us every day
than we dare to claim,
and our grateful voices say,
'Glory to your name!'

3 If you call us to a cross
and its shadows come
turning all our gain to loss,
shrouding heart and home,
let us think how your dear Son
to his triumph came,
then through pain and tears pray on,
'Glory to your name!'

4 If in mercy you prepare
joyful years ahead,
if through days serene and fair
peaceful paths we tread;
then, whatever life may bring,
let our lips proclaim
and our glad hearts ever sing,
'Glory to your name!'

258
<small>H. Downton</small>
<small>© in this version Jubilate Hymns†</small>

1 For your mercy and your grace
faithful through another year,
hear our song of thankfulness,
Saviour and Redeemer, hear.

2 All our sins on you we cast,
you, our perfect Sacrifice;
and, forgetting what is past,
press towards our glorious prize.

3 Dark the future – let your light
guide us, bright and morning Star;
fierce the battles we must fight –
arm us, Saviour, for the war!

4 In our weakness and distress,
be our Rock, O Lord, we pray;
in the pathless wilderness,
be our true and living Way.

5 Keep us faithful, keep us pure,
keep us evermore your own;
help, O help us to endure,
make us fit to wear the crown!

259
<small>© David Mowbray†</small>

1 Lord of our growing years,
with us from infancy,
laughter and quick-dried tears,
freshness and energy:
your grace surrounds us all our days –
for all your gifts we bring our praise.

2 Lord of our strongest years,
stretching our youthful powers,
lovers and pioneers
when all the world seems ours:
your grace surrounds us . . .

3 Lord of our middle years,
giver of steadfastness,
courage that perseveres
when there is small success:
your grace surrounds us . . .

4 Lord of our older years,
steep though the road may be,
rid us of foolish fears,
bring us serenity:
your grace surrounds us . . .

5 Lord of our closing years,
always your promise stands;
hold us when death appears,
safely within your hands:
your grace surrounds us . . .

260

T. O. Chisholm, in this version Jubilate Hymns
© 1925 and 1951 Hope Publishing Company

1 Great is your faithfulness, O God my Father,
  you have fulfilled all your promise to me;
  you never fail and your love is unchanging –
  all you have been you for ever will be.
    Great is your faithfulness,
    great is your faithfulness,
    morning by morning new mercies I see;
    all I have needed your hand has provided –
    great is your faithfulness, Father, to me.

2 Summer and winter,
      and springtime and harvest,
  sun, moon and stars in their courses above
  join with all nature in eloquent witness
  to your great faithfulness, mercy and love.
    Great is your faithfulness . . .

3 Pardon for sin, and a peace everlasting,
  your living presence to cheer and to guide;
  strength for today,
      and bright hope for tomorrow –
  these are the blessings your love will provide.
    Great is your faithfulness . . .

261 © David Mowbray†

1 Lord of the changing year,
  patterns and colours bright;
  all that we see and hear,
  sunrise and starlit night:
  the seasons, Lord, in splendour shine,
  your never-failing wise design.

2 Lord of the winter scene,
  hard-frozen ice and snow;
  death where once life has been,
  nothing is seen to grow;
  few creatures roam, few birds will fly
  across the clouded Christmas sky:

3 Lord of unfolding spring,
  promise of life to come;
  nature begins to sing
  where once her tongue was dumb;
  the crocus blooms, the hedgerows wake,
  and Easter day is soon to break:

4 Lord of the summer days,
  spreading and green the trees;
  songthrush lifts high your praise,
  gulls light on deep-blue seas;
  the warmth and welcome of the sun
  brings happiness to everyone:

5 Lord of the autumn gold,
  reaping and harvest home,
  sheep safely in the fold,
  turn of the year has come:
  the seasons, Lord, in splendour shine,
  your never-failing wise design.

262 © Michael Perry†

1 O Christ of all the ages, come!
  we fear to journey on our own;
  without you near we cannot face
  the future months, the years unknown.

2 Afflicted, tempted, tried like us,
  you match our moments of despair;
  with us you watch the desert hours,
  and in our sorrows you are there.

3 O Saviour, fastened to a cross
  by tearing nails – our selfish ways;
  the grieving, caring Lord of love,
  you bear the sins of all our days.

4 Triumphant from the grave you rise –
  the morning breaks upon our sight;
  and with its dawning, future years
  will shine with your unending light.

5 O Christ of all the ages, come!
  the days and months and years go by:
  accept our praise, redeem our lives –
  our strength for all eternity! (Amen.)

263 © Timothy Dudley-Smith

1 O Christ the same,
      through all our story's pages –
  our loves and hopes,
      our failures and our fears;
  eternal Lord, the king of all the ages,
  unchanging still amid the passing years:
  O living Word, the source of all creation,
  who spread the skies and set the stars ablaze;
  O Christ the same,
      who wrought our whole salvation,
  we bring our thanks for all our yesterdays.

2 O Christ the same,
    the friend of sinners, sharing
our inmost thoughts,
    the secrets none can hide;
still as of old upon your body bearing
the marks of love, in triumph glorified:
O Son of Man,
    who stooped for us from heaven –
O Prince of life, in all your saving power;
O Christ the same,
    to whom our hearts are given:
we bring our thanks for this the present hour.

3 O Christ the same,
    secure within whose keeping
our lives and loves,
    our days and years remain;
our work and rest,
    our waking and our sleeping,
our calm and storm,
    our pleasure and our pain:
O Lord of love, for all our joys and sorrows,
for all our hopes,
    when earth shall fade and flee;
O Christ the same,
    beyond our brief tomorrows,
we bring our thanks for all that is to be.

264   T. Ken
© in this version Jubilate Hymns†

Part 1

1 Awake, my soul, and with the sun
your daily stage of duty run;
shake off your sleep, and joyful rise
to make your morning sacrifice.

2 Redeem your mis-spent time that's past
and live this day as if your last;
improve your talent with due care,
for God's great Day yourself prepare.

3 Let all your speaking be sincere,
your conscience as the noonday clear;
think how all-seeing God surveys
your secret thoughts and all your ways.

Part 2

4 Give praise to God, who safely kept
and well refreshed me while I slept:
grant, Lord, that when from death I wake
I may of endless life partake.

5 To you my vows I here renew:
disperse my sins as morning dew;
guard my first springs of thought and will,
and with your love my spirit fill.

6 Direct, control, suggest this day
all I desire or do or say;
that all my powers with all their might
for your sole glory may unite.

Doxology

7 Praise God, from whom all blessings flow
in heaven above and earth below;
one God, three persons, we adore –
to him be praise for evermore!

265   Eleanor Farjeon
© David Higham Associates Ltd

1 Morning has broken like the first morning;
blackbird has spoken like the first bird:
praise for the singing, praise for the morning,
praise for them springing
    fresh from the word!

2 Sweet the rain's new fall, sunlit from heaven,
like the first dew fall on the first grass:
praise for the sweetness of the wet garden,
sprung in completeness where his feet pass.

3 Mine is the sunlight, mine is the morning
born of the one light Eden saw play:
praise with elation, praise every morning,
God's re-creation of the new day!

266   C. Wesley

1 Christ whose glory fills the skies,
Christ the true, the only light;
Sun of righteousness, arise,
triumph over shades of night:
    Dayspring from on high, be near;
    Daystar, in my heart appear!

2 Dark and cheerless is the dawn
till your mercy's beams I see;
joyless is the day's return
till your glories shine on me:
    as they inward light impart,
    cheer my eyes and warm my heart.

3 Visit then this soul of mine,
pierce the gloom of sin and grief;
fill me, radiancy divine,
scatter all my unbelief:
    more and more yourself display,
    shining to the perfect day!

267   from Psalm 5, Brian Foley
© Faber Music Ltd

1 Lord, as I wake I turn to you,
yourself the first thought of my day;
my king, my God, whose help is sure,
yourself the help for which I pray.

2 There is no blessing, Lord, from you
  for those who make their will their way,
  no praise for those who will not praise,
  no peace for those who will not pray.

3 Your loving gifts of grace to me,
  those favours I could never earn,
  call for my thanks in praise and prayer,
  call me to love you in return.

4 Lord, make my life a life of love,
  keep me from sin in all I do;
  Lord, make your law my only law,
  your will my will, for love of you.

268 © Timothy Dudley-Smith

1 Lord, as the day begins
  lift up our hearts in praise;
  take from us all our sins,
  guard us in all our ways:
  our every step direct and guide
  that Christ in all be glorified!

2 Christ be in work and skill,
  serving each other's need;
  Christ be in thought and will,
  Christ be in word and deed:
  our minds be set on things above
  in joy and peace, in faith and love.

3 Grant us the Spirit's strength,
  teach us to walk his way;
  so bring us all at length
  safe to the close of day:
  from hour to hour sustain and bless,
  and let our song be thankfulness.

4 Now as the day begins
  make it the best of days;
  take from us all our sins,
  guard us in all our ways:
  our every step direct and guide
  that Christ in all be glorified!

269 H. W. Baker
© in this version Jubilate Hymns†

1 My Father, for another night
  of quiet sleep and rest;
  for all the joy of morning light,
  your holy name be blessed.

2 Now with the new-born day I give
  myself to you again;
  that gladly I for you may live,
  and you within me reign.

3 In every action, great or small,
  in every thought and aim;
  your glory may I seek in all,
  do all in Jesus' name.

4 My Father, for his sake, I pray,
  your child accept and bless;
  and lead me by your grace today
  in paths of righteousness.

270 J. Keble

1 New every morning is the love
  our waking and uprising prove:
  through sleep and darkness safely brought,
  restored to life and power and thought.

2 New mercies, each returning day,
  surround your people as they pray:
  new dangers past, new sins forgiven,
  new thoughts of God, new hopes of heaven.

3 If in our daily life our mind
  be set to honour all we find,
  new treasures still, of countless price,
  God will provide for sacrifice.

4 The trivial round, the common task,
  will give us all we ought to ask:
  room to deny ourselves, a road
  to bring us daily nearer God.

5 Prepare us, Lord, in your dear love
  for perfect rest with you above,
  and help us, this and every day,
  to grow more like you as we pray.

271 © Michael Perry†

1 We share a new day's dawn with Christ,
  our lives refreshed and hopes restored:
  this is the day to serve our Lord!
  And with this new day's dawn we rise
  and lift our hearts up to the skies.

2 For heaven's grace we turn to prayer,
  for truth and strength we read Christ's word:
  here is the grace to serve our Lord!
  And so by heaven's grace this day
  we'll learn to walk in Jesus' way.

3 Our song shall be of perfect love –
  of Christ's redemption, faith's reward:
  this is love's service to our Lord!
  And perfect love shall be our song
  till all our days to Christ belong.

272 © Michael Saward†

1 Welcome to another day!
   night is blinded:
   'Welcome', let creation say;
   darkness ended.
   Comes the sunshine after dew,
   time for labour;
   time to love my God anew
   and my neighbour.

2 Welcome to the day of prayer
   with God's people;
   welcome is the joy we share
   at his table.
   Bread and wine from heaven fall:
   come, receive it
   that the Christ may reign in all
   who believe it.

3 Welcome is the peace that's given,
   sure for ever;
   welcome is the hope of heaven
   when life's over.
   As we work and as we pray,
   trust God's story:
   come then, as the dawning day
   heralds glory!

273 from the Gelasian and Leonine sacramentaries
© Christopher Idle†

1 Almighty Lord, the holy One
   whose reign in glory we await:
   look down from your eternal throne
   and our dark world illuminate;
   from sons and daughters of the light
   dispel the shameful deeds of night.

2 Defend us from all evil powers;
   our weakness and fatigue replace
   through all the silent sleeping hours
   with sweet refreshing by your grace;
   forgive our sins, our hope renew,
   that we may rest and rise with you.

274 T. Ken
© in this version Jubilate Hymns†

1 Glory to you, my God, this night
   for all the blessings of the light;
   keep me, O keep me, King of kings,
   beneath your own almighty wings.

2 Forgive me, Lord, through your dear Son,
   the wrong that I this day have done,
   that peace with God and man may be,
   before I sleep, restored to me.

3 Teach me to live, that I may dread
   the grave as little as my bed;
   teach me to die, that so I may
   rise glorious at the awesome day.

4 O may my soul on you repose
   and restful sleep my eyelids close;
   sleep that shall me more vigorous make
   to serve my God when I awake.

5 If in the night I sleepless lie,
   my mind with peaceful thoughts supply;
   let no dark dreams disturb my rest,
   no powers of evil me molest.

6 Praise God from whom all blessings flow
   in heaven above and earth below;
   one God, three persons, we adore –
   to him be praise for evermore!

275 from *Phos Hilaron*, J. Keble
© in this version Jubilate Hymns†

1 Hail, gladdening Light,
         of his pure glory poured
   who is the immortal Father,
         heavenly, blessed,
   Holiest of holies, Jesus Christ our Lord.

2 Now we have come to the sun's hour of rest;
   the lights of evening round us shine;
   we hymn the Father, Son,
         and Holy Spirit divine.

3 Worthiest are you at all times to be sung
   with uncorrupted tongue,
   Son of our God, giver of life alone;
   therefore in all the world
   we make your glories known.

276 from the Latin
© in this version Jubilate Hymns†

1 Before the ending of the day,
   Creator of the world, we pray:
   protect us by your mighty grace,
   grant us your mercy and your peace:

2 Bless us in sleep, that we may find
   no terrors to disturb our mind;
   our cunning enemy restrain –
   guard us from sin and all its stain.

3 O Father, may your will be done
   through Jesus Christ your only Son;
   whom with the Spirit we adore,
   one God, both now and evermore.

277
from *Phos Hilaron*
© Christopher Idle†

1 Light of gladness, Lord of glory,
  Jesus Christ our king most holy,
  shine among us in your mercy:
      earth and heaven join their hymn.

2 Let us sing at sun's descending
  as we see the lights of evening,
  Father, Son, and Spirit praising
      with the holy seraphim.

3 Son of God, through all the ages
  worthy of our holiest praises,
  yours the life that never ceases,
      light which never shall grow dim.

278
© Timothy Dudley-Smith

1 Lighten our darkness now the day is ended –
  Father in mercy,
      guard your children sleeping;
  from every evil, every harm defended,
  safe in your keeping:

2 To that last hour,
      when heaven's day is dawning,
  far spent the night
      that knows no earthly waking;
  keep us as watchmen,
      longing for the morning,
  till that day's breaking.

279
W. Romanis
© in this version Jubilate Hymns†

1 Round me falls the night –
  Saviour, be my light:
  through the hours in darkness shrouded
  let me see your face unclouded;
  let your glory shine
  in this heart of mine.

2 When my work is done
  and my rest begun,
  peaceful sleep and silence seeking
  let me hear you softly speaking;
  to my inward ear
  whisper 'I am near.'

3 Holy, heavenly Light,
  shining through earth's night,
  joy and life and inspiration,
  love enfolding every nation:
  be with me tonight,
  Saviour, be my light.

280
J. Ellerton
© in this version Jubilate Hymns†

1 The day you gave us, Lord, is ended,
  the sun is sinking in the west;
  to you our morning hymns ascended,
  your praise shall sanctify our rest.

2 We thank you that your church, unsleeping
  while earth rolls onward into light,
  through all the world her watch is keeping
  and rests not now by day or night.

3 As to each continent and island
  the dawn proclaims another day,
  the voice of prayer is never silent,
  nor dies the sound of praise away.

4 The sun that bids us rest is waking
  your church beneath the western sky;
  fresh voices hour by hour are making
  your mighty deeds resound on high.

5 So be it, Lord: your throne shall never,
  like earth's proud empires, pass away;
  your kingdom stands, and grows for ever,
  until there dawns that glorious day.

281
J. Ellerton

1 Saviour, again to your dear name we raise
  with one accord our parting hymn of praise;
  we give you thanks
      before our worship cease –
  then, in the silence, hear your word of peace.

2 Give us your peace, Lord,
      on our homeward way:
  with you began, with you shall end the day;
  guard now the lips from sin,
      the hearts from shame,
  that in this house have called upon your name.

3 Give us your peace, Lord,
      through the coming night,
  turn all our darkness to your perfect light;
  then, through our sleep,
      our hope and strength renew,
  for dark and light are both alike to you.

4 Give us your peace
      throughout our earthly life:
  comfort in sorrow, courage in the strife;
  then, when your voice
      shall make our conflict cease,
  call us, O Lord, to your eternal peace.

282 © John Arlott

1 God whose farm is all creation,
take the gratitude we give;
take the finest of our harvest,
crops we grow that all may live.

2 Take our ploughing, seeding, reaping,
hopes and fears of sun and rain,
all our thinking, planning, waiting,
ripened in this fruit and grain.

3 All our labour, all our watching,
all our calendar of care
in these crops of your creation,
take, O God – they are our prayer.

283 Cecil F. Alexander

All things bright and beautiful,
all creatures great and small,
all things wise and wonderful –
the Lord God made them all.

1 Each little flower that opens,
each little bird that sings –
he made their glowing colours,
he made their tiny wings.
All things bright . . .

2 The purple-headed mountain,
the river running by,
the sunset, and the morning
that brightens up the sky:
All things bright . . .

3 The cold wind in the winter,
the pleasant summer sun,
the ripe fruits in the garden –
he made them every one.
All things bright . . .

4 He gave us eyes to see them,
and lips that we might tell
how great is God almighty,
who has made all things well!
All things bright . . .

284 H. Alford
© in this version Jubilee Hymns†

1 Come, you thankful people, come,
raise the song of harvest home!
fruit and crops are gathered in
safe before the storms begin:
God our maker will provide
for our needs to be supplied;
come, with all his people, come,
raise the song of harvest home!

2 All the world is God's own field,
harvests for his praise to yield;
wheat and weeds together sown
here for joy or sorrow grown:
first the blade and then the ear,
then the full corn shall appear –
Lord of harvest, grant that we
wholesome grain and pure may be.

3 For the Lord our God shall come
and shall bring his harvest home;
he himself on that great day,
worthless things shall take away,
give his angels charge at last
in the fire the weeds to cast,
but the fruitful ears to store
in his care for evermore.

4 Even so, Lord, quickly come –
bring your final harvest home!
gather all your people in
free from sorrow, free from sin,
there together purified,
ever thankful at your side –
come, with all your angels, come,
bring that glorious harvest home!

285 W. Whiting
© in this version Jubilee Hymns†

1 Eternal Father, strong to save,
whose arm restrains the restless wave,
who told the mighty ocean deep
its own appointed bounds to keep:
we cry, O God of majesty,
for those in peril on the sea.

2 O Christ, whose voice the waters heard
and hushed their raging at your word,
who walked across the surging deep
and in the storm lay calm in sleep:
we cry, O Lord of Galilee,
for those in peril on the sea.

3 Creator Spirit, by whose breath
were fashioned sea and sky and earth:
who made the stormy chaos cease
and gave us life and light and peace:
we cry, O Spirit strong and free,
for those in peril on the sea.

4 O Trinity of love and power,
preserve their lives in danger's hour;
from rock and tempest, flood and flame,
protect them by your holy name,
and to your glory let there be
glad hymns of praise from land and sea.

286
F. Pratt Green
© Stainer & Bell Ltd

1 For the fruits of his creation,
   thanks be to God;
for his gifts to every nation,
   thanks be to God;
for the ploughing, sowing, reaping,
silent growth while we are sleeping,
future needs in earth's safe-keeping,
   thanks be to God.

2 In the just reward of labour,
   God's will is done;
in the help we give our neighbour,
   God's will is done;
in our worldwide task of caring
for the hungry and despairing,
in the harvests we are sharing,
   God's will is done.

3 For the harvests of his Spirit,
   thanks be to God;
for the good we all inherit,
   thanks be to God;
for the wonders that astound us,
for the truths that still confound us,
most of all, that love has found us,
   thanks be to God.

287
C. Wordsworth
© in this version Jubilate Hymns†

1 O Lord of heaven and earth and sea,
to you all praise and glory be,
who loved us from eternity
   and gave us all.

2 The golden sunshine, gentle air,
sweet flowers and fruit, your love declare;
when harvests ripen you are there –
   you give us all.

3 For peaceful homes and healthful days,
for all the blessings earth displays,
we owe you thankfulness and praise –
   you give us all.

4 Freely you gave your only Son,
who on the cross salvation won;
and in the life through him begun
   you give us all.

5 You sent your Spirit from above
as wind and fire and gentle dove;
and in his gifts of power and love
   you gave us all.

6 For souls redeemed, for sins forgiven,
for means of grace and hopes of heaven,
to you, O Lord what can be given?
   you give us all.

7 We lose what on ourselves we spend;
we have as treasure without end
whatever, Lord, to you we lend –
   you give us all.

8 Father, from whom we all derive
our life, our gifts, our power to give:
O may we ever with you live;
   you give us all.

288
Brian Wren
© Oxford University Press

1 Praise God for the harvest of farm and of field,
praise God for the people
   who gather their yield,
the long hours of labour, the skills of a team,
the patience of science,
   the power of machine.

2 Praise God for the harvest
   that's sent from afar,
from market and harbour,
   from tropical shore:
foods packed and transported,
   and planted and grown
by God-given neighbours,
   unseen and unknown.

3 Praise God for the harvest
   that comes from the ground,
by drill or by mineshaft, by opencast mound;
for oil and for iron, for tinplate and coal,
praise God, who in love has provided
   them all.

4 Praise God for the harvest of science
   and skill,
the urge to discover, create and fulfil:
for all new inventions that promise to gain
a future more hopeful, a world more humane.

5 Praise God for the harvest of conflict
   and love,
for leaders and peoples who struggle
   and serve
to conquer oppression,
   earth's plenty increase,
and gather God's harvest of justice
   and peace.

289
© Michael Perry†

1 Roar the waves, the waters praising
God who saves; and from beneath
creatures rise in shapes amazing
to our eyes – he gives them breath:
God who set the planets blazing
holds us yet in life or death.

2 Cries a bird at break of morning –
  music heard when life began;
  Christ was there at day's first dawning,
  son to share a father's plan:
  Jesus, born our hope and warning,
  shall return – the Son of Man.

3 Sing the trees, the branches calling
  in the breeze; the Spirit's song
  sweeps the grass, the flowers falling.
  Look! he passes all along:
  wind of God whose strength appalling
  mocks the proud and bends the strong.

4 Sound the praise of God the Father,
  voices raise to Christ the Son;
  in the Spirit Christians gather –
  speak his merit everyone:
  not in vain words glory – rather
  tell again what God has done!

290

from Psalm 65
© Michael Saward†

1 The earth is yours, O God –
  you nourish it with rain;
  the streams and rivers overflow,
  the land bears seed again.

2 The soil is yours, O God –
  the shoots are moist with dew;
  and ripened by the burning sun
  the corn grows straight and true.

3 The hills are yours, O God –
  their grass is lush and green,
  providing pastures for the flocks
  which everywhere are seen.

4 The whole rich land is yours
  for fodder or for plough;
  and so, for rain, sun, soil and seed,
  O God, we thank you now.

291

after W. C. Dix
© in this version Word & Music†

1 To you, O Lord, our hearts we raise
  in hymns of adoration:
  accept our sacrifice of praise,
  our shouts of exultation;
  for by your hand our souls are fed –
  what joys your love has given!
  You give to us our daily bread,
  so give us bread from heaven!

2 And now on this our festal day,
  your love to us expressing
  our gifts before you, Lord, we lay,
  the firstfruits of your blessing:
  bright robes of gold the fields adorn,
  the hills with joy are ringing;
  the valleys stand so thick with corn
  that even they are singing.

3 Yet in your presence we confess,
  O Lord of earth and heaven,
  our pride, our greed and selfishness –
  we ask to be forgiven:
  and where the hungry suffer still
  because of our ambition,
  there let our riches serve your will
  your love be our commission.

4 There is a country bright as day
  beyond the crystal river,
  where hunger will be done away
  and thirst be gone for ever;
  where praises ring out loud and strong
  that now with ours are blending;
  where we shall sing the harvest-song
  that never has an ending.

292

after M. Claudius
Jane M. Campbell

1 We plough the fields, and scatter
  the good seed on the land;
  but it is fed and watered
  by God's almighty hand:
  he sends the snow in winter,
  the warmth to swell the grain;
  the breezes and the sunshine
  and soft refreshing rain.
    All good gifts around us
    are sent from heaven above:
    then thank the Lord, O thank the Lord
    for all his love.

2 He only is the maker
  of all things near and far;
  he paints the wayside flower,
  he lights the evening star:
  the winds and waves obey him,
  by him the birds are fed;
  much more, to us his children
  he gives our daily bread.
    All good gifts . . .

3 We thank you, then, our Father,
  for all things bright and good;
  the seed-time and the harvest,
  our life, our health, our food:
  accept the gifts we offer
  for all your love imparts;
  and that which you most welcome
  our humble, thankful hearts!
    All good gifts . . .

293 from *Deus Misereatur* (Psalm 67)
H. F. Lyte

1 God of mercy, God of grace,
   show the brightness of your face:
   shine upon us, Saviour, shine,
   fill your church with light divine,
   and your saving health extend
   to the earth's remotest end.

2 Let the people praise you, Lord!
   be by all who live adored:
   let the nations shout and sing
   glory to their saviour king,
   at your feet their tribute pay,
   and your holy will obey.

3 Let the people crown you king!
   then shall earth her harvest bring,
   God to us his blessing give,
   we to God devoted live;
   all below and all above,
   one in joy and light and love.

294 J. E. Seddon
© Mrs. M. Seddon†

1 Jesus the Lord of love and life,
   draw near to bless this man and wife;
   as they are now in love made one,
   let your good will for them be done.

2 Give them each day your peace and joy,
   let no dark clouds these gifts destroy;
   in growing trust may love endure,
   to keep their marriage-bond secure.

3 As they have vowed to have and hold,
   each by the other be consoled;
   in wealth or want, in health or pain,
   till death shall part, let love remain.

4 Deepen, O Lord, their love for you,
   and in that love, their own renew;
   each in the other find delight,
   as lives and interests now unite.

5 Be to them both a guide and friend,
   through all the years their home defend;
   Jesus the Lord of love and life,
   stay near and bless this man and wife.

295 H. C. A. Gaunt
© Oxford University Press

1 Eternal Father, Lord of life,
   you have in every nation
   bestowed on loving man and wife
   a share in your creation:
   for this you formed the family,
   the cradle of all living,
   and that this wonder still should be,
   today we make thanksgiving.

2 Help us to keep our sacred vow
   of faithfulness, unbroken;
   in all our words and works to show
   each other love unspoken:
   grant us your wisdom day by day;
   through us may grace be flowing
   to help our children on their way,
   in truth and freedom growing.

3 And when the dangerous days come by
   of doubt and fear and blindness,
   then strengthen every family
   with courage, faith and kindness;
   that we, alert, your love may share
   alike with friend and stranger,
   and be the channels of your care,
   and draw the sting of danger.

4 May we with joy our tasks fulfil
   as father, child, or mother,
   that families may learn your will
   in loving one another;
   until at last that day may be
   when all, the truth perceiving,
   will know themselves your family,
   in Jesus Christ believing.

296 © Timothy Dudley-Smith

1 Father on high to whom we pray
   and lift our thankful hearts above,
   for all your mercies day by day,
   for gifts of hearth and home and love:
      protect them still beneath your care –
      Lord, in your mercy, hear our prayer.

2 O Christ who came as man to earth,
   and chose in Egypt's land to be
   a homeless child of alien birth,
   an exile and a refugee:
      for homeless people everywhere –
      Lord, in your mercy, hear our prayer.

3 Spirit divine, whose work is done
   in souls renewed and lives restored:
   strive in our hearts to make us one,
   one faith, one family, one Lord;
      till at the last one home we share –
      Lord, in your mercy, hear our prayer.

297 © Michael Perry†

1 Lord Jesus Christ, invited guest and saviour,
with tender mercy hear us as we pray;
grant our desire
for those who seek your favour,
come with your love
and bless them both today.

2 Give them your strength
for caring and for serving,
give them your graces –
faithfulness and prayer;
make their resolve to follow you unswerving,
make their reward
your peace beyond compare.

3 Be their delight in joy, their hope in sorrow,
be their true friend in pleasure as in pain;
guest of today and guardian of tomorrow,
turn humble water into wine again!

298 F. S. Pierpoint

1 For the beauty of the earth,
for the beauty of the skies,
for the love which from our birth
over and around us lies,
Christ our God, to you we raise
this our sacrifice of praise.

2 For the beauty of each hour
of the day and of the night,
hill and vale, and tree and flower,
sun and moon and stars of light,
Christ our God . . .

3 For the joy of ear and eye,
for the heart and mind's delight,
for the mystic harmony
linking sense to sound and sight,
Christ our God . . .

4 For the joy of human love,
brother, sister, parent, child,
friends on earth and friends above,
pleasures pure and undefiled,
Christ our God . . .

5 For each perfect gift divine
to our race so freely given,
joys bestowed by love's design,
flowers of earth and fruits of heaven,
Christ our God . . .

299 © Alan Gaunt

1 Great God, we praise the mighty love
which urges us to rise above
constricting doubts and fears;
whose purpose is to set us free
to live our lives creatively
throughout the coming years.

2 We praise you for the love we see
in man and wife and family,
in friends and neighbours too;
the love which nurtured us from birth,
the love which teaches human worth
and leads our minds to you.

3 We praise you most for love supreme
which breaks through pain and death
to stream
in unrestricted light;
which from Christ's resurrection dawn
has shone, and never been withdrawn,
to make our future bright.

4 For by your perfect love refined
our own will not be undermined
by futile guilt and shame;
but through disaster, grief or strife
we'll re-affirm the joy of life
and glorify your name.

300 after K. P. J. Spitta
© Honor Mary Thwaites

1 Happy the home that welcomes you,
Lord Jesus,
truest of friends, most honoured guest of all;
where hearts and eyes
are bright with joy to greet you,
your slightest wishes eager to fulfil.

2 Happy the home
where man and wife together
are of one mind, believing in your love;
through love and pain,
prosperity and hardship,
through good and evil days
your care they prove.

3 Happy the home, O loving friend of children,
where they are given to you
with hands of prayer;
where at your feet they early learn to listen
to your own words,
and thank you for your care.

4 Happy the home
where work is done to please you,
in tasks both great and small,
that you may see
each family doing all as you would wish them
as members of your household, glad and free.

5 Happy the home
      that knows your healing comfort,
where, unforgotten, every joy you share;
until each one,
      their work on earth completed,
comes to your Father's house
      to meet you there.

301 © Christopher Porteous†

1 His eyes will guide my footsteps
when faltering age is near;
his light will lift my darkness
and help my ears to hear:
in faith I claim the promise
of Jesus' love for me;
the Lord of hope and healing
who made the blind to see.

2 When others fail or leave me,
he comes to me in prayer;
when life no longer needs me
I find my comfort here:
his promises are faithful –
he lives, my closest friend;
I know that he will keep me
until my days shall end.

3 He comes when I am weary,
in pain or in distress;
with patient understanding
and perfect gentleness:
he was far more forsaken
than I shall ever be;
the presence of my saviour
is everything to me.

302 © Basil Bridge

1 Jesus, Lord, we pray,
be our guest today!
gospel story has recorded
how your glory was afforded
to a wedding day –
be our guest, we pray.

2 Lord of love and life,
blessing man and wife:
as they stand, their need confessing,
may your hand take theirs in blessing;
you will share their life –
bless this man and wife.

3 Lord of hope and faith,
faithful unto death:
let the ring serve as a token
of a love sincere, unbroken,
love more strong than death –
Lord of hope and faith!

303 Anna B. Warner

1 Jesus loves me! – this I know,
for the Bible tells me so;
little ones to him belong –
they are weak, but he is strong.
    Yes, Jesus loves me,
    yes, Jesus loves me,
    yes, Jesus loves me –
    the Bible tells me so.

2 Jesus loves me! – he who died,
heaven's gate to open wide;
he will wash away my sin,
let his little child come in.
    Yes, Jesus loves me . . .

3 Jesus loves me! He will stay
close beside me all the way,
till he takes his little one
to be with him near his throne.
    Yes, Jesus loves me . . .

304 after A. Midlane
© in this version Jubilate Hymns†

1 There's a song for all the children
that makes the heavens ring,
a song that even angels
can never, never sing;
they praise the Lord their maker
and see him glorified,
but we can call him Saviour
because for us he died.

2 There's a place for all the children
where Jesus reigns in love,
a place of joy and freedom
that nothing can remove;
a home that is more friendly
than any home we know,
where Jesus makes us welcome
because he loves us so.

3 There's a friend for all the children
to guide us every day,
whose care is always faithful
and never fades away;
there's no-one else so loyal –
his friendship stays the same;
he knows us and he loves us,
and Jesus is his name.

305 Jane Leeson

1 Loving Shepherd of your sheep,
   keep your lamb, in safety keep;
   nothing can your power withstand,
   none can tear me from your hand.

2 Loving Lord, you chose to give
   your own life that we might live;
   and your hands outstretched to bless
   bear the cruel nails' impress.

3 Help me praise you every day,
   gladly serve you and obey;
   like your glorious ones above,
   happy in your precious love.

4 Loving Shepherd ever near,
   teach your lamb your voice to hear;
   let my footsteps never stray
   from the true and narrow way.

5 Where you lead me I will go,
   walking in your steps below;
   till, before my Father's throne,
   I shall know as I am known.

306 C. Wesley

1 Forth in your name, O Lord, I go
   my daily labour to pursue;
   you, Lord, alone I choose to know
   in all I think or speak or do.

2 The task your wisdom has assigned
   here let me cheerfully fulfil;
   in all my work your presence find
   and prove your good and perfect will.

3 You I would set at my right hand
   whose eyes my inmost secrets view;
   and labour on at your command
   and offer all my work to you.

4 Help me to bear your easy yoke
   and every moment watch and pray;
   and still to things eternal look
   and hasten to that glorious day.

5 Gladly for you may I employ
   all that your generous grace has given;
   and run my earthly course with joy,
   and closely walk with you to heaven.

307 F. Pott

1 Angel voices ever singing
      round your throne of light,
   angels' music ever ringing
      rests not day or night;
   thousands only live to bless you
      and confess you Lord of might.

2 Lord beyond our mortal sight,
      in glory far away,
   can it be that you delight
      in sinners' songs today;
   may we know that you are near us
      and will hear us? Yes, we may!

3 Yes, we know your heart rejoices
      in each work divine,
   using minds and hands and voices
      in your great design;
   craftsman's art and music's measure
      for your pleasure all combine.

4 Here to you, great God, we offer
      praise in harmony,
   and for your acceptance proffer
      all unworthily
   hearts and minds and hands and voices
      in our choicest psalmody.

5 Honour, glory, might and merit
      for your works and ways,
   Father, Son and Holy Spirit,
      God through endless days;
   with the best that you have given
      earth and heaven render praise.

308 David Mowbray

1 Come to us, creative Spirit,
   in our Father's house;
   every human talent hallow,
   hidden skills arouse,
   that within your earthly temple,
   wise and simple,
   may rejoice.

2 Poet, painter, music-maker
   all your treasures bring;
   craftsman, actor, graceful dancer
   make your offering;
   join your hands in celebration:
   let creation
   shout and sing!

3 Word from God eternal springing
fill our minds, we pray;
and in all artistic vision
give integrity:
may the flame within us burning
kindle yearning
day by day.

4 In all places and forever
glory be expressed
to the Son, with God the Father
and the Spirit blessed:
in our worship and our living
keep us striving
for the best.

309 © Timothy Dudley-Smith

1 Jesus is the Lord of living,
all creation's bright array;
hearts for loving and forgiving,
ordered round of work and play –
    Jesus is the Lord of living,
    year by year and day by day.

2 Jesus is the man for others,
love of God in man made plain;
those whom God created brothers
now in Christ are one again –
    Jesus is the man for others,
    ours the pardon, his the pain.

3 Jesus is the prince of glory,
love and praise to him be shown:
love for our salvation's story,
praise for his eternal throne –
    Jesus is the prince of glory,
    glory be to him alone!

310 C. Kingsley
© in this version Word & Music†

1 From you all skill and science flow,
all pity, care and love,
all calm and courage, faith and hope –
O pour them from above!

2 And share them, Lord, to each and all,
as each and all have need;
so let your gifts return to you
in noble thought and deed.

3 And hasten, Lord, that perfect day
when pain and death shall cease,
and your just rule shall fill the earth
with health and light and peace:

4 When ever green the grass shall be,
and ever blue the skies,
and our destruction shall no more
deface your paradise.

311 P. Dearmer

1 God is love – his the care,
tending each, everywhere;
God is love – all is there!
Jesus came to show him,
that we all might know him:
    Sing aloud, loud, loud;
    sing aloud, loud, loud:
    God is good,
    God is truth, God is beauty – praise him!

2 Jesus shared all our pain,
lived and died, rose again,
rules our hearts, now as then –
for he came to save us
by the truth he gave us:
    Sing aloud . . .

3 To our Lord praise we sing –
light and life, friend and king,
coming down love to bring,
pattern for our duty,
showing God in beauty:
    Sing aloud . . .

312 © David Mowbray†

1 Let creation bless the Father,
glorify his name on high!
In him all things have their being,
live and move unceasingly:
angels and archangels praise him,
all the hosts of earth and heaven;
power and might are his for ever
who the Son to us has given.

2 Let creation greet in Jesus
God the Father's promised Christ,
seek and find in him salvation,
Lamb of God once sacrificed;
raised from death, in glory seated
at the Father's side again:
all God's children wait the moment
for the coming of his reign.

3 Let creation bless the Spirit,
present through all time and space
in the work of life's unfolding,
source of order, truth and grace:
all the wealth of words and music,
art and science, quest of faith –
these are signs that God is with us,
that his Spirit fills the earth.

4 Father, Son and Holy Spirit,
undivided and supreme;
filling all things, yet descending
to our lives, to dwell within:
through the church, let every creature
learn to love and not destroy;
let creation, reaching upward,
scale the heights of peace and joy!

313 © Edward Burns

1 O God, who gives to humankind
a searching heart and questing mind:
grant us to find your truth and laws,
and wisdom to perceive their cause.

2 In all our learning give us grace
to bow ourselves before your face;
as knowledge grows, Lord, keep us free
from self-destructive vanity.

3 Sometimes we think we understand
all workings of your mighty hand;
then through your Son help us to know
those truths which you alone can show.

4 Teach us to joy in things revealed,
to search with care all yet concealed;
as through Christ's light your truth we find
and worship you with heart and mind.

314 A. F. Bayly
© Oxford University Press

1 O Lord of every shining constellation
that wheels in splendour
through the midnight sky:
grant us your Spirit's true illumination
to read the secrets of your work on high.

2 You, Lord, have made
the atom's hidden forces;
your laws its mighty energies fulfil:
teach us, to whom you give
such rich resources,
in all we use, to serve your holy will.

3 O Life, awaking life in cell and tissue;
from flower to bird,
from beast to humankind:
help us to trace, from birth to final issue,
the sure unfolding purpose of your mind.

4 You, Lord, have stamped your image
on your creatures
and, though they mar that image,
love them still:
lift up our eyes to Christ, that in his features
we may discern the beauty of your will.

5 Great Lord of nature, shaping and renewing,
you made us more than nature's child to be;
you help us tread,
with grace our souls enduing,
the road to life and immortality.

315 H. Twells
© in this version Jubilate Hymns†

1 At evening, when the sun had set,
the sick, O Lord, around you lay:
in what distress and pain they met,
but in what joy they went away!

2 Once more the evening comes, and we
oppressed with various ills draw near;
and though your form we cannot see,
we know and feel that you are here.

3 O Saviour Christ, our fears dispel –
for some are sick and some are sad,
and some have never loved you well,
and some have lost the love they had.

4 And none, O Lord, have perfect rest,
for none are wholly free from sin;
and those who long to serve you best
are conscious most of wrong within.

5 O Saviour Christ, the Son of Man,
you have been troubled, tested, tried;
your kind but searching glance can scan
the very wounds that shame would hide.

6 Your touch has still its ancient power;
no word from you can fruitless fall:
meet with us in this evening hour
and in your mercy heal us all!

316 after Synesius, A. W. Chatfield
© in this version Jubilate Hymns†

1 Lord Jesus, think of me
and take away my fear;
in my depression, may I be
assured that you are near.

2 Lord Jesus, think of me
by many cares oppressed;
in times of great anxiety
give me your promised rest.

3 Lord Jesus, think of me
when darker grows the day;
and in my sad perplexity
show me the heavenly way.

4 Lord Jesus, think of me
when night's dark shadows spread;
restore my lost serenity,
and show me light ahead.

5 Lord Jesus, think of me,
that when the night is past
I may the glorious morning see
and share your joy at last!

317 © Michael Perry†

1 When Jesus walked upon this earth
his word was peace;
he spoke of fellowship with God,
he brought the prisoners release;
and all his caring
witnessed to his peaceful word.

2 When Jesus walked upon this earth
his touch was grace;
they came with stretcher, bandage, crutch
from east and west to seek his face;
and all his healing
witnessed to his gracious touch.

3 When Jesus walked upon this earth
his heart was love;
he came to take the humblest part,
among the penitent to move;
and all his serving
witnessed to his loving heart.

4 When Jesus walked upon this earth
his name was king;
to fight demonic powers he came
and bring his glorious kingdom in:
let all our praising
witness to his kingly name!

318 © Michael Perry†

1 We give God thanks for those who knew
the touch of Jesus' healing love;
they trusted him to make them whole,
to give them peace, their guilt remove.

2 We offer prayer for all who go
relying on his grace and power,
to help the anxious and the ill,
to heal their wounds, their lives restore.

3 We dedicate our skills and time
to those who suffer where we live,
to bring such comfort as we can
to meet their need, their pain relieve.

4 So Jesus' touch of healing grace
lives on within our willing care;
by thought and prayer and gifts we prove
his mercy still, his love we share.

319 © Michael Perry†

1 Heal me, hands of Jesus,
and search out all my pain;
restore my hope, remove my fear
and bring me peace again.

2 Cleanse me, blood of Jesus,
take bitterness away;
let me forgive as one forgiven
and bring me peace today.

3 Know me, mind of Jesus,
and show me all my sin;
dispel the memories of guilt
and bring me peace within.

4 Fill me, joy of Jesus:
anxiety shall cease
and heaven's serenity be mine,
for Jesus brings me peace!

320 D. W. Hughes
© Mary Hughes

1 Creator of the earth and skies,
to whom all truth and power belong:
grant us your truth to make us wise,
grant us your power to make us strong.

2 We have not known you: to the skies
our monuments of folly soar;
and all our self-wrought miseries
have made us trust ourselves the more.

3 We have not loved you: far and wide
the wreckage of our hatred spreads;
and evils wrought by human pride
recoil on unrepentant heads.

4 We long to end this worldwide strife:
how shall we follow in your way?
Speak to us all your words of life
until our darkness turns to day!

321 F. Pratt Green
© Stainer & Bell Ltd

1 Christ is the world's light, he and none other;
born in our darkness,
   he became our brother –
if we have seen him, we have seen the Father:
   Glory to God on high!

2 Christ is the world's peace,
   he and none other;
no man can serve him
   and despise his brother –
who else unites us, one in God the Father?
   Glory to God on high!

3 Christ is the world's life, he and none other;
sold once for silver, murdered here,
   our brother –
he, who redeems us,
   reigns with God the Father:
   Glory to God on high!

4 Give God the glory, God and none other;
give God the glory, Spirit, Son and Father;
give God the glory, God in man my brother:
   Glory to God on high!

322 from a line by W. A. Dunkerley
© Michael Perry†

1 In Christ there is no east or west,
in him no pride of birth;
the chosen family God has blessed
now spans the whole wide earth.

2 For God in Christ has made us one
from every land and race;
he reconciled us through his Son
and met us with his grace.

3 It is by grace we are assured
that we belong to him:
the love we share in Christ our Lord,
the Spirit's work within.

4 So brothers, sisters, praise his name
who died to set us free
from sin, division, hate and shame,
from spite and enmity!

5 In Christ there is no east or west –
he breaks all barriers down;
by Christ redeemed, by Christ possessed,
in Christ we live as one.

323 G. W. Briggs
© Oxford University Press

1 Christ is the world's true light,
its captain of salvation,
our daystar clear and bright,
desire of every nation:
new life, new hope awakes
where we accept his way;
freedom her bondage breaks
and night is turned to day.

2 In Christ all races meet,
their ancient feuds forgetting,
the whole round world complete
from sunrise to its setting:
when Christ is known as Lord
all shall forsake their fear,
to ploughshare beat the sword,
to pruning-hook the spear.

3 One Lord, in one great name
unite all who have known you,
cast out our pride and shame
that hinder to enthrone you:
the world has waited long,
has laboured long in pain;
to heal its ancient wrong
come, Prince of peace, and reign!

324 H. E. Fosdick
© Elinor F. Downs

1 God of grace and God of glory,
come among us in your power;
crown your ancient church's story,
bring her bud to glorious flower.
   Grant us wisdom,
   grant us courage
for the facing of this hour.

2 See the hosts of evil round us
scorn your Christ, attack his ways!
Fears and doubts too long have bound us –
free our hearts to work and praise.
   Grant us wisdom,
   grant us courage
for the living of these days.

3 Save us from weak resignation
to the evils we deplore;
let the search for your salvation
be our glory evermore.
   Grant us wisdom,
   grant us courage
serving you whom we adore.

4 Heal your children's warring madness,
 bend our pride to your control;
 shame our wanton, selfish gladness,
 rich in things and poor in soul.
   Grant us wisdom,
   grant us courage
 lest we miss your kingdom's goal.

325 © Michael Perry†

1 God save and bless our nation,
   be all our inspiration;
 in every generation
   make hatred cease:
 let love and justice guide us,
   nor fear nor greed divide us;
 come, Lord, and walk beside us –
   grant us your peace!

2 Lord, be our true confession,
   our hope, our faith's possession;
 so hear our intercession,
   help us to stand:
 not by the strength you gave us,
   nor pride that you forgave us,
 but for your glory save us –
   God bless our land!

326 unknown, © in this version Jubilate Hymns†
(see also traditional version, 592)

1 God save our gracious Queen,
 God bless and guard our Queen,
   long live the Queen!
 Guard us in liberty,
 bless us with unity,
 save us from tyranny:
   God save the Queen!

2 Lord be our nation's light,
 guide us in truth and right:
   in you we stand;
 give us your faithfulness,
 keep us from selfishness,
 raise us to godliness:
   God save our land!

3 Spirit of love and life,
 healing our nation's strife,
   on you we call:
 teach us your better way,
 grant us your peace today;
 God bless our Queen, we pray,
   God save us all!

327 J. E. Seddon
© Mrs. M. Seddon†

1 Here, Lord, we come to you,
 the fount of life,
 eternal love:
 so in this faithless world
 our faith renew.

2 Lord, all things come from you
 for every life
 in every land:
 that we may share your gifts,
 our love renew.

3 Here, Lord, we bring to you
 each lonely life,
 each hungry child:
 in all who want and wait,
 their hope renew.

4 Lord, we confess to you
 our selfish ease,
 our lack of love:
 now through your Spirit's touch
 your church renew.

5 So, Lord, we come to you,
 we are all one,
 of humankind:
 so in our common need
 our life renew –

6 Help us to do your will,
 turn prayer to deed,
 stir heart and mind,
 and through our grateful lives
 your world renew.

328 © Timothy Dudley-Smith

1 Lord, for the years your love
   has kept and guided,
 urged and inspired us,
   cheered us on our way,
 sought us and saved us,
   pardoned and provided:
 Lord of the years, we bring our thanks today.

2 Lord, for that word,
   the word of life which fires us,
 speaks to our hearts
   and sets our souls ablaze,
 teaches and trains,
   rebukes us and inspires us:
 Lord of the word,
   receive your people's praise.

3 Lord, for our land in this our generation,
  spirits oppressed by pleasure,
    wealth and care:
for young and old,
  for commonwealth and nation,
Lord of our land,
  be pleased to hear our prayer,

4 Lord, for our world;
  when we disown and doubt him,
loveless in strength, and comfortless in pain,
hungry and helpless, lost indeed without him:
Lord of the world,
  we pray that Christ may reign.

5 Lord for ourselves;
  in living power remake us –
self on the cross and Christ upon the throne,
past put behind us, for the future take us:
Lord of our lives, to live for Christ alone.

329 H. S. Holland
© in this version Jubilate Hymns†

1 Judge eternal, throned in splendour,
Lord of lords and King of kings,
with your living fire of judgement
purge this realm of bitter things;
comfort all its wide dominion
with the healing of your wings.

2 Weary people still are longing
for the hour that brings release,
and the city's crowded clamour
cries aloud for sin to cease;
and the countryside and woodlands
plead in silence for their peace.

3 Crown, O Lord, your own endeavour,
cleave our darkness with your sword,
cheer the faint and feed the hungry
with the richness of your word;
cleanse the body of this nation
through the glory of the Lord.

330 from *Deus Misereatur* (Psalm 67)
© Michael Baughen†

1 May God be gracious to us!
that your way may be known upon earth
and your power to save among nations:
  Let the peoples praise you, O God,
  let all the peoples praise you!

2 Let nations sing with gladness
for your judgement of peoples is fair
and you guide the earth's many nations:
  Let the peoples praise you . . .

3 See how the earth is fruitful,
for the blessing of God has been given:
may the whole wide world now revere him!
  Let the peoples praise you . . .

331 R. Bridges
© in this version Jubilate Hymns†

1 Rejoice, O land, in God your Lord,
obey his will and keep his word;
for you the saints lift up their voice:
fear not, O land, in God rejoice!

2 Glad shall you be, with blessing crowned,
and joy and peace shall clothe you round;
yes, love with you shall make a home
until you see God's kingdom come.

3 He shall forgive your sins untold –
remember now his love of old;
walk in his way, his word adore,
and keep his truth for evermore.

332 © Timothy Dudley-Smith

1 Remember, Lord, the world you made,
for Adam's race to find
the life of heaven on earth displayed,
a home for humankind.

2 A home of peace: but war and strife
and hatred we confess;
where death is in the midst of life
and children fatherless.

3 A home of freedom: yet the flame
burns low for liberty;
and few will serve in Jesus' name
that all men may be free.

4 A home of plenty: clothed and fed
our sturdy children play;
while other children cry for bread
not half the world away.

5 Renew our love, O Lord, and touch
our hearts to feel and care
that we who seem to have so much
so little seem to share.

6 For those who have no prayers to say,
who in despair are dumb,
teach us to live as well as pray
'O Lord, your kingdom come!'

333
B. Rees
© Mrs. M. E. Rees

1 The kingdom of God
　　　is justice and joy;
　for Jesus restores
　　　what sin would destroy.
　God's power and glory
　　　in Jesus we know;
　and here and hereafter
　　　the kingdom shall grow.

2 The kingdom of God
　　　is mercy and grace;
　the captives are freed,
　　　the sinners find place,
　the outcast are welcomed
　　　God's banquet to share;
　and hope is awakened
　　　in place of despair.

3 The kingdom of God
　　　is challenge and choice:
　believe the good news,
　　　repent and rejoice!
　His love for us sinners
　　　brought Christ to his cross:
　our crisis of judgement
　　　for gain or for loss.

4 God's kingdom is come,
　　　the gift and the goal;
　in Jesus begun,
　　　in heaven made whole.
　The heirs of the kingdom
　　　shall answer his call;
　and all things cry 'Glory!'
　　　to God all in all.

334
L. Hensley

1 Your kingdom come, O God!
　your rule, O Christ, begin;
　break with your iron rod
　the tyrannies of sin.

2 Where is your reign of peace
　and purity and love?
　When shall all hatred cease
　as in the realms above?

3 When comes the promised time,
　the end of strife and war;
　when lust, oppression, crime
　and greed shall be no more?

4 O Lord our God, arise
　and come in your great might!
　revive our longing eyes
　which languish for your sight.

5 As rebels scorn your name
　and wolves devour your fold,
　by many deeds of shame
　we learn that love grows cold.

6 On nations near and far
　thick darkness gathers yet:
　arise, O Morning Star,
　arise and never set!

335
Brian Wren
© Oxford University Press

1 When Christ was lifted from the earth,
　his arms stretched out above,
　through every culture, every birth,
　to draw an answering love.

2 Still east and west his love extends,
　and always, near or far,
　he calls and claims us as his friends
　and loves us as we are.

3 Where generation, class or race
　divide us to our shame,
　he sees not labels but a face,
　a person and a name.

4 Thus freely loved, though fully known,
　may I in Christ be free
　to welcome and accept his own
　as Christ accepted me.

336
from Psalms 149 and 150
© Michael Perry†

1 Bring to the Lord a glad new song,
　children of grace extol your king;
　worship and praise to God belong –
　to instruments of music, sing!
　Let those be warned who spurn his name,
　nations and kings attend his word;
　God's justice shall bring tyrants shame:
　let every creature praise the Lord!

2 Praise him within these hallowed walls,
　praise him beneath the dome of heaven;
　by cymbals' sounds and trumpets' calls
　let praises fit for God be given:
　with strings and brass and wind rejoice –
　then, join his praise with full accord
　all living things with breath and voice:
　let every creature praise the Lord!

337
R. Robinson
© in this version Jubilate Hymns†

1 Come, O Fount of every blessing,
tune my heart to sing your grace:
streams of mercy never ceasing
call for songs of loudest praise.

2 Jesus sought me when a stranger
wandering far away from God,
and, to rescue me from danger,
he redeemed me by his blood.

3 Prone to wander – Lord, I feel it;
prone to leave the God I love!
take my heart; in mercy seal it,
guard it for the realms above.

4 Lord, my joy, my consolation,
all my days to you belong;
as your grace is my salvation,
so your grace shall be my song.

338
R. Heber
© in this version Jubilate Hymns†

1 Brightest and best of the suns of the morning,
dawn on our darkness and come to our aid;
star of the east, the horizon adorning,
guide where our infant redeemer is laid!

2 What shall we give him, in costly devotion?
Shall we bring incense and offerings divine,
gems of the mountain and pearls of the ocean,
myrrh from the forest or gold from the mine?

3 Vainly we offer each lavish oblation,
vainly with gifts would his favour secure;
richer by far is the heart's adoration,
dearer to God are the prayers of the poor.

4 Brightest and best of the suns of the morning,
dawn on our darkness and come to our aid;
star of the east, the horizon adorning,
guide where our infant redeemer is laid!

339
after Alcuin
© Christopher Idle†

1 Eternal light, shine in my heart,
eternal hope, lift up my eyes;
eternal power, be my support,
eternal wisdom, make me wise.

2 Eternal life, raise me from death,
eternal brightness, help me see;
eternal Spirit, give me breath,
eternal Saviour, come to me:

3 Until by your most costly grace,
invited by your holy word,
at last I come before your face
to know you, my eternal God.

340
from *Te Deum*
© Timothy Dudley-Smith

1 God of gods, we sound his praises,
highest heaven its homage brings;
earth and all creation raises
glory to the King of kings:
holy, holy, holy, name him,
Lord of all his hosts proclaim him;
to the everlasting Father
every tongue in triumph sings.

2 Christians in their hearts enthrone him,
tell his praises wide abroad;
prophets, priests, apostles own him
martyrs' crown and saints' reward.
Three-in-One his glory sharing,
earth and heaven his praise declaring,
praise the high majestic Father,
praise the everlasting Lord!

3 Hail the Christ, the king of glory,
he whose praise the angels cry;
born to share our human story,
love and labour, grieve and die:
by his cross his work completed,
sinners ransomed, death defeated;
in the glory of the Father
Christ ascended reigns on high.

4 Lord, we look for your returning;
teach us so to walk your ways,
hearts and minds your will discerning,
lives alight with joy and praise:
in your love and care enfold us,
by your constancy uphold us;
may your mercy, Lord and Father,
keep us now and all our days!

341
from *Te Deum*
© Christopher Idle†

1 God, we praise you! God, we bless you!
God, we name you sovereign Lord!
Mighty King whom angels worship,
Father, by your church adored:
all creation shows your glory,
heaven and earth draw near your throne
singing 'Holy, holy, holy,'
Lord of hosts, and God alone!

2 True apostles, faithful prophets,
saints who set their world ablaze,
martyrs, once unknown, unheeded,
join one growing song of praise,
while your church on earth confesses
one majestic Trinity:
Father, Son, and Holy Spirit,
God, our hope eternally.

3 Jesus Christ, the king of glory,
everlasting Son of God,
humble was your virgin mother,
hard the lonely path you trod:
by your cross is sin defeated,
hell confronted face to face,
heaven opened to believers,
sinners justified by grace.

4 Christ, at God's right hand victorious,
you will judge the world you made;
Lord, in mercy help your servants
for whose freedom you have paid:
raise us up from dust to glory,
guard us from all sin today;
King enthroned above all praises,
save your people, God, we pray.

342 G. Herbert

1 Let all the world in every corner sing,
'My God and King!'
The heavens are not too high,
his praise may thither fly;
the earth is not too low,
his praises there may grow:
let all the world in every corner sing,
'My God and King!'

2 Let all the world in every corner sing,
'My God and King!'
The church with psalms must shout –
no door can keep them out;
but above all, the heart
must bear the longest part:
let all the world in every corner sing,
'My God and King!'

343 from *Cantate Domino* (Psalm 98), E. R. Routley
© 1974 by Agape, Carol Stream, IL 60187.

1 New songs of celebration render
to him who has great wonders done:
Love sits enthroned in ageless splendour –
come and adore the mighty one!
He has made known his great salvation
which all his friends with joy confess;
he has revealed to every nation
his everlasting righteousness.

2 Joyfully, heartily resounding,
let every instrument and voice
peal out the praise of grace abounding,
calling the whole world to rejoice.
Trumpets and organs, set in motion
such sounds as make the heavens ring;
all things that live in earth and ocean,
make music for your mighty king.

3 Rivers and seas and torrents roaring,
honour the Lord with wild acclaim;
mountains and stones look up adoring
and find a voice to praise his name.
Righteous, commanding, ever-glorious,
praises be his that never cease:
just is our God, whose truth victorious
establishes the world in peace.

344 J. S. B. Monsell

1 O worship the Lord in the beauty of holiness,
bow down before him, his glory proclaim;
with gold of obedience
and incense of lowliness,
kneel and adore him – the Lord is his name.

2 Low at his feet
lay your burden of carefulness,
high on his heart he will bear it for you,
comfort your sorrows
and answer your prayerfulness,
guiding your steps in the way that is true.

3 Fear not to enter his courts in the slenderness
of the poor wealth
you would count as your own;
truth in its beauty and love in its tenderness –
these are the offerings to bring to his throne.

4 These, though we bring them
in trembling and fearfulness,
he will accept for the name that is dear;
mornings of joy
give for evenings of tearfulness,
trust for our trembling and hope for our fear.

5 O worship the Lord in the beauty of holiness,
bow down before him, his glory proclaim;
with gold of obedience
and incense of lowliness,
kneel and adore him – the Lord is his name.

345 H. F. Lyte

1 Praise the Lord, his glories show,   Alleluia,
all that lives on earth below;   alleluia,
angels round his throne above,   alleluia,
all who see and share his love.   alleluia!

2 Earth to heaven and heaven to earth   Alleluia,
tell his wonders, sing his worth;   alleluia,
age to age, and shore to shore,   alleluia,
praise him, praise him evermore.   alleluia!

3 Praise the Lord, his mercies trace,   Alleluia,
praise his providence and grace;   alleluia,
all that he for us has done,   alleluia,
all he gives us in his Son!   alleluia!

346 after N. F. S. Grundtvig
© Michael Saward†

1 Praise we offer, Lord of glory,
for your coming to our earth;
called to be the child of Mary,
taking manhood by your birth:
praise we offer, Lord of glory
for your coming to our earth.

2 Praise we offer, Lord of glory,
for your passion and your death;
called to suffer for us sinners,
faithful till your final breath:
praise we offer, Lord of glory
for your passion and your death.

3 Praise we offer, Lord of glory,
for your conquest of the grave;
called to break the chains which bound us,
rising, faithful souls to save:
praise we offer, Lord of glory
for your conquest of the grave.

4 Praise we offer, Lord of glory,
for your Spirit's touch of power;
called to give our lives new radiance,
filling us from hour to hour;
praise we offer, Lord of glory
for your Spirit's touch of power.

5 Praise we offer, Lord of glory,
for the hope which all our days,
called to being by your labours,
turns our thought to endless praise:
praise we offer, Lord of glory –
endless songs of joyful praise!

347 H. W. Baker

1 Rejoice today with one accord,
sing out with jubilation;
rejoice, and praise our mighty Lord
his arm has brought salvation:
his works of love proclaim
the greatness of his name;
for he is God alone,
his mercy he has shown –
let all his saints adore him!

2 When in distress to him we cried,
he heard our sad complaining:
O trust in him, our faithful guide –
his love is all-sustaining:
to him our hearts shall raise
triumphant songs of praise;
now every voice shall sing,
'O praise our God and king!'
let all his saints adore him!

348 © David Mowbray†

1 Shout for joy, loud and long,
God be praised with a song!
to the Lord we belong –
children of the Father,
God the great life-giver!
Shout for joy, joy, joy;
shout for joy, joy, joy!
God is love, God is light,
God is everlasting!

2 By God's word all was made,
heaven and earth, light and shade,
nature's wonders displayed,
man to rule creation
from its first foundation.
Shout for joy . . .

3 Yet our pride makes us fall!
so Christ came for us all –
not the righteous to call –
by his cross and passion,
bringing us salvation!
Shout for joy . . .

4 Now has Christ truly risen
and his Spirit is given
to all those under heaven
who will walk beside him,
though they once denied him!
Shout for joy . . .

349 from *Cantate Domino* (Psalm 98)
© Timothy Dudley-Smith

1 Sing a new song to the Lord,
he to whom wonders belong;
rejoice in his triumph and tell of his power –
O sing to the Lord a new song!

2 Now to the ends of the earth
see his salvation is shown;
and still he remembers his mercy and truth,
unchanging in love to his own.

3 Sing a new song and rejoice,
publish his praises abroad;
let voices in chorus, with trumpet and horn,
resound for the joy of the Lord!

4 Join with the hills and the sea
thunders of praise to prolong:
in judgement and justice
he comes to the earth –
O sing to the Lord a new song!

350 J. Montgomery

1 Songs of praise the angels sang,
heaven with alleluias rang
when creation was begun;
when God spoke, and it was done.

2 Songs of praise announced the dawn
when the Prince of peace was born;
songs of praise arose when he
captive led captivity.

3 Heaven and earth must pass away –
songs of praise shall crown that day!
God will make new heavens and earth –
songs of praise shall greet their birth!

4 And must we alone be dumb
till that glorious kingdom come?
No! the church delights to raise
psalms and hymns and songs of praise.

5 Saints below, with heart and voice
still in songs of praise rejoice;
learning here by faith and love
songs of praise to sing above.

6 Hymns of glory, songs of praise,
Father, these to you we raise;
Saviour, Jesus, risen Lord,
with the Spirit be adored.

351 J. Montgomery

1 Stand up and bless the Lord,
you people of his choice;
stand up and praise the Lord your God
with heart and soul and voice.

2 Though high above all praise,
above all blessing high,
who would not fear his holy name,
give thanks and glorify?

3 O for the living flame
from his own altar brought,
to touch our lips, our minds inspire,
and wing to heaven our thought!

4 God is our strength and song,
and his salvation ours;
then be his love in Christ proclaimed
with all our ransomed powers.

5 Stand up and bless the Lord,
the Lord your God adore;
stand up and praise his glorious name
both now and evermore.

352 from *Cantate Domino* (Psalm 98)
© Michael Baughen†

1 Sing to God new songs of worship –
all his deeds are marvellous;
he has brought salvation to us
with his hand and holy arm:
he has shown to all the nations
righteousness and saving power;
he recalled his truth and mercy
to his people Israel.

2 Sing to God new songs of worship –
earth has seen his victory;
let the lands of earth be joyful
praising him with thankfulness:
sound upon the harp his praises,
play to him with melody;
let the trumpets sound his triumph,
show your joy to God the king!

3 Sing to God new songs of worship –
let the sea now make a noise;
all on earth and in the waters
sound your praises to the Lord:
let the hills rejoice together,
let the rivers clap their hands,
for with righteousness and justice
he will come to judge the earth.

353 R. Baxter
© in this version Jubilate Hymns†

1 You holy angels bright
who wait at God's right hand,
or through the realms of light
fly at your Lord's command:
assist our song,
or else the theme
too high will seem
for mortal tongue.

2 You faithful souls at rest,
who ran this earthly race,
and now from sin released
behold the saviour's face:
his praises sound
and all unite
in sweet delight
to see him crowned.

3 You saints who serve below,
adore your heavenly king,
and as you onward go
your joyful anthems sing:
take what he gives
and praise him still
through good and ill,
who ever lives.

4 So take, my soul, your part;
   triumph in God above,
   and with a well-tuned heart
   sing out your songs of love:
       with joy proclaim
       through all your days
       in ceaseless praise
       his glorious name!

354

H. W. Baker
© in this version Jubilate Hymns†

1 Sing praise to the Lord!
   praise him in the height;
   rejoice in his word
   you angels of light:
   you heavens, adore him
   by whom you were made,
   and worship before him
   in brightness arrayed.

2 Sing praise to the Lord!
   praise him upon earth
   in tuneful accord,
   you saints of new birth:
   praise him who has brought you
   his grace from above;
   praise him who has taught you
   to sing of his love.

3 Sing praise to the Lord!
   all things that give sound,
   each jubilant chord
   re-echo around:
   loud organs, his glory
   proclaim in deep tone,
   and sweet harp, the story
   of what he has done.

4 Sing praise to the Lord!
   thanksgiving and song
   to him be outpoured
   all ages along:
   for love in creation,
   for heaven restored,
   for grace of salvation,
   sing praise to the Lord!

   Amen, amen.

355

Charlotte Elliott
© in this version Jubilate Hymns†

1 Christian, seek not yet repose,
   cast your dreams of ease away:
   you are in the midst of foes –
       watch and pray.

2 Wicked forces, evil powers,
   gathered in unseen array,
   wait for your unguarded hours –
       watch and pray.

3 Put your heavenly armour on,
   wear it always night and day;
   ambushed lies the evil one –
       watch and pray.

4 Hear, above all, hear your Lord;
   love him, serve him and obey,
   treasure in your heart his word –
       watch and pray.

5 Watch, as if on that alone
   hung the issue of the day;
   pray that victory shall be won –
       watch and pray.

356

J. G. Whittier
© in this version Jubilate Hymns†

1 Dear Lord and Father of mankind,
   forgive our foolish ways:
   reclothe us in our rightful mind;
   in purer lives your service find,
       in deeper reverence praise,
       in deeper reverence praise.

2 In simple trust like theirs who heard,
   beside the Syrian sea,
   the gracious calling of the Lord –
   let us, like them, obey his word:
       'Rise up and follow me,
       rise up and follow me!'

3 O sabbath rest by Galilee!
   O calm of hills above,
   when Jesus shared on bended knee
   the silence of eternity
       interpreted by love,
       interpreted by love!

4 With that deep hush subduing all
   our words and works that drown
   the tender whisper of your call,
   as noiseless let your blessing fall
       as fell your manna down,
       as fell your manna down.

5 Drop your still dews of quietness,
   till all our strivings cease;
   take from our souls the strain and stress,
   and let our ordered lives confess
       the beauty of your peace,
       the beauty of your peace.

6 Breathe through the heats of our desire
   your coolness and your balm;
   let sense be dumb, let flesh retire,
   speak through the earthquake, wind, and fire,
       O still small voice of calm,
       O still small voice of calm!

357 from Ephesians 3
© Christopher Idle†

1 Father and God,
    from whom our world derives
all fatherhood in every family,
we bow our knees for power to fill our lives –
your mighty grace, your Spirit's energy:

2 For Christ to make his home in every heart,
to plant and build us
    in his love's pure strength;
to help his church to grasp in every part
love's boundless height and depth,
    and breadth and length.

3 With all God's fulness let us now be filled,
and know the splendour
    of his love unknown;
expect the gifts a father gives his child
and see the trophies that our king has won.

4 To God be praise! His power in us can do
far more than we can ask or understand;
through Jesus Christ
    who by his church makes new
for every age the glories God has planned.

358 from *The Lord's Prayer*, J. E. Seddon
© Mrs. M. Seddon†

1 Father God in heaven,
    Lord most high:
hear your children's prayer,
    Lord most high:
hallowed be your name,
    Lord most high –
O Lord, hear our prayer.

2 May your kingdom come
    here on earth;
may your will be done
    here on earth,
as it is in heaven
    so on earth –
O Lord, hear our prayer.

3 Give us daily bread
    day by day,
and forgive our sins
    day by day,
as we too forgive
    day by day –
O Lord, hear our prayer.

4 Lead us in your way,
    make us strong;
when temptations come
    make us strong;
save us all from sin,
    keep us strong –
O Lord, hear our prayer.

5 All things come from you,
    all are yours –
kingdom, glory, power,
    all are yours;
take our lives and gifts,
    all are yours –
O Lord, hear our prayer.

359 E. Cooper

1 Father of heaven, whose love profound
a ransom for our souls has found:
before your throne we sinners bend –
to us your pardoning love extend.

2 Almighty Son, incarnate Word,
our prophet, priest, redeemer, Lord:
before your throne we sinners bend –
to us your saving grace extend.

3 Eternal Spirit, by whose breath
the soul is raised from sin and death:
before your throne we sinners bend –
to us your living power extend.

4 Jehovah – Father, Spirit, Son –
mysterious Godhead, Three-in-One:
before your throne we sinners bend –
grace, pardon, life to us extend.

360 Love M. Willis

1 Father, hear the prayer we offer –
not for ease our prayer shall be,
but for strength that we may ever
live our lives courageously.

2 Not for ever in green pastures
do we ask our way to be;
but the steep and rugged pathway
may we tread rejoicingly.

3 Not for ever by still waters
would we idly rest and stay;
but would strike the living fountains
from the rocks along our way.

4 Be our strength in hours of weakness,
in our wanderings be our guide;
through endeavour, failure, danger,
Father, be there at our side.

361
H. W. Baker
© in this version Jubilate Hymns†

1 God made me for himself, to serve him here
with love's pure service and in filial fear;
to show his praise, to labour for him now,
then see his glory where the angels bow.

2 All needful grace was mine
through his dear Son
whose life and death my full salvation won;
grace that would give me strength
and hold me fast,
grace that would seal and crown my work
at last.

3 And I, poor sinner, threw it all away,
lived for the work or pleasure of each day –
as if no Christ had shed his precious blood,
as if I owed no homage to my God.

4 O Holy Spirit, with your fire divine
melt into tears this thankless heart of mine:
teach me to love what once I seemed to hate
and live to God before it is too late.

362
Brian Foley
© Faber Music Ltd

1 How can we sing with joy to God,
how can we pray to him,
when we are far away from God
in selfishness and sin?

2 How can we claim to do God's will
when we have turned away
from things of God to things of earth,
and willed to disobey?

3 How can we praise the love of God
which all his works make known,
when all our works turn from his love
to choices of our own?

4 God knows the sinful things we do,
the Godless life we live,
yet in his love he calls to us,
so ready to forgive.

5 So we will turn again to God –
his ways will be our ways,
his will our will, his love our love,
and he himself our praise!

363
J. Newton

1 Great Shepherd of your people, hear!
your presence now display;
as you have given a place for prayer,
so give us hearts to pray.

2 Within these walls let holy peace
and love and friendship dwell;
here give the troubled conscience ease,
the wounded spirit heal.

3 May we in faith receive your word,
in faith present our prayers;
and in the presence of our Lord
unburden all our cares.

4 The hearing ear, the seeing eye,
the contrite heart bestow;
and shine upon us from on high,
that we in grace may grow.

364
W. Pennefather

1 Jesus, stand among us
in your risen power;
let this time of worship
be a hallowed hour.

2 Breathe the Holy Spirit
into every heart;
bid the fears and sorrows
from each soul depart.

3 Thus with quickened footsteps
we'll pursue our way,
watching for the dawning
of the eternal day.

365
from Psalm 61, J. E. Seddon
© Mrs. M. Seddon†

1 Listen to my prayer, Lord,
hear my humble cry;
when my heart is fainting,
to your throne I fly.

2 In earth's farthest corner
you will hear my voice:
set me on your rock, Lord,
then I shall rejoice.

3 You have been my shelter
when the foe was near,
as a tower of refuge
shielding me from fear.

4 I will rest for ever
in your care and love,
guarded and protected
as by wings above.

5 All that I have promised,
help me to fulfil;
and in all who love you
work your perfect will.

6 May your truth and mercy
  keep me all my days;
  let my words and actions
  be my songs of praise!

5 Patience to watch and weep and wait,
  whatever you may send;
  courage that will not hesitate
  to trust you to the end.

6 Give these, and then your will be done;
  thus, strengthened with all might,
  we through your Spirit and your Son
  shall pray, and pray aright.

366 H. M. Butler

1 'Lift up your hearts!' We lift them to the Lord,
  and give to God our thanks with one accord;
  it is our joy and duty, all our days
  to lift our hearts in grateful thanks and praise.

2 Above the level of the former years,
  the mire of sin, the slough of guilty fears,
  the mist of doubt, the blight of love's decay –
  O Lord of light, lift all our hearts today!

3 Above the swamps of subterfuge and shame,
  the deeds, the thoughts,
    that honour may not name,
  the halting tongue
    that dares not tell the whole –
  O Lord of truth, lift every Christian soul!

4 Above the storms that darken human life –
  pride, jealousy and envy, rage and strife;
  where cold mistrust
    holds friend and friend apart –
  O Lord of love, lift every Christian heart!

5 Then, with the trumpet call as Christ appears,
  'Lift up your hearts!' rings, pealing in our ears;
  still shall our hearts respond with full accord –
  'We lift them up, we lift them to the Lord!'

368 W. Cowper
© in this version Jubilate Hymns†

1 O for a closer walk with God,
  the calm of sins forgiven,
  a light to shine upon the road
  that leads at last to heaven.

2 O gentle Messenger, return –
  return, O holy Dove;
  I hate the sins that made you mourn
  and grieved your heart of love.

3 Restore the happiness I knew
  when first I saw the Lord;
  refresh me with the radiant view
  of Jesus and his word!

4 From every idol I have known
  now set my spirit free;
  O make me worship you alone,
  and reign supreme in me.

5 So shall my walk be close with God,
  my wanderings be forgiven;
  so shall his light mark out the road
  that leads at last to heaven.

367 J. Montgomery

1 Lord, teach us how to pray aright
  with reverence and with fear:
  though dust and ashes in your sight,
  we may, we must draw near.

2 We perish if we cease from prayer:
  O grant us power to pray;
  and when to meet you we prepare,
  Lord, meet us by the way.

3 O God of love, before your face
  we come with contrite heart
  to ask from you these gifts of grace –
  truth in the inward part:

4 Faith in the only Sacrifice
  that can for sin atone;
  to found our hopes, to fix our eyes
  on Christ, and Christ alone:

369 F. W. Faber
© in this version Jubilate Hymns†

1 My God, how wonderful you are,
  your majesty how bright;
  how beautiful your mercy-seat
  in depths of burning light!

2 Creator from eternal years
  and everlasting Lord,
  by holy angels day and night
  unceasingly adored!

3 How wonderful, how beautiful
  the sight of you must be –
  your endless wisdom, boundless power,
  and awesome purity!

4 O how I fear you, living God,
  with deepest, tenderest fears,
  and worship you with trembling hope
  and penitential tears!

5 But I may love you too, O Lord,
  though you are all-divine,
  for you have stooped to ask of me
  this feeble love of mine.

6 Father of Jesus, love's reward,
  great king upon your throne,
  what joy to see you as you are
  and know as I am known!

370 J. Newton

1 May the grace of Christ our saviour
  and the Father's boundless love,
  with the Holy Spirit's favour,
  rest upon us from above.

2 So may we remain in union
  with each other and the Lord,
  and possess, in sweet communion,
  joys which earth cannot afford.

371 W. Cowper

1 Lord Jesus, when your people meet
  they come before your mercy-seat;
  where you are sought, you shall be found,
  and every place is holy ground.

2 Your presence, by no walls confined,
  is known within the humble mind;
  the meek will bring you where they come,
  and going take you to their home.

3 Great Shepherd of your chosen few,
  your former mercies here renew;
  here to our waiting hearts proclaim
  the greatness of your saving name.

4 Here may we prove the power of prayer
  to strengthen faith and sweeten care;
  to teach our faint desires to rise
  and bring all heaven before our eyes.

5 Lord, we are few, but you are near,
  your arm can save, your ear can hear:
  break through the heavens,
      come quickly down,
  and make a thousand hearts your own!

372 J. Montgomery
© in this version Jubilate Hymns†

1 Prayer is the soul's supreme desire
  expressed in thought or word;
  the burning of a hidden fire,
  a longing for the Lord.

2 Prayer is the simplest sound we teach
  when children learn God's name;
  and yet it is the noblest speech
  that human lips can frame.

3 Prayer is the secret battleground
  where victories are won;
  by prayer the will of God is found
  and work for him begun.

4 Prayer is the Christian's vital breath,
  the Christian's native air,
  our watchword at the gates of death;
  we enter heaven with prayer.

5 Prayer is the church's glorious song,
  our task and joy supreme;
  we name our Lord in every tongue,
  and praise is all our theme.

6 Jesus, by whom we come to God,
  the true and living way,
  the humble path of prayer you trod,
  Lord, teach us how to pray.

373 J. M. Scriven

1 What a friend we have in Jesus,
  all our sins and griefs to bear;
  what a privilege to carry
  everything to God in prayer!
  O what peace we often forfeit,
  O what needless pain we bear,
  all because we do not carry
  everything to God in prayer.

2 Have we trials and temptations,
  is there trouble anywhere?
  We should never be discouraged:
  take it to the Lord in prayer.
  Can we find a friend so faithful
  who will all our sorrows share?
  Jesus knows our every weakness –
  take it to the Lord in prayer.

3 Are we weak and heavy-laden,
  burdened with a load of care?
  Jesus is our mighty saviour:
  he will listen to our prayer.
  Do your friends despise, forsake you?
  take it to the Lord in prayer;
  in his arms he will enfold you
  and his love will shield you there.

374 from Psalm 17, I. Williams
© in this version Jubilate Hymns†

1 O Lord our guardian and our guide,
be near us when we call;
uphold us when our footsteps slide,
and raise us when we fall.

2 The world, the flesh and Satan dwell
around the path we tread;
O save us from the snares of hell,
Deliverer from the dead!

3 And if we tempted are to sin,
and evil powers are strong;
be present, Lord, keep watch within
and save our souls from wrong.

4 Still let us always watch and pray,
and know that we are frail;
that if the tempter cross our way,
yet he shall not prevail.

375 C. Wesley

1 Come, let us with our Lord arise!
our Lord who made both earth and skies,
who died to save the world he made
and rose triumphant from the dead:
he rose, the prince of life and peace,
and stamped the day for ever his.

2 This is the day the Lord has made
that all may see his love displayed,
may feel his resurrection's power
and rise again to fall no more,
in perfect righteousness renewed
and filled with all the life of God.

3 Then let us render him his own,
with solemn prayer approach the throne,
with meekness hear the gospel word,
with thanks his dying love record,
our joyful hearts and voices raise
and fill his courts with songs of praise.

376 © David Mowbray†

1 First of the week and finest day,
when God commanded light to shine:
cast darkness and its works away
to celebrate with bread and wine!

2 First of the week was Easter morn
when Christ the Lord from death was raised;
new life, fresh hope that day was born
and God in heaven and earth was praised.

3 First of the week the Spirit came
to fill the church with grace and power;
the rushing wind and tongues of flame
were heralds of that promised hour.

4 First of the week we set aside
to meet, to learn, to give, to pray;
to spread Christ's gospel far and wide –
in truth, this is the Lord's own day!

377 I. Watts

1 Sweet is the work, my God, my King,
to praise your name, give thanks and sing;
to show your love by morning light,
and talk of all your truth at night.

2 Sweet is the day, the first and best,
on which I share your sacred rest;
so let my heart in tune be found,
like David's harp of joyful sound.

3 My heart shall triumph in the Lord
and bless his works, and bless his word:
God's works of grace, how bright they shine –
how deep his counsels, how divine!

4 Soon I shall see and hear and know
all I desired on earth below,
and all my powers for God employ
in that eternal world of joy.

378 © Michael Saward†

1 Ring from your steeple, bells of gladness!
this is the day the world was born;
God's voice rang out across the darkness,
light filled the sky that primal morn.

2 Ring from your steeple, bells of victory!
this is the day death's sting was drawn;
God's voice rang out, the tomb was empty,
hope sprang alive that Easter morn.

3 Ring from your steeple, bells of power!
this is the day when, at the dawn,
God's voice rang out through wind and fire,
hearts became strong that Whitsun morn.

4 Ring from your steeple, bells of heaven!
this is the day when none shall mourn;
God's voice rings out this one-in-seven,
joy fills his church this Sunday morn.

379 I. Watts

1 This is the day the Lord has made,
he calls the hours his own:
let heaven rejoice, let earth be glad,
and praise surround the throne.

2 Today he rose and left the dead,
and Satan's empire fell;
today the saints his triumphs spread,
and all his wonders tell.

3 Hosanna to the anointed king,
to David's holy Son!
help us, O Lord; descend and bring
salvation from your throne.

4 Blessed be the Lord, who freely came
to save our sinful race;
he comes, in God his Father's name,
with words of truth and grace.

5 Hosanna in the highest strains
the church on earth can raise!
the highest heaven in which he reigns
shall give him nobler praise.

380 J. Ellerton

1 This is the day of light –
let there be light today!
Arise, O Christ, to end our night
and chase its gloom away.

2 This is the day of rest –
our inner strength renew;
on lives by many cares oppressed
send your refreshing dew.

3 This is the day of peace –
with peace our spirits fill;
bid all the blasts of discord cease,
the waves of strife be still.

4 This is the day of prayer
let earth to heaven draw near!
Lift up our hearts to seek you there;
come down to meet us here.

5 This is the first of days:
come, with your living breath
and wake dead souls to love and praise,
O Victor over death!

381 © Michael Saward†

1 Baptized in water,
sealed by the Spirit,
cleansed by the blood of Christ our king;
heirs of salvation,
trusting his promise –
faithfully now God's praise we sing.

2 Baptized in water,
sealed by the Spirit,
dead in the tomb with Christ our king;
one with his rising,
freed and forgiven
thankfully now God's praise we sing.

3 Baptized in water,
sealed by the Spirit,
marked with the sign of Christ our king;
born of one Father,
we are his children –
joyfully now God's praise we sing.

382 © Michael Perry†

1 Born of the water,
born of the Spirit –
called by the wind and the fire;
sealed with his promise,
we shall inherit
more than the most we desire.

2 One through redemption,
one with the Father –
children of grace and of heaven;
joyfully sharing
faith with each other,
sinners whose sins are forgiven.

3 Glory, all glory,
glory to Jesus –
die we in him and we live!
friends for his service,
heirs to the treasures
God, and God only, can give.

383 © John Bowers

Christians, lift up your hearts,
and make this a day of rejoicing;
God is our strength and song –
glory and praise to his name!

1 Here God's life-giving word
once more is proclaimed to his people,
uplifting those who are down,
challenging all with its truth:
Christians, lift up your hearts . . .

2 All those baptized into Christ
share the glory of his resurrection,
dying with him unto sin,
walking in newness of life:
    Christians, lift up your hearts,
    and make this a day of rejoicing;
    God is our strength and song –
    glory and praise to his name!

3 Summoned by Christ's command
his people draw near to his table,
gladly to greet their Lord
known in the breaking of bread:
    Christians, lift up your hearts . . .

384 © Timothy Dudley-Smith

1 Father, now behold us
and this child, we pray;
in your love enfold us,
wash our sins away.

2 Christ's eternal blessing
for this life we claim:
faith, by ours, professing;
signed in Jesus' name.

3 By the Spirit tended,
childhood grow to youth;
from all ill defended,
full of grace and truth.

4 God of all creation,
stoop from heaven's throne,
and by Christ's salvation
make this child your own!

385 © Basil Bridge

1 God the Father, name we treasure,
each new generation draws
from the past that you have given
for the future that is yours:
may these children, in your keeping,
love your ways, obey your laws.

2 Christ, the name that Christians carry;
Christ, who from the Father came,
calling us to share your sonship,
for these children grace we claim:
may they be your true disciples,
yours in deed as well as name.

3 Holy Spirit, from the Father
on the friends of Jesus poured:
may our children share those graces
promised to them in the word,
and their gifts find rich fulfilment,
dedicated to our Lord.

386 © Michael Saward†

1 Have you not heard? Do you not know
that Christ has died for you?
that through his death he conquered death
to pay the ransom due.

2 What shall we say? How shall we live?
since through his word revealed
he calls on us to die with him,
deep in his tomb concealed.

3 Is there no hope? Is there no joy?
Yes! Bursting from the grave,
baptized in him we rise to life
freed by his power to save.

4 One in his death, one in his life,
in baptism restored,
we trust his promise, know his power
and serve our mighty Lord.

387 © Michael Saward†

1 My trust I place in God's good grace
his promises believing,
for now I see Christ died for me
my pardon thus achieving.

2 By water's sign this gift is mine,
my guilt has gone for ever;
for Christ the Son and I are one –
this bond no power can sever.

3 His word is true, my heart is new,
my life is joy unbounded,
for he will save me from the grave
while Satan stands confounded.

4 So now I sing of Christ my king,
his holy name confessing
who by this deed gives all I need
and fills me with his blessing.

388 © Michael Saward†

1 This is the truth which we proclaim,
God makes a promise firm and sure;
marked by this sign made in his name,
here, for our sickness, God's own cure.

2 This is the grave in which we lie:
pierced to the heart by sin's sharp sword,
risen with Christ, to self we die
and live to praise our reigning Lord.

3 This is the sacrament of birth:
sealed by a Saviour's death for sin,
trust in his mercy all on earth,
open your hearts and let him in!

4 This is the covenant of grace –
God to the nations shows his love;
people of every tribe and race,
born by his Spirit from above.

5 This is the badge we proudly wear:
washed by our God, the Three-in-One;
welcomed in fellowship, we share
hope of eternal life begun.

389 © John Geyer

1 We know that Christ is raised
and dies no more;
embraced by futile death he broke its hold,
and our despair he turned to blazing joy:
Alleluia!

2 We share by water in his saving death;
this union brings to being one new cell,
a living and organic part of Christ:
Alleluia!

3 The Father's splendour
clothes the Son with life,
the Spirit's fission shakes the church of God;
baptized we live with God the Three-in-One:
Alleluia!

4 A new creation comes to life and grows
as Christ's new body
takes on flesh and blood;
the universe restored and whole will sing:
Alleluia! (Amen.)

390 © Michael Perry†

1 Now through the grace of God we claim
this life to be his own,
baptized with water in the name
of Father, Spirit, Son.

2 For Jesus Christ the crucified,
who broke the power of sin,
now lives to plead for those baptized
in unity with him.

3 So let us act upon his word,
rejoicing in our faith,
until we rise with Christ our Lord
and triumph over death!

391 © Angela Tilby

1 All-holy Father, king of endless glory,
faithful creator, look on your creation:
singing we praise you in this banquet given
for our salvation.

2 Now we remember how your servant Jesus
fed his companions,
bread and wine supplying,
gave them his presence in these holy tokens,
pledge of his dying.

3 Father, we bless you in this celebration:
praise for the body broken for our healing,
praise for the sacred blood
of our redemption,
mercy revealing.

4 Hear our petitions which we bring before you:
guard us in weakness – comfort the forsaken,
strengthen the tempted; give to all the faithful
victory unshaken.

392 W. Bright
© in this version Jubilate Hymns†

1 And now, O Father, mindful of the love
which bought us once for all
on Calvary's tree,
and having with us Christ who reigns above,
we celebrate with joy for all to see
that only offering perfect in your eyes:
the one true, pure, immortal sacrifice.

2 Look, Father, look on his anointed face,
and only look on us as found in him;
look not on our misusings of your grace,
our prayer so feeble and our faith so dim;
for, set between our sins and their reward,
we see the cross of Christ, your Son, our Lord.

3 And so we come: O draw us to your feet,
most patient Saviour, who can love us still;
and by this food, so awesome and so sweet,
deliver us from every touch of ill;
for your glad service, Master, set us free,
and make of us what you would have us be.

393 Fred Kaan
© 1968 Galliard Ltd/Stainer & Bell Ltd

1 As we break the bread
and taste the life of wine,
we bring to mind our Lord,
man of all time.

2 Grain is sown to die;
it rises from the dead,
becomes through human toil
our common bread.

3 Pass from hand to hand
the living love of Christ!
machine and man provide
bread for this feast.

4 Jesus binds in one
our daily life and work;
he is of all mankind
symbol and mark.

5 Having shared the bread
that died to rise again,
we rise to serve the world,
scattered as grain.

394 © David Mowbray†

1 At the supper, Christ the Lord
gathered friends and said the blessing;
bread was broken, wine was poured,
faith in Israel's God expressing:
signs of the forthcoming passion,
tokens of a great salvation.

2 After supper, Jesus knelt,
taking towel and bowl of water;
washing the disciples' feet,
servant now as well as master:
'You,' said he, 'have my example –
let your way of life be humble!'

3 In the fellowship of faith
Christ himself with us is present;
supper of the Lord in truth,
host and master all-sufficient!
From this table, gladly sharing,
send us, Lord, to love and caring.

395 from J. and C. Wesley's *Hymns on the Lord's Supper* © in this version Jubilate Hymns†

1 Author of life divine,
we see your table spread
with drink – the mystic wine,
and food – the eternal bread:
preserve the life that you have given
that we may eat with you in heaven.

2 Our hungry souls sustain
with fresh supplies of love,
till all your life we gain
and all your strength we prove;
till we receive your perfect grace
and rise to see you face to face.

396 R. Heber

1 Bread of the world in mercy broken,
wine of the soul in mercy shed;
by whom the words of life were spoken
and in whose death our sins are dead:

2 Look on the heart by sorrow broken,
look on the tears by sinners shed,
and make your feast to us the token
that by your grace our souls are fed.

397 unknown © in this version Jubilate Hymns†

1 Behold the eternal King and Priest
here brings for me the bread and wine;
himself the master of the feast,
his flesh and blood the food divine.

2 Lord Christ, I come, I hear your call,
I eat and drink at your command;
low at your feet I humbly fall –
O touch me with your nail-pierced hand!

3 Wash clean my heart and make it new,
to beat with love for you alone;
so let me find my life in you,
and have no will except your own.

4 In strength or weakness, be my rest,
in joy or sorrow, be my friend:
so all my life I shall be blessed,
and by your mercy, gain my end.

398 J. Conder © in this version Jubilate Hymns†

1 Bread of heaven, on you we feed,
for your flesh is food indeed;
always may our souls be fed
with this true and living bread;
day by day our strength supplied
through your life, O Christ, who died.

2 Vine of heaven, your precious blood
seals today our peace with God;
Lord, your wounds our healing give,
to your cross we look and live:
Jesus, with your power renew
those who live by faith in you!

399
G. W. Briggs, © Oxford University Press
and in this version Jubilate Hymns

1 Come, risen Lord, as guest among your own!
come and preside that we with you may dine;
here at your table
    make your presence known
in this our sacrament of bread and wine.

2 We meet as in that upper room they met,
here with your word of blessing
    now you stand;
this is your body: you are with us yet –
faith still receives the cup as from your hand.

3 We are one body, for we all partake –
one church united in communion blessed;
one name we bear,
    one bread of life we break,
with all your saints on earth and saints at rest.

4 One with each other, Lord, and one in you –
Jesus, our saviour and our living head;
we are your people: come, our faith renew,
be known to us in breaking of the bread.

400
after J. Franck, Catherine Winkworth
© in this version Jubilate Hymns†

1 Deck yourself, my soul, with gladness;
leave the gloomy haunts of sadness.
Come into the daylight's splendour,
there with joy your praises render
to the Lord whose grace unbounded
has this royal banquet founded:
though all other powers excelling,
with my soul he makes his dwelling.

2 Lord, I bow before you lowly,
filled with joy most deep and holy,
as with trembling awe and wonder
all your mighty works I ponder –
how, by mystery surrounded,
depth no-one has ever sounded,
none may dare to pierce unbidden
secrets that in you are hidden.

3 Shining sun, my life you brighten,
radiance, you my soul enlighten;
joy, the best of all our knowing,
fountain, swiftly in me flowing:
at your feet I kneel, my Maker –
let me be a fit partaker
of this sacred food from heaven,
for our good, your glory, given.

4 Jesus, Bread of life, I pray you,
let me gladly here obey you;
never to my hurt invited,
always by your love delighted:
from this banquet let me measure,
Lord, how vast and deep its treasure;
through the gifts your hands have given
let me be your guest in heaven.

401
from the Latin, after J. M. Neale
© in this version Jubilate Hymns†

1 Draw near and take the body of the Lord
and drink by faith
    the blood for you outpoured:

2 Saved by that body and that holy blood,
with souls refreshed
    give humble thanks to God.

3 Christ our redeemer, God's eternal Son,
once by his cross and blood the victory won:

4 He gave his life for greatest as for least;
himself the victim and himself the priest.

5 Victims were offered by the law of old –
shadows themselves,
    of Jesus' death they told:

6 Lord of all life and saviour of our race,
Christ has restored our hope
    and brought us grace.

7 Approach him now
    with trusting hearts sincere
and take the pledges of salvation here:

8 Christ who in this life all his saints defends,
gives to believers life that never ends.

9 He feeds the hungry
    with the bread of heaven
to those who thirst
    his living streams are given:

10 Judge of the nations, all to him must bow,
the king of ages, he is with us now.

402
after W. H. H. Jervois
© Michael Saward†

1 Father almighty, we your humble servants,
fed by the blood and body of our saviour,
offer ourselves, our souls and bodies to you –
    thanking you always.

2 We, as a living sacrifice, now ask you:
send us to work, empowered by your Spirit,
that we may live to bring you praise
    and glory –
    so let it be, Lord.

403 L. F. Benson

1 For the bread which you have broken,
for the wine which you have poured,
for the words which you have spoken,
now we give you thanks, O Lord.

2 By these pledges that you love us,
by your gift of peace restored,
by your call to heaven above us,
consecrate our lives, O Lord:

3 In your service, Lord, defend us,
help us to obey your word;
in the world to which you send us
let your kingdom come, O Lord!

404 C. V. Pilcher
© F. E. V. Pilcher

1 Here, Lord, we take the broken bread
and drink the wine, believing
that by your life our souls are fed,
your parting gifts receiving.

2 As you have given, so we would give
ourselves for others' healing;
as you have lived, so we would live
the Father's love revealing.

405 © Christopher Porteous
and in this version Jubilate Hymns†

1 He gave his life in selfless love,
for sinners once he came;
he had no stain of sin himself
but bore our guilt and shame:
he took the cup of pain and death,
his blood was freely shed;
we see his body on the cross,
we share the living bread.

2 He did not come to call the good
but sinners to repent;
it was the lame, the deaf, the blind
for whom his life was spent:
to heal the sick, to find the lost –
it was for such he came,
and round his table all may come
to praise his holy name.

3 They heard him call his Father's name –
then 'Finished!' was his cry;
like them we have forsaken him
and left him there to die:
the sins that crucified him then
are sins his blood has cured;
the love that bound him to a cross
our freedom has ensured.

4 His body broken once for us
is glorious now above;
the cup of blessing we receive,
a sharing of his love:
as in his presence we partake,
his dying we proclaim
until the hour of majesty
when Jesus comes again.

406 H. Bonar

1 Here, O my Lord, I see you face to face,
here faith can touch and handle
things unseen;
here I will grasp with firmer hand your grace
and all my weariness upon you lean.

2 Here I will feed upon the bread of God,
here drink with you the royal wine of heaven;
here I will lay aside each earthly load,
here taste afresh the calm of sin forgiven.

3 I have no help but yours, nor do I need
another arm but yours to lean upon;
it is enough, my Lord, enough indeed,
my hope is in your strength,
your strength alone.

4 Mine is the sin, but yours the righteousness;
mine is the guilt,
but yours the cleansing blood:
here is my robe, my refuge, and my peace;
your blood, your righteousness,
O Lord my God.

5 Too soon we rise, the symbols disappear;
the feast, though not the love, is past
and done:
gone are the bread and wine,
but you are here,
nearer than ever, still my shield and sun.

6 Feast after feast thus comes and passes by,
yet, passing, points to that glad feast above;
giving sweet foretaste of the festal joy,
the Lamb's great bridal feast of bliss and love.

407 H. W. Baker
© in this version Jubilate Hymns†

1 I am not worthy, holy Lord,
that you should come to me:
but speak the word! – one gracious word
can set the sinner free.

2 I am not worthy – cold and bare
the lodging of my soul:
how can you stoop to enter here?
Lord, speak and make me whole.

3 I am not worthy; yet, my God,
shall I turn you away
when you have given your flesh and blood
my ransom price to pay?

4 Come, feed me now with food divine
in the appointed hour,
and this unworthy heart of mine
fill with your love and power!

408 Brian Wren
© Oxford University Press

1 I come with joy to meet my Lord,
forgiven, loved, and free;
in awe and wonder to recall
his life laid down for me.

2 I come with Christians far and near
to find, as all are fed,
the new community of love
in Christ's communion bread.

3 As Christ breaks bread and bids us share,
each proud division ends;
the love that made us, makes us one,
and strangers now are friends.

4 And thus with joy we meet our Lord;
his presence, always near,
is in such friendship better known:
we see and praise him here.

5 Together met, together bound,
we'll go our different ways;
and as his people in the world
we'll live and speak his praise.

409 J. S. B. Monsell

1 I hunger and I thirst,
Jesus, my manna be:
O living waters, burst
out of the rock for me!

2 O bruised and broken bread,
my life-long needs supply:
as living souls are fed,
so feed me, or I die.

3 O true lifegiving vine,
let me your goodness prove:
by your life sweeten mine,
refresh my soul with love.

4 Rough paths my feet have trod
since first their course began:
renew me, bread of God,
restore me, Son of man.

5 For still the desert lies
behind me and before:
O living waters, rise
within me evermore!

410 after J. Montgomery
© in this version Jubilate Hymns†

1 O Lord, you gave in love divine
your body and your blood;
that living bread, that heavenly wine
is our immortal food:

2 You met with us in breaking bread;
so as we now depart,
O Saviour, stay with us and spread
your table in our heart.

411 Constance Coote

1 In the quiet consecration
of this glad communion hour,
here we rest in you, Lord Jesus,
taste your love and touch your power.

2 Here we learn through sacred symbol
all your grace can be and do,
by this wonderful indwelling –
you in us, and we in you.

3 Christ the living bread from heaven,
Christ whose blood is drink indeed,
here by faith and with thanksgiving
in our hearts on you we feed.

4 By your death for sin atoning,
by your resurrection-life,
hold us fast in joyful union,
strengthen us to face the strife.

5 While afar in solemn radiance
shines the feast that is to come –
after conflict, heaven's glory,
your great feast of love and home.

412 T. Cotterill

1 In memory of the Saviour's love
we keep the sacred feast,
where every humble contrite heart
is made a welcome guest.

2 By faith we take the bread of life
by which our souls are fed,
and drink the token of his blood
that was for sinners shed.

3 Around his table here we sing
   the wonders of his love,
   and so anticipate by faith
   the heavenly feast above.

413 from the Latin
R. Palmer

1 Jesus, the joy of loving hearts,
   true source of life, our lives sustain:
   from the best bliss that earth imparts
   we turn unfilled to you again.

2 Your truth unchanged has ever stood,
   you rescue those who on you call:
   to those yet seeking, you are good –
   to those who find you, all-in-all.

3 We taste of you, the living bread,
   and long to feast upon you still;
   we drink from you, the fountain-head,
   our thirsty souls from you we fill.

4 Our restless spirits long for you,
   whichever way our lot is cast,
   glad when your gracious smile we view,
   blessed when our faith can hold you fast.

5 Jesus, for ever with us stay,
   make all our moments calm and bright;
   chase the dark night of sin away,
   spread through the world your holy light.
      (Amen.)

414 Fred Kaan
© Stainer & Bell Ltd

1 Let us talents and tongues employ,
   reaching out with a shout of joy:
   bread is broken, the wine is poured,
   Christ is spoken and seen and heard.
      Jesus lives again,
      earth can breathe again,
      pass the Word around:
      loaves abound!

2 Christ is able to make us one,
   at the table he sets the tone,
   teaching people to live to bless,
   love in word and in deed express.
      Jesus lives again . . .

3 Jesus calls us in, sends us out
   bearing fruit in a world of doubt,
   gives us love to tell, bread to share:
   God Emmanuel everywhere!
      Jesus lives again . . .

415 © Basil Bridge

1 The Son of God proclaim!
   the Lord of time and space,
   the God who bade the light break forth
   now shines in Jesus' face.

2 He, God's creative Word,
   the church's Lord and head,
   here bids us gather as his friends
   and share his wine and bread.

3 The Lord of life and death
   with wondering praise we sing;
   we break the bread at his command
   and name him God and king.

4 We take this cup in hope,
   for he who gladly bore
   the shameful cross, is risen again
   and reigns for evermore.

416 G. Bourne

1 Lord, enthroned in heavenly splendour,
   glorious first-born from the dead,
   you alone our strong defender
   lifting up your people's head:
      Alleluia, alleluia,
   Jesus, true and living bread!

2 Prince of life, for us now living,
   by your body souls are healed;
   Prince of peace, your pardon giving,
   by your blood our peace is sealed:
      Alleluia, alleluia,
   Word of God in flesh revealed.

3 Paschal Lamb! your offering finished,
   once for all, when you were slain;
   in its fulness undiminished
   shall for evermore remain:
      Alleluia, alleluia,
   cleansing souls from every stain.

4 Great High Priest of our profession,
   through the veil you entered in,
   by your mighty intercession
   grace and mercy there to win:
      Alleluia, alleluia,
   only sacrifice for sin.

5 Life-imparting heavenly Manna,
   stricken rock, with streaming side;
   heaven and earth, with loud hosanna,
   worship you, the Lamb who died:
      Alleluia, alleluia,
   risen, ascended, glorified!

417 Patrick Appleford
© 1960 Josef Weinberger Ltd

1 Lord Jesus Christ, you have come to us,
   you are one with us, Mary's son;
   cleansing our souls from all their sin,
   pouring your love and goodness in:
   Jesus, our love for you we sing –
      living Lord!

At communion, this may be sung:
2 Lord Jesus Christ, now and every day
   teach us how to pray, Son of God;
   you have commanded us to do
   this in remembrance, Lord, of you:
   into our lives your power breaks through –
      living Lord!

3 Lord Jesus Christ, you have come to us,
   born as one of us, Mary's son;
   led out to die on Calvary,
   risen from death to set us free:
   living Lord Jesus, help us see
      you are Lord!

4 Lord Jesus Christ, I would come to you,
   live my life for you, Son of God;
   all your commands I know are true,
   your many gifts will make me new:
   into my life your power breaks through –
      living Lord!

418 P. Doddridge
© in this version Jubilate Hymns†

1 My God, now is your table spread,
   your cup with love still overflows:
   so may your children here be fed
   as Christ to us his goodness shows.

2 This holy feast, which Jesus makes
   a banquet of his flesh and blood
   how glad each one who comes and takes
   this sacred drink, this royal food!

3 His gifts that richly satisfy
   are yet to some in vain displayed:
   did not for them the saviour die –
   may they not share the children's bread?

4 My God, here let your table be
   a place of joy for all your guests,
   and may each one salvation see
   who now its sacred pledges tastes.

419 Fred Kaan
© 1968 Galliard Ltd/Stainer & Bell Ltd

1 Now let us from this table rise
   renewed in body, mind and soul;
   with Christ we die and live again,
   his selfless love has made us whole.

2 With minds alert, upheld by grace,
   to spread the word in speech and deed,
   we follow in the steps of Christ,
   at one with us in hope and need.

3 To fill each human house with love,
   it is the sacrament of care;
   the work that Christ began to do
   we humbly pledge ourselves to share.

4 Then give us courage, Father God,
   to choose again the pilgrim way,
   and help us to accept with joy
   the challenge of tomorrow's day!

420 W. H. Turton, © Hymns Ancient & Modern Ltd
and in this version Jubilate Hymns

1 O Christ, at your first eucharist you prayed
   that all your church might be for ever one;
   at every eucharist this prayer is made
   with longing heart and soul,
      'Your will be done':
   O may we all one bread, one body be
   through this blessed sacrament of unity.

2 For all your church, O Lord, we intercede
   that you will make our sad divisions cease:
   O draw us nearer each to each, we plead,
   by drawing all to you, the prince of peace.
      Thus may we all one bread, one body be
   through this blessed sacrament of unity.

3 We pray for those who wander
      from your fold:
   O bring them back,
      great Shepherd of the sheep
   back to the faith which saints believed of old,
   the faith for all your holy church to keep.
      Soon may we all one bread, one body be
   through this blessed sacrament of unity.

4 So, Lord, at length
      when sacraments shall cease,
   may we be one with all your church above;
   one with your saints in one unbroken peace,
   one with your saints in one unbounded love:
      Far happier then, in peace and love to be
   one with the Trinity-in-Unity!

421 E. Osler
© in this version Jubilate Hymns†

1 O God, unseen yet ever near,
your presence may we feel;
and thus, inspired with holy fear,
around your table kneel.

2 Here may your faithful people know
the blessings of your love,
the streams that through the desert flow,
the manna from above.

3 We come, obedient to your word,
to feast on heavenly food;
to eat the body of the Lord,
and drink his precious blood.

4 O living Bread, enduring Vine,
your words we shall obey,
and go, renewed with strength divine,
rejoicing on our way.

422 after C. H. Boutflower
© in this version Word & Music†

1 O joy of God, we seek you in the morning
and long to see the glory of your face:
rise on our darkness
with your sun's new dawning –
flood all our being in this feast of grace.

2 O life of God, for you our spirits hunger –
unless we feed on you we surely die:
with love and faith renewed
and hope grown younger
send us from here to serve you,
Lord most high.

3 O peace of God,
you pass our understanding –
safe through each moment
keep us every day:
with joy divine and mercy never ending,
direct our path and prosper all our way.

423 from a Syriac liturgy, J. M. Neale
C. Humphreys and P. Dearmer

1 Strengthen for service, Lord, the hands
that holy things have taken;
let ears that now have heard your songs
to clamour never waken.

2 Lord, may the tongues which 'Holy' sang
keep free from all deceiving;
the eyes which saw your love be bright,
the glorious hope perceiving:

3 The feet that tread your holy courts
from light be never banished;
the bodies by your Body fed,
be with new life replenished.

424 © Michael Saward†

1 O Sacrifice of Calvary,
O Lamb whose sacred blood was shed,
O great High Priest on heaven's throne,
O Victor from the dead!
here I recall your agony,
here see again your bloodstained brow;
beyond the sign of bread and wine
I know your presence now.

2 Your royal presence intercedes
eternally for me above,
and here my hungry spirit feeds
upon these gifts of love;
before your holy table laid
I kneel once more in hope and peace,
your blood and flesh my soul refresh
with joy that shall not cease.

425 H. F. Lyte

1 Abide with me, fast falls the eventide;
the darkness deepens: Lord, with me abide.
When other helpers fail and comforts flee,
help of the helpless, O abide with me.

2 Swift to its close ebbs out life's little day;
earth's joys grow dim, its glories pass away.
Change and decay in all around I see –
you never change, O Lord: abide with me!

3 I need your presence every passing hour:
what but your grace
can foil the tempter's power?
Who like yourself
my guide and strength can be?
Through cloud and sunshine,
Lord, abide with me!

4 I have no fear with you at hand to bless;
ills have no weight and tears no bitterness.
Where is death's sting?
Where, grave, your victory?
I triumph still if you abide with me.

5 Hold now your cross before my closing eyes;
shine through the gloom
and point me to the skies!
Heaven's morning breaks
and earth's vain shadows flee:
in life, in death, O Lord, abide with me!

426 © Elizabeth Cosnett

1 Can we by searching find out God
   or formulate his ways?
   Can numbers measure what he is
   or words contain his praise?

2 Although his being is too bright
   for human eyes to scan,
   his meaning lights our shadowed world
   through Christ, the Son of Man.

3 Our boastfulness is turned to shame,
   our profit counts as loss,
   when earthly values stand beside
   the manger and the cross.

4 We there may recognise his light,
   may kindle in its rays,
   find there the source of penitence,
   the starting-point for praise.

5 There God breaks in upon our search,
   makes birth and death his own:
   he speaks to us in human terms
   to make his glory known.

427 © Michael Perry†

1 God the Father of creation,
   master of the realms sublime,
   Lord of light and life's foundation:
      we believe and trust in him.

2 Christ who came from highest heaven,
   God from God before all time,
   Son for our redemption given:
      we believe and trust in him.

3 Spirit, God in us residing,
   power of life and love supreme,
   intercessor – pleading, guiding:
      we believe and trust in him.

4 Trinity of adoration!
   earth responds to heaven's theme;
   one the church's acclamation:
      we believe and trust in him!

428 © Ivor Jones

1 Christ, our king before creation,
   Life before all life began,
   crowned in deep humiliation
   by your partners in God's plan:
   make us humble in believing,
   and, believing, bold to pray
      'Lord, forgive our self-deceiving,
      come and reign in us today!'

2 Lord of time and Lord of history,
   giving, when the world despairs,
   faith to wrestle with the mystery
   of a God who loves and cares:
   make us humble in believing,
   and, believing, bold to pray
      'Lord, by grace beyond conceiving,
      come and reign in us today!'

3 Word that ends our long debating,
   Life of God which sets us free,
   through your body recreating
   Life as life is meant to be:
   make us humble in believing,
   and, believing, bold to pray
      'Lord, in us your aim achieving,
      come and reign in us today!'

429 J. H. Newman
© in this version Jubilate Hymns†

1 Firmly I believe and truly
   God is Three and God is One;
   and I next acknowledge duly
   manhood taken by the Son.

2 And I trust and hope most fully
   in that manhood crucified;
   and each thought and deed unruly
   do to death, for he has died.

3 Simply to his grace and wholly
   light and life and strength belong;
   and I love supremely, solely,
   Christ the holy, Christ the strong.

4 And I make this affirmation
   for the love of Christ alone:
   holy Church is his creation
   and his teachings are her own.

5 Honour, glory, power, and merit
   to the God of earth and heaven,
   Father, Son, and Holy Spirit –
   praise for evermore be given!

430 R. Keen
© in this version Jubilate Hymns†

1 How firm a foundation, you people of God,
   is laid for your faith in his excellent word!
   What more can he say to you than he has said
   to everyone trusting in Jesus our head?

2 Since Jesus is with you, do not be afraid;
   since he is your Lord,
      you need not be dismayed:
   he strengthens you, guards you,
      and helps you to stand,
   upheld by his righteous, omnipotent hand.

3 When through the deep waters
        he calls you to go,
the rivers of trouble shall not overflow;
the Lord will be with you, to help and to bless,
and work for your good
        through your deepest distress.

4 When through fiery trials
        your pathway shall lead,
his grace shall sustain you
        with all that you need;
the flames shall not hurt you – his only design
your dross to consume
        and your gold to refine.

5 Whoever has come to believe in his name
will not be deserted, and not put to shame;
though hell may endeavour
        that Christian to shake
his Lord will not leave him, nor ever forsake.

431 B. Rees
© Mrs. M. E. Rees

1 Have faith in God, my heart,
trust and be unafraid;
God will fulfil in every part
each promise he has made.

2 Have faith in God, my mind,
although your light burns low;
God's mercy holds a wiser plan
than you can fully know.

3 Have faith in God, my soul,
his cross for ever stands;
and neither life nor death can pluck
his children from his hands.

4 Lord Jesus, make me whole;
grant me no resting place
until I rest, heart, mind, and soul,
the captive of your grace.

432 Dorothy Greenwell

1 I am not skilled to understand
what God has willed, what God has planned;
I only know at his right hand
stands one who is my saviour.

2 I take him at his word and deed:
'Christ died to save me,' this I read;
and in my heart I find a need
of him to be my saviour.

3 That he should leave his place on high
and come for sinners here to die;
you find it strange? So once did I,
before I knew my saviour.

4 I hope that Christ my Lord may see
fulfilment of his work in me;
and with his child contented be,
as I with my dear saviour.

5 Yes, living, dying, let me bring
my strength, my comfort, from this spring:
that he who lives to be my king
once died to be my saviour.

433 Frances R. Havergal

1 I am trusting you, Lord Jesus,
you have died for me;
trusting you for full salvation
great and free.

2 I am trusting you for pardon –
at your feet I bow;
for your grace and tender mercy,
trusting now.

3 I am trusting you for cleansing,
Jesus, Son of God;
trusting you to make me holy
by your blood.

4 I am trusting you to guide me –
you alone shall lead;
every day and hour supplying
all my need.

5 I am trusting you for power –
yours can never fail;
words which you yourself shall give me
must prevail.

6 I am trusting you, Lord Jesus –
never let me fall;
I am trusting you for ever,
and for all.

434 © Michael Perry†

1 I believe in God the Father
who created heaven and earth;
holding all things in his power,
bringing light and life to birth.

2 I believe in God the Saviour,
Son of Man and Lord most high,
crucified to be redeemer,
raised to life that death may die.

3 I believe in God the Spirit,
wind of heaven and flame of fire,
pledge of all that we inherit,
sent to comfort and inspire.

4 Honour, glory, might and merit
be to God, and God alone!
Father, Son and Holy Spirit,
One-in-Three and Three-in-One.

435
H. Bonar
© in this version Jubilate Hymns†

1 I bless the Christ of God,
I rest on love divine,
and with unfaltering voice and heart
I call this Saviour mine.

2 For nothing I have done
can save my guilty soul;
no burden that my flesh has borne
can make my spirit whole.

3 Not what I feel or do –
no toil, nor pain nor blood,
not all my prayers and sighs and tears
can give me peace with God.

4 Your work alone, O Christ,
can ease this weight of sin;
your blood alone, O Lamb of God,
can give me peace within.

5 Not love for you, O Lord,
but your great love for me
can rid me of this dark unrest
and set my spirit free.

6 Your voice alone, O God,
can speak the word of grace
to calm the tempests in my heart
and make its raging cease.

7 And so I bless your name,
I trust your love divine;
by grace, for all eternity,
I dare to call you mine.

436
H. Bonar
© in this version Jubilate Hymns†

1 I hear the words of love,
I trust in Jesus' blood,
I see the mighty sacrifice –
and I have peace with God.

2 This everlasting peace,
as certain as his name,
is sure as God's eternal throne –
unchangeably the same.

3 Though love is sometimes cold,
and joy still ebbs and flows,
yet peace with God remains secure –
such faithfulness he shows.

4 I change, but he does not:
his truth can never lie;
his love, not mine, upholds my faith –
for Jesus shall not die.

437
W. T. Matson
© in this version Jubilate Hymns†

1 Lord, I was blind; I could not see
in your marred visage any grace:
but now the beauty of your face
in radiant vision dawns on me.

2 Lord, I was deaf; I could not hear
the thrilling music of your voice:
but now I hear you and rejoice,
and all your spoken words are dear.

3 Lord, I was dumb; I could not speak
the grace and glory of your name:
but now as touched with living flame
my lips will speak for Jesus' sake.

4 Lord, I was dead; I could not move
my lifeless soul from sin's dark grave:
but now the power of life you gave
has raised me up to know your love.

5 Lord, you have made the blind to see,
the deaf to hear, the dumb to speak,
the dead to live – and now I break
the chains of my captivity!

438
C. Wesley

1 Jesus, lover of my soul,
let me to your presence fly,
while the gathering waters roll,
while the tempest still is high.
Hide me, O my Saviour, hide,
till the storm of life is past;
safe into the haven, guide
and receive my soul at last.

2 Other refuge have I none,
all my hope in you I see:
leave, O leave me, not alone;
still support and comfort me.
All my trust on you is stayed,
all my help from you I bring:
cover my defenceless head
with the shadow of your wing.

3 You, O Christ, are all I want,
more than all in you I find:
raise the fallen, cheer the faint,
heal the sick and lead the blind.
Just and holy is your name,
I am all unworthiness;
false and full of sin I am,
you are full of truth and grace.

4 Plenteous grace with you is found,
  grace to wash away my sin:
  let the healing streams abound;
  make and keep me clean within.
  Living Fountain, now impart
  all your life and purity;
  spring for ever in my heart,
  rise to all eternity!

439 I. Watts
© in this version Jubilate Hymns†

1 What offering shall we give
  or what atonement bring
  to God by whom alone we live,
  high heaven's eternal king?

2 For all the blood of beasts
  on Jewish altars slain
  could never give the conscience peace
  or wash away its stain:

3 But Christ, the heavenly Lamb,
  takes all our sins away –
  a sacrifice of nobler name
  and richer blood than they.

4 In faith I lay my hand
  upon his head divine
  while as a penitent I stand
  and there confess my sin.

5 So I look back to see
  the weight he chose to bear
  when hanging on the cross for me –
  because my guilt was there.

6 Believing, we rejoice
  to know our sins forgiven;
  we bless the Lamb with heart and voice
  and join the praise of heaven.

440 Charlotte Elliott
© in this version Jubilate Hymns†

1 Just as I am, without one plea
  but that you died to set me free,
  and at your bidding 'Come to me!'
    O Lamb of God, I come.

2 Just as I am, without delay
  your call of mercy I obey –
  your blood can wash my sins away:
    O Lamb of God, I come.

3 Just as I am, though tossed about
  with many a conflict, many a doubt,
  fightings within and fears without,
    O Lamb of God, I come.

4 Just as I am, poor, wretched, blind!
  Sight, riches, healing of the mind –
  all that I need, in you to find:
    O Lamb of God, I come.

5 Just as I am! You will receive,
  will welcome, pardon, cleanse, relieve:
  because your promise I believe,
    O Lamb of God, I come.

6 Just as I am! Your love unknown
  has broken every barrier down:
  now to be yours, yes, yours alone,
    O Lamb of God, I come.

7 Just as I am! Of that free love
  the breadth, length, depth and height
    to prove,
  here for a time and then above,
    O Lamb of God, I come.

441 C. Wesley
© in this version Jubilate Hymns†

1 O come, our all-victorious Lord,
  your power to us make known;
  strike with the hammer of your word
  and break these hearts of stone.

2 If only we might all begin
  our foolishness to mourn,
  to turn at once from every sin
  and to our saviour turn!

3 Ourselves and God we need to know
  in this your gracious day;
  repentance, faith, and life bestow,
  and take our sins away.

4 Convict us first of unbelief,
  and freely then release;
  fill every soul with sacred grief
  and then with sacred peace.

5 Lord, make us poor; help us believe,
  and so make rich the poor;
  the knowledge of our sickness give,
  and knowledge of its cure.

6 The healthy sense of guilt impart
  and then remove the load;
  disturb, and then set free the heart
  by your atoning blood.

7 Our desperate state through sin declare,
  then speak our sins forgiven;
  for perfect holiness prepare
  and take us into heaven.

442 P. Doddridge
© in this version Jubilate Hymns†

1 O happy day that fixed my choice
on you, my Saviour and my God!
well may this grateful heart rejoice
and tell of Christ's redeeming blood.

2 It's done, the great transaction's done!
I am my Lord's, and he is mine;
he led me, and I followed on
responding to the voice divine.

3 Now rest, my long-divided heart,
in Jesus Christ who loves you, rest
and never from your Lord depart –
enriched in him, by him possessed!

4 So God, who heard my solemn vow,
in daily prayer shall hear my voice
till in my final breath I bow
and bless the day that fixed my choice.

443 F. W. Faber
© in this version Jubilate Hymns†

1 Restless souls, why do you scatter
like a flock of frightened sheep?
Doubting hearts, why do you wander
from a love so true and deep?

2 There's a wideness in God's mercy
like the wideness of the sea;
there's a kindness in his justice
which is more than liberty.

3 There is no place where earth's sorrows
are more keenly felt than heaven;
there is no place where earth's failings
have such gracious judgement given.

4 There is plentiful redemption
through the blood that Christ has shed;
there is joy for all the members
in the sorrows of the head.

5 For the love of God is broader
than the measure of our mind,
and the heart of the eternal
is most wonderfully kind.

6 If our love were but more simple
we should take him at his word,
and our lives would find fulfilment
in the goodness of the Lord.

444 A. M. Toplady
© in this version Jubilate Hymns†
(see also traditional version, 593)

1 Rock of ages, cleft for me,
hide me now, my refuge be;
let the water and the blood
from your wounded side which flowed,
be for sin the double cure,
cleanse me from its guilt and power.

2 Not the labours of my hands
can fulfil your law's demands;
could my zeal no respite know,
could my tears for ever flow,
all for sin could not atone:
you must save and you alone.

3 Nothing in my hand I bring,
simply to your cross I cling;
naked, come to you for dress,
helpless, look to you for grace;
stained by sin, to you I cry:
'Wash me, Saviour, or I die!'

4 While I draw this fleeting breath,
when my eyelids close in death,
when I soar through realms unknown,
bow before the judgement throne:
hide me then, my refuge be,
Rock of ages, cleft for me.

445 from Psalm 91
© Timothy Dudley-Smith

1 Safe in the shadow of the Lord,
beneath his hand and power,
I trust in him,
I trust in him,
my fortress and my tower.

2 My hope is set on God alone
though Satan spreads his snare;
I trust in him,
I trust in him
to keep me in his care.

3 From fears and phantoms of the night,
from foes about my way,
I trust in him,
I trust in him
by darkness as by day.

4 His holy angels keep my feet
secure from every stone;
I trust in him,
I trust in him,
and unafraid go on.

5 Strong in the everlasting name,
and in my Father's care,
I trust in him,
I trust in him
who hears and answers prayer.

6 Safe in the shadow of the Lord,
   possessed by love divine,
     I trust in him,
     I trust in him,
   and meet his love with mine.

446 Edith G. Cherry
© in this version Jubilee Hymns†

1 We trust in you, our shield and our defender;
   we do not fight alone against the foe:
   strong in your strength,
     safe in your keeping tender,
   we trust in you, and in your name we go.
   Strong in your strength . . .

2 We trust in you, O Captain of salvation!
   in your dear name, all other names above:
   Jesus our righteousness, our sure foundation,
   our prince of glory and our king of love.
   Jesus, our righteousness . . .

3 We go in faith,
     our own great weakness feeling,
   and needing more each day
     your grace to know;
   yet from our hearts a song of triumph pealing,
   'We trust in you, and in your name we go.'
   Yet from our hearts . . .

4 We trust in you, our shield and our defender:
   yours is the battle – yours shall be the praise!
   when passing through
     the gates of dazzling splendour,
   victors, we rest in you through endless days.
   When passing through . . .

447 from 2 Corinthians 4
© Timothy Dudley-Smith

1 Out of darkness let light shine!
   Formless void its Lord obeyed;
   at his word, by his design,
   sun and moon and stars were made.

2 Still his brightness shines abroad,
   darkened lives his light have known;
   all the glories of the Lord
   in the face of Christ are shown.

3 New creation's second birth
   bids eternal night depart;
   as the dawn of dawn on earth
   morning breaks within the heart.

4 Out of darkness let light shine,
   as it shone when light began;
   earth be filled with light divine,
   Christ be light for everyman!

448 I. Watts
© in this version Jubilee Hymns†

1 I'm not ashamed to name my Lord,
   or to defend his cause,
   maintain the honour of his word,
   the glory of his cross.

2 Jesus, my God! – I know his name,
   his name is all my trust;
   he will not put my soul to shame
   nor let my hope be lost.

3 Firm as his throne his promise stands,
   and he can well secure
   what he entrusted to my hands
   until that final hour.

4 Then he'll make known my worthless name
   before his Father's face,
   and in the new Jerusalem
   appoint to me a place.

449 A. Toplady

1 A debtor to mercy alone,
   of covenant-mercy I sing;
   nor fear, with your righteousness on,
   my person and offering to bring:
   the terrors of law and of God
   with me can have nothing to do;
   my saviour's obedience and blood
   hide all my transgressions from view.

2 The work which his goodness began,
   the arm of his strength will complete;
   his promise is 'Yes' and 'Amen',
   and never was forfeited yet:
   things future, nor things that are now,
   nor all things below or above,
   can make him his purpose forgo,
   or sever my soul from his love.

3 Eternity will not erase
   my name from the palms of his hands;
   in marks of indelible grace
   impressed on his heart it remains:
   yes, I to the end shall endure,
   as sure as the promise is given;
   more happy, but not more secure
   the glorified spirits in heaven.

450 J. Hart

1 How good is the God we adore!
  our faithful, unchangeable friend:
  his love is as great as his power
  and knows neither measure nor end.

2 For Christ is the first and the last;
  his Spirit will guide us safe home:
  we'll praise him for all that is past
  and trust him for all that's to come.

451 after J. Neander
        R. Bridges

1 All my hope on God is founded,
  all my trust he shall renew;
  he, my guide through changing order,
  only good and only true:
      God unknown,
      he alone,
  calls my heart to be his own.

2 Human pride and earthly glory,
  sword and crown betray his trust;
  what with care and toil we fashion,
  tower and temple, fall to dust;
      but God's power
      hour by hour
  is my temple and my tower.

3 Day by day our mighty giver
  grants to us his gifts of love;
  in his will our souls find pleasure,
  leading to our home above:
      Love shall stand
      at his hand,
  joy shall wait for his command.

4 Still from earth to God eternal
  sacrifice of praise be done;
  high above all praises praising
  for the gift of Christ his Son:
      Hear Christ's call
      one and all –
  we who follow shall not fall.

452 C. Wesley, © in this version Jubilate Hymns†
        (see also traditional version, 588)

1 And can it be that I should gain
  an interest in the Saviour's blood?
  Died he for me, who caused his pain;
  for me, who him to death pursued?
  Amazing love! – how can it be
  that you, my God, should die for me?

2 What mystery here! – the Immortal dies;
  who can explore his strange design?
  In vain the first-born seraph tries
  to sound the depths of love divine.
  Such mercy this! – let earth adore;
  let angel minds enquire no more.

3 He left his Father's throne above –
  so free, so infinite his grace –
  emptied himself of all but love,
  and bled for Adam's helpless race.
  What mercy this, immense and free,
  for, O my God, it found out me!

4 Long my imprisoned spirit lay,
  fast bound in sin and nature's night:
  your sunrise turned that night to day;
  I woke – the dungeon flamed with light.
  My chains fell off, your voice I knew;
  I rose, went out and followed you!

5 No condemnation now I dread;
  Jesus, and all in him, is mine!
  Alive in him, my living head,
  and clothed in righteousness divine,
  bold I approach the eternal throne
  and claim the crown through Christ my own.

453 Charitie L. de Chenez

1 Before the throne of God above
  I have a strong, a perfect plea:
  a great high priest, whose name is Love,
  who ever lives and pleads for me.

2 My name is written on his hands,
  my name is hidden in his heart;
  I know that while in heaven he stands
  no power can force me to depart.

3 When Satan tempts me to despair
  and tells me of the guilt within,
  upward I look, and see him there
  who made an end of all my sin.

4 Because the sinless Saviour died,
  my sinful soul is counted free;
  for God, the just, is satisfied
  to look on him and pardon me.

5 Behold him there! the risen Lamb,
  my perfect, sinless Righteousness,
  the great unchangeable I AM,
  the King of glory and of grace!

6 One with my Lord, I cannot die:
  my soul is purchased by his blood,
  my life is safe with Christ on high,
  with Christ, my saviour and my God.

454 T. Binney

1 Eternal light, eternal light!
how pure the soul must be
when, placed within your searching sight,
it does not fear, but with delight
can face such majesty.

2 The spirits who surround your throne
may bear that burning bliss;
but that is surely theirs alone,
since they have never, never known
a fallen world like this.

3 There is a way for us to rise
to that sublime abode:
an offering and a sacrifice,
a Holy Spirit's energies,
an advocate with God.

4 Such grace prepares us for the sight
of holiness above;
the child of ignorance and night
may dwell in the eternal light
through the eternal love.

455 John Eddison
© Scripture Union

1 Father, although I cannot see
the future you have planned,
and though the path is sometimes dark
and hard to understand:
yet give me faith, through joy and pain,
to trace your loving hand.

2 When I recall that in the past
your promises have stood
through each perplexing circumstance
and every changing mood,
I rest content that all things work
together for my good.

3 Whatever, then, the future brings
of good or seeming ill,
I ask for strength to follow you
and grace to trust you still;
and I would look for no reward,
except to do your will.

456 © Ernest Palfrey

1 It was
a man who was born
when no one expected it,
a king above all
though no one suspected it.
My God pledged his love,
my joy has reflected it.
So it was.

2 It was
as though I'd been born
when no one expected it,
released from a past
though no one suspected it;
the future a gift,
my joy has reflected it.
So it is.

457 from Romans 8
© Michael Perry†

1 He lives in us, the Christ of God,
his Spirit joins with ours;
he brings to us the Father's grace
with powers beyond our powers.
And if enticing sin grows strong,
when human nature fails,
God's Spirit in our inner self
fights with us, and prevails.

2 Our pangs of guilt and fears of death
are Satan's stratagems –
by Jesus Christ who died for us
God pardons; who condemns?
And when we cannot feel our faith,
nor bring ourselves to pray,
the Spirit pleads with God for us
in words we could not say.

3 God gave his Son to save us all –
no other love like this!
then shall he ever turn away
from those he marks as his?
And God has raised him from the grave,
in this we stand assured;
so none can tear us from his love
in Jesus Christ our Lord.

458 Anna L. Waring
© in this version Jubilate Hymns†

1 In heavenly love abiding,
  no change my heart shall fear:
  and safe is such confiding,
  for nothing changes here:
  the storm may roar around me,
  my heart may low be laid;
  my Father's arms surround me,
  how can I be afraid?

2 Wherever he may guide me
  no want shall turn me back;
  my shepherd is beside me
  and nothing can I lack:
  his wisdom is for ever,
  his sight is never dim;
  his love deserts me never
  and I will walk with him.

3 Green pastures are before me,
  which yet I have not seen;
  bright skies will shine with glory
  where threatening clouds have been:
  my hope I cannot measure,
  my path to life is free;
  my saviour has my treasure,
  and he will walk with me.

459 © David Mowbray†

1 In Christ shall all be made alive, we sing!
  in him God's children into life shall spring;
  though seed of Adam, creatures of the dust,
  we rise again through Christ
      in whom we trust.

2 This Christ shall reign,
      and sin and death defeat,
  beside the Father he will take his seat;
  then shall God's children share that victory
  and stand, new-clothed with immortality.

3 Yet here and now this faith is far from vain
  for in God's Son a forward glimpse we gain;
  in life's distress,
      with no fresh strength to draw,
  we rise, through him,
      to heights undreamed before.

4 In Christ shall all be made alive, we sing!
  with him God's faithful servants he will bring;
  gathered with joy before the Father's throne,
  there we shall know,
      as we ourselves are known.

460 after N. L. von Zinzendorf, J. Wesley
© in this version Jubilate Hymns†

1 Jesus, your blood and righteousness
  my beauty are, my glorious dress!
  mid flaming worlds, in these arrayed
  with joy shall I lift up my head.

2 Bold shall I stand in that great day,
  and none condemn me, try who may:
  fully absolved through Christ I am
  from sin and fear, from guilt and shame.

3 This stainless robe its beauty wears
  when all else fades with passing years;
  no age can change its glorious hue –
  the robe of Christ is ever new.

4 When from the dust of death I rise
  to claim my home beyond the skies,
  then this shall be my only plea –
  that Jesus died and lives for me!

5 O let the dead now hear your voice,
  let those once lost in sin rejoice!
  their beauty this, their glorious dress:
  Jesus, your blood and righteousness.

461 after J. Franck, Catherine Winkworth
© in this version Jubilate Hymns†

1 Jesus, priceless treasure,
  source of purest pleasure,
  friend most sure and true:
  long my heart was burning,
  fainting much and yearning,
  thirsting, Lord, for you:
  yours I am, O spotless Lamb,
  so will I let nothing hide you,
  seek no joy beside you!

2 Let your arms surround me:
  those who try to wound me
  cannot reach me here;
  though the world is shaking,
  earth and nations quaking,
  Jesus calms my fear:
  Satan's force must run its course
  and his bitter storms assail me;
  Jesus will not fail me.

3 Banish thoughts of sadness
  for the Lord of gladness,
  Jesus, enters in;
  though the clouds may gather,
  those who love the saviour
  still have peace within:
  though I bear much sorrow here
  still in you lies purest pleasure,
  Jesus, priceless treasure!

462
E. Mote
© in this version Jubilate Hymns†

1 My hope is built on nothing less
than Jesus' blood and righteousness;
no merit of my own I claim,
but wholly trust in Jesus' name.
 On Christ, the solid rock, I stand –
 all other ground is sinking sand.

2 When weary in this earthly race,
I rest on his unchanging grace;
in every wild and stormy gale
my anchor holds and will not fail.
 On Christ, the solid rock . . .

3 His vow, his covenant and blood
are my defence against the flood;
when earthly hopes are swept away
he will uphold me on that day.
 On Christ, the solid rock . . .

4 When the last trumpet's voice shall sound,
O may I then in him be found!
clothed in his righteousness alone,
faultless to stand before his throne.
 On Christ the solid rock . . .

463
Frances R. Havergal
© in this version Jubilate Hymns†

1 Like a river glorious
is God's perfect peace,
over all victorious,
in its bright increase:
perfect, yet still flowing
fuller every day;
perfect, yet still growing
deeper all the way.
 Trusting in the Father
 hearts are fully blessed,
 finding as he promised
 perfect peace and rest.

2 Hidden in the hollow
of his mighty hand
where no harm can follow,
in his strength we stand:
we may trust him fully
all for us to do;
those who trust him wholly
find him wholly true.
 Trusting in the Father . . .

464
verse 1 C. Wesley
verses 2 and 3 after P. Gerhardt
J. Wesley, © in this version Jubilate Hymns†

1 Still near me, O my Saviour, stand
and guard me in temptation's hour;
within the hollow of your hand
uphold me by your saving power:
no force in earth or hell shall move
or ever tear me from your love.

2 Still let your love point out my way –
what gifts of grace your love has brought!
still counsel me from day to day,
direct my work, inspire my thought:
and if I fall, soon let me hear
your voice, and know that love is near.

3 In suffering, let your love be peace,
in weakness let your love be power:
and when the storms of life shall cease,
Jesus, in that tremendous hour,
through death to life still be my guide
and save me then, for whom you died!

465
S. T. Francis
© in this version Jubilate Hymns†

1 Oh the deep, deep love of Jesus,
vast, unmeasured, boundless, free,
rolling as a mighty ocean
in its fulness over me!
Underneath me, all around me,
is the current of his love;
leading onward, leading homeward
to that glorious rest above.

2 Oh the deep, deep love of Jesus –
spread his praise from shore to shore!
he who loves us, ever loves us,
changes never, nevermore:
he who died to save his loved ones
intercedes for them above;
he who called them his own people
watches over them in love.

3 Oh the deep, deep love of Jesus,
love of every love the best;
vast the ocean of his blessing,
sweet the haven of his rest!
Oh the deep, deep love of Jesus –
for my Heaven of heavens is he;
this my everlasting glory –
Jesus' mighty love for me!

466 after B. S. Ingemann, S. Baring-Gould
© in this version Jubilate Hymns†

1 Through the night of doubt and sorrow
   onward goes the pilgrim band,
   singing songs of expectation,
   marching to the promised land.

2 One the hymn a thousand voices
   sing as from the heart of one;
   one the conflict, one the danger,
   one the march in God begun:

3 One the object of our journey,
   one the faith that never tires,
   one the urgent looking forward,
   one the hope our God inspires:

4 Courage, therefore, Christian pilgrims;
   with the cross before your eyes,
   bear its shame, and fight its battle –
   die with Christ, with Christ arise!

5 Soon shall come the great awakening,
   soon the bursting of the tomb;
   then the scattering of all shadows,
   and the end of tears and gloom.

467 E. H. Bickersteth
© in this version Jubilate Hymns†

1 Peace, perfect peace,
      in this dark world of sin?
   the blood of Jesus gives us peace within.

2 Peace, perfect peace,
      by troubled thoughts oppressed?
   to do the will of Jesus, this is rest.

3 Peace, perfect peace,
      when loved ones are in need?
   in Jesus' keeping we are safe indeed.

4 Peace, perfect peace,
      the future all unknown?
   we know that Jesus reigns upon the throne.

5 Peace, perfect peace,
      death shadowing us and ours?
   Christ Jesus conquered death
      and all its powers.

6 Jesus is Lord!
      Earth's struggles soon shall cease,
   and we shall come to heaven's perfect peace.

468 H. Bonar

1 Beloved, let us love: for love is of God;
   in God alone love has its true abode.

2 Beloved, let us love: for those who love,
   they only, are his children from above.

3 Beloved, let us love: for love is rest,
   and those who do not love cannot be blessed.

4 Beloved, let us love: for love is light,
   and those who do not love still live in night.

5 Beloved, let us love: for only thus
   shall we see God, the Lord, who first loved us.

469 W. J. Sparrow-Simpson and Jubilate Hymns
© amended text Novello and Company Ltd

1 All for Jesus, all for Jesus!
   this our song shall ever be:
   you our only hope, our saviour,
   yours the love that sets us free!

2 All for Jesus: you will give us
   strength to serve you hour by hour:
   none can move us from your presence
   while we trust your grace and power.

3 All for Jesus – you have loved us,
   all for Jesus – you have died,
   all for Jesus – you are with us;
   all for Jesus crucified.

4 All for Jesus, all for Jesus,
   all our talents and our powers,
   all our thoughts and words and actions,
   all our passing days and hours.

5 All for Jesus, all for Jesus!
   this the church's song shall be
   till at last her children gather,
   one in him eternally.

470 © Timothy Dudley-Smith

1 As water to the thirsty,
   as beauty to the eyes,
   as strength that follows weakness,
   as truth instead of lies,
   as songtime and springtime
   and summertime to be,
      so is my Lord,
      my living Lord,
   so is my Lord to me.

2 Like calm in place of clamour,
like peace that follows pain,
like meeting after parting,
like sunshine after rain,
like moonlight and starlight
and sunlight on the sea,
   so is my Lord,
    my living Lord,
so is my Lord to me.

3 As sleep that follows fever,
as gold instead of grey,
as freedom after bondage,
as sunrise to the day;
as home to the traveller
and all we long to see,
   so is my Lord,
    my living Lord,
so is my Lord to me.

471 Mary Shekleton
© in this version Jubilate Hymns†

1 Beyond all knowledge is your love divine,
my Saviour, Jesus! Yet this soul of mine
would of your love,
   in all its breadth and length,
its height and depth, and everlasting strength,
   know more and more.

2 Beyond all telling is your love divine,
my Saviour, Jesus! Yet this voice of mine
would gladly share with sinners far and near
your love which can remove all guilty fear
   and give love birth.

3 Beyond all praising is your love divine,
my Saviour, Jesus! Yet this heart of mine
would sing your love, so full, so rich, so free,
which brings a rebel sinner, such as me,
   back home to God.

4 O fill me, Saviour, Jesus, with your love!
renew me with your Spirit from above;
to you in simple faith let me draw near
to know, to tell, to sing your love so dear,
   my Lord and king.

472 W. Cowper
© in this version Jubilate Hymns†

1 Christian, do you hear the Lord?
Jesus speaks his gracious word;
gently sounds the saviour's call,
'Do you love me best of all?'

2 'I delivered you when bound,
and when bleeding, healed your wound;
saw you wandering, set you right,
turned your darkness into light.'

3 'Can a mother's tenderness
for her own dear child grow less?
Though she may forgetful be,
you are always dear to me.'

4 'Mine is an unchanging love,
higher than the heights above,
deeper than the depths beneath,
free and faithful, strong as death.'

5 'You shall see my glory soon,
when the work of grace is done;
crowned with splendour you shall be:
Christian, come and follow me!'

6 Lord, it is my chief complaint
that my love is weak and faint;
yet I love you, and adore –
O for grace to love you more!

473 after C. Coffin
R. Bridges

1 Happy are they, they who love God,
whose hearts have Christ confessed;
who by his cross have found their life,
beneath his yoke, their rest.

2 Glad is the praise, sweet are the songs,
when they together sing;
and strong the prayers that bow the ear
of heaven's eternal king.

3 Christ gives their homes pleasure and peace
and makes their loves his own;
but O what weeds the evil one
has in God's garden sown!

4 Sad were our life, evil this earth
did not its sorrows prove
the path by which the sheep may find
the fold of Jesus' love.

5 Then they shall know, they who love him,
how good shall come from pain;
and death itself cannot unbind
their happiness again.

474 from 1 Corinthians 13, C. Wordsworth
© in this version Jubilate Hymns†

1 Holy Spirit, gracious guest,
hear and grant our heart's request
for that gift supreme and best:
   holy heavenly love.

2 Faith that mountains could remove,
tongues of earth or heaven above,
knowledge, all things, empty prove
   if I have no love.

3 Though I as a martyr bleed,
   give my goods the poor to feed,
   all is vain if love I need:
      therefore give me love.

4 Love is kind and suffers long,
   love is pure and thinks no wrong,
   love than death itself more strong:
      therefore give us love.

5 Prophecy will fade away,
   melting in the light of day;
   love will ever with us stay:
      therefore give us love.

6 Faith and hope and love we see
   joining hand in hand agree –
   but the greatest of the three,
      and the best, is love.

2 Jesus, too late I searched for you
   to pay the debt of love I owe:
   how can I sing your worthy fame,
   the glorious beauty of your name?
      Jesus, my Lord . . .

3 Jesus, how strong your love must be
   that you should come to die for me;
   how great the joy that you have brought,
   so far exceeding hope or thought!
      Jesus, my Lord . . .

4 Jesus, your love shall be my song –
   to you my heart and soul belong:
   my life is yours, O Lord divine,
   and you, dear Saviour, you are mine:
      Jesus, my Lord . . .

475 from Psalm 18
© Christopher Idle†

1 I love you, O Lord, you alone,
   my refuge on whom I depend;
   my maker, my saviour, my own,
   my hope and my trust without end:
   the Lord is my strength and my song,
   defender and guide of my ways;
   my master to whom I belong,
   my God who shall have all my praise.

2 The dangers of death gathered round,
   the waves of destruction came near;
   but in my despairing I found
   the Lord who released me from fear:
   I called for his help in my pain,
   to God my salvation I cried;
   he brought me his comfort again,
   I live by the strength he supplied.

3 My hope is the promise he gives,
   my life is secure in his hand;
   I shall not be lost, for he lives!
   he comes to my aid – I shall stand!
   Lord God, you are powerful to save,
   your Spirit will spur me to pray;
   your Son has defeated the grave.
   I trust and I praise you today!

476 H. Collins
© in this version Jubilate Hymns†

1 Jesus, my Lord, my God, my all –
   hear me, O Saviour, when I call;
   hear me, and from your dwelling-place
   pour down the riches of your grace:
      Jesus, my Lord, whom I adore,
      help me to love you more and more.

477 after Augustine
© Timothy Dudley-Smith

1 Light of the minds that know him,
      may Christ be light to mine!
   my sun in risen splendour,
      my light of truth divine;
   my guide in doubt and darkness,
      my true and living way,
   my clear light ever shining,
      my dawn of heaven's day.

2 Life of the souls that love him,
      may Christ be ours indeed!
   the living bread from heaven
      on whom our spirits feed;
   who died for love of sinners
      to bear our guilty load,
   and make of life's brief journey
      a new Emmaus road.

3 Strength of the wills that serve him,
      may Christ be strength to me,
   who stilled the storm and tempest,
      who calmed the tossing sea;
   his Spirit's power to move me,
      his will to master mine,
   his cross to carry daily
      and conquer in his sign.

4 May it be ours to know him
      that we may truly love,
   and loving, fully serve him
      as serve the saints above;
   till in that home of glory
      with fadeless splendour bright,
   we serve in perfect freedom
      our strength, our life, our light.

478 from the Latin, E. Caswall
© in this version Jubilate Hymns†

1 Jesus, the very thought of you
   makes every moment blessed,
   until we come where all is new
   and in your presence rest.

2 No ear can hear, no voice proclaim,
   nor can the heart recall
   a sweeter sound than Jesus' name,
   the saviour of us all.

3 Hope of each contrite, humble mind,
   joy of the poor and meek;
   to those who falter, you are kind,
   and good to those who seek!

4 But what to those who find? Ah, this
   no tongue nor pen can show!
   The love of Jesus – what it is
   none but his loved ones know.

5 Jesus, be all our glory here,
   our joy and prize alone;
   our all-in-all when we draw near
   to your eternal throne.

479 from the Latin, E. Caswall
© in this version Jubilate Hymns†

1 My God, I love you; not because
   I hope for heaven thereby,
   nor yet because if I do not
   I shall for ever die.

2 But you, Lord Jesus, on the cross
   once suffered in my place;
   for me you bore the nails and spear,
   the darkness and disgrace:

3 And griefs and torments numberless
   and sweat of agony,
   and even death itself, for one
   who was your enemy.

4 Then why, O Saviour Jesus Christ,
   should I not love you well?
   not for the sake of winning heaven
   nor of escaping hell:

5 Not with the thought of seeking gain
   nor working for reward,
   but as you gave yourself for me,
   O ever-loving Lord.

6 So now I love you, and will love,
   and in your praise will sing,
   solely because you are my God
   and my eternal king.

480 Brian Wren
© Oxford University Press

1 Lord God, your love has called us here
   as we, by love, for love were made;
   your living likeness still we bear,
   though marred, dishonoured, disobeyed.
       We come, with all our heart and mind
       your call to hear, your love to find.

2 We come with self-inflicted pains
   of broken trust and chosen wrong,
   half-free, half-bound by inner chains,
   by social forces swept along,
       by powers and systems close confined
       yet seeking hope for humankind.

3 Lord God, in Christ you call our name
   and then receive us as your own
   not through some merit, right or claim
   but by your gracious love alone.
       We strain to glimpse your mercy seat
       and find you kneeling at our feet.

4 Then take the towel, and break the bread,
   and humble us, and call us friends;
   suffer and serve till all are fed
   and show how grandly love intends
       to work till all creation sings,
       to fill all worlds, to crown all things.

5 Lord God, in Christ you set us free
   your life to live, your joy to share:
   give us your Spirit's liberty
   to turn from guilt and dull despair,
       and offer all that faith can do
       while love is making all things new.

481 L. Connaughton
© McCrimmon Publishing Co Ltd

1 Love is his word, love is his way,
   feasting with all, fasting alone,
   living and dying, rising again,
   love, only love, is his way:
       Richer than gold is the love of my Lord,
       better than splendour and wealth.

2 Love is his way, love is his mark,
   sharing his last Passover feast,
   Christ at his table, host to the twelve,
   love, only love, is his mark:
       Richer than gold . . .

3 Love is his mark, love is his sign,
   bread for our strength, wine for our joy,
   'This is my body, this is my blood' –
   love, only love, is his sign:
       Richer than gold . . .

4 Love is his sign, love is his news,
  'Do this,' he said, 'lest you forget
  all my deep sorrow, all my dear blood' –
  love, only love, is his news:
      Richer than gold . . .

5 Love is his news, love is his name,
  we are his own, chosen and called,
  family, brethren, cousins and kin,
  love, only love, is his name:
      Richer than gold . . .

6 Love is his name, love is his law,
  hear his command, all who are his:
  'Love one another, I have loved you' –
  love, only love, is his law.
      Richer than gold . . .

7 Love is his law, love is his word:
  love of the Lord, Father and Word,
  love of the Spirit, God ever one,
  love, only love, is his word:
      Richer than gold . . .

482 G. W. Robinson

1 Loved with everlasting love,
  led by grace that love to know;
  Spirit, breathing from above,
  you have taught me it is so:
  O what full and perfect peace,
  joy and wonder all divine!
  In a love which cannot cease,
  I am his and he is mine.
      In a love . . .

2 Heaven above is softer blue,
  earth around is richer green;
  something lives in every hue,
  Christless eyes have never seen:
  songs of birds in sweetness grow,
  flowers with deeper beauties shine,
  since I know, as now I know,
  I am his and he is mine.
      Since I know . . .

3 His for ever, his alone!
  who the Lord from me shall part?
  With what joy and peace unknown
  Christ can fill the loving heart!
  Heaven and earth may pass away,
  sun and stars in gloom decline,
  but of Christ I still shall say:
  I am his and he is mine.
      But of Christ . . .

483 C. Wesley

1 O for a heart to praise my God –
  a heart from sin set free,
  a heart that's sprinkled with the blood
  so freely shed for me.

2 A heart resigned, submissive, meek,
  my great redeemer's throne;
  where only Christ is heard to speak,
  where Jesus reigns alone.

3 A humble, lowly, contrite heart,
  believing, true, and clean,
  which neither life nor death can part
  from him who dwells within.

4 A heart in every thought renewed,
  and full of love divine;
  perfect and right and pure and good –
  your life revealed in mine.

5 Your nature, gracious Lord, impart –
  come quickly from above,
  write your new name upon my heart,
  your new best name of love!

484 from the Latin, E. Caswall
© in this version Jubilate Hymns†

1 O Jesus, king most wonderful
  and conqueror renowned;
  O sweetness inexpressible
  in whom all joys are found!

2 When you draw near and touch the heart
  then truth begins to shine;
  then this world's vanities depart,
  then kindles love divine.

3 O Jesus, light of all below,
  the fount of living fire,
  surpassing all the joys we know
  and all we can desire.

4 Jesus, may all confess your name,
  your tender love adore,
  and seeking you, themselves inflame
  to seek you more and more.

5 O Jesus whom our voices bless,
  whom we would love alone;
  for ever let our lives express
  the image of your own.

485 after J. Scheffler, J. Wesley
© in this version Jubilate Hymns†

1 O Lord my love, my strength, my tower,
O Lord my hope, my joy, my crown:
O let me love with all my power
your works, yourself and you alone;
and love until your sacred fire
shall fill my soul with pure desire.

2 I thank you, uncreated Sun,
that in my heart your radiance shined,
that Satan's power was overthrown,
that you restored my wounded mind;
I welcome your life-giving voice,
and in your freedom I rejoice.

3 Support me in the strenuous race
and do not let my footsteps stray;
still strengthen me with heavenly grace
to persevere upon your way;
to serve you, Lord, with all my might
and make your glory my delight.

4 O Lord my love, my strength, my tower,
O Lord my hope, my joy, my crown:
O let me love you in the hour
of joy or pain – your smile or frown;
and when my flesh and heart decay,
that love shall flower in endless day.

486 G. Matheson
© in this version Word & Music†

1 O love that will not let me go,
revive your loveliness in me:
I give you back the life I owe
that in your ocean depths its flow
    may richer, fuller be.

2 O light that follows all my way,
renew your radiance in me:
I welcome your life-giving ray
that in your sunshine's blaze each day
    may brighter, fairer be.

3 O joy that seeks for me through pain,
restore your hopefulness to me;
I trace the rainbow through the rain
and trust your promise once again:
    that dawn shall tearless be.

4 O cross that raises up my head,
remove the sinfulness from me:
I lay in dust life's glory dead,
and from the ground there blossoms red,
    life that shall endless be.

487 T. Monod
© in this version Jubilate Hymns†

1 Oh the bitter shame and sorrow
that a time could ever be
when I let the Saviour's pity
plead in vain, and proudly answered,
'None of you and all of me!'

2 Yet you found me; there I saw you
dying and in agony,
heard you pray, 'Forgive them, Father',
and my wistful heart said faintly,
'Some of you and some of me.'

3 Day by day your tender mercy,
healing, helping, full and free,
firm and strong, with endless patience
brought me lower, while I whispered,
'More of you and less of me.'

4 Higher than the highest heaven,
deeper than the deepest sea,
Lord, your love at last has conquered:
grant me now my spirit's longing,
'All of you and none of me!'

488 © Alan Gaunt

1 Praise for the mighty love
which God through Christ made known;
love which for others lived,
died on the cross alone;
the love which heightens all our powers,
the love which makes the future ours.

2 Courage to face the worst
that others do or say,
eloquence, faith or skill,
fortunes to give away;
the means to feed the human race
or power to fathom farthest space:

3 Left unrefined by love
all these are empty noise,
like instruments untuned
or useless, broken toys:
but he who died for love outlives
ambition's greatest victories.

4 Love makes the future bright,
transcending greed and pride;
life's possibilities
by love are opened wide;
and heights which seemed impossible
by love are made accessible.

5 Love is the life of God
lived in our lives again;
this is the life for us,
worth all its hurt and pain;
and in the power of love we'll live
to greet the future God will give!

489 © Michael Saward†

1 All-creating heavenly Giver,
bringing light and life to birth;
all-sustaining heavenly Father
of the families of earth:
    We, your children, lift our voices
    singing gladly of your love:
    never-ending are the praises
    rising to your throne above.

2 Ever-living Lord and Saviour,
breaking chains of sin and shame;
ever-loving Intercessor,
all shall triumph in your name:
    We, your servants liberated
    at a fearful ransom-price,
    in your kingdom are united
    by that mighty sacrifice.

3 Life-conceiving Wind of heaven,
breathing gifts upon us all;
life-enhancing Spirit, given
to enrich us, great and small:
    We, whose talents widely differ,
    now restore to you your own,
    and in true thanksgiving offer
    all we are before the throne.

4 Father, Son and Holy Spirit,
blessing all within your hand:
full the cup that we inherit,
firm the ground on which we stand:
    We, your people, undeserving
    of the grace you freely give,
    now and ever, in thanksgiving
    to your praise and glory live.

490 from 1 Thessalonians 5
© Christopher Idle†

1 As sons of the day and daughters of light,
no longer we sleep like creatures of night:
for Jesus has died that with him we may live;
by all that he gave us, we learn how to give.

2 One body in Christ, let all play their part:
the lazy be warned, the timid take heart;
let those who are hurt
    never pay back with wrong,
but serve one another: together be strong!

3 Be constant in prayer, at all times rejoice,
in all things give thanks –
    let God hear your voice!
alive to his Spirit, alert to his word,
test all things,
    and hold to what pleases the Lord.

4 May God who first called, gave peace
    and made whole,
preserve us from fault in body and soul:
our Lord Jesus Christ
    keep us firm in his grace
until at his coming we meet face to face.

491 C. Wesley
© in this version Jubilate Hymns†

1 Christ, from whom all blessings flow,
by whose grace your people grow;
Christ whose nature now we share,
work in us, your body here.

2 Send your Spirit from above
and unite us in your love;
still for more to you we call –
with your fulness fill us all.

3 Move and motivate and guide,
varying gifts for each provide;
placed according to your will,
let us all our work fulfil.

4 Gladly may we all agree,
bound in one community;
kindly for each other care –
all our joys and sorrows share.

5 Love has all our strife destroyed,
rendered all divisions void;
sects and names and parties fall:
you, O Christ, are all in all.

492 G. K. A. Bell
© Oxford University Press

1 Christ is the king! O friends rejoice;
brothers and sisters, with one voice
let the world know he is your choice.
    Alleluia, alleluia, alleluia!

2 O magnify the Lord, and raise
anthems of joy and holy praise
for Christ's brave saints of ancient days.
    Alleluia . . .

3 They with a faith for ever new
followed the king, and round him drew
thousands of servants brave and true.
    Alleluia . . .

4 O Christian women, Christian men,
all the world over, seek again
the way disciples followed then.
    Alleluia . . .

5 Christ through all ages is the same:
place the same hope in his great name;
with the same faith his word proclaim.
    Alleluia . . .

6 Let Love's unconquerable might
your scattered companies unite
in service to the Lord of light.
Alleluia, alleluia, alleluia!

7 So shall God's will on earth be done,
new lamps be lit, new tasks begun,
and the whole church at last be one.
Alleluia . . .

4 Saviour, since of Zion's city
I through grace a member am,
let the world deride or pity,
I will glory in your name:
fading are the world's best pleasures,
all its boasted pomp and show;
solid joys and lasting treasures
none but Zion's children know.

493
William Reid, junior
© 1959 by The Hymn Society of America/
Hope Publishing Company

1 Help us, O Lord, to learn
the truths your word imparts,
to study that your laws may be
inscribed upon our hearts.

2 Help us, O Lord, to live
the faith which we proclaim,
that all our thoughts and words and deeds
may glorify your name.

3 Help us, O Lord, to teach
the beauty of your ways,
that yearning souls may find the Christ
and sing aloud his praise.

494 J. Newton

1 Glorious things of you are spoken,
Zion, city of our God;
he whose word cannot be broken
formed you for his own abode:
on the rock of ages founded,
what can shake your sure repose?
with salvation's walls surrounded
you may smile at all your foes.

2 See, the streams of living waters
springing from eternal love!
well supply your sons and daughters
and all fear of want remove:
who can faint while such a river
ever flows their thirst to assuage?
grace, which like the Lord the giver
never fails from age to age.

3 Round each habitation hovering
see the cloud and fire appear
for a glory and a covering,
showing that the Lord is near:
thus they march, the pillar leading,
light by night and shade by day;
daily on the manna feeding
which he gives them when they pray.

495
E. Merrington
in © Christian Conference of Asia Hymnal
and in this version Jubilate Hymns

1 God of eternity, Lord of the ages,
Father and Saviour and Spirit you reign;
yours is the glory of time's numbered pages,
yours is the power to revive us again.

2 Thankful, we come to you, Lord of the nations,
praising your faithfulness, mercy, and grace
shown through the story of past generations,
pledge of your love to each people and race.

3 Wherever home may be, parted by oceans,
there is Jerusalem, there God adored;
we lift our hearts in united devotions –
ends of the earth, join in praise to the Lord!

4 Yours is the heritage, generous Giver!
brightly the heavens your glory declare;
bright streams the sunlight
on mountain and river,
bright shines the cross
over fields rich and fair.

5 Pardon our sinfulness, God of all pity,
call to remembrance your mercies of old;
strengthen your church to stand firm as a city
set on a hill as a light for the world.

6 Head of the church on earth, risen, ascended,
yours is the honour that lives in this place;
as you have blessed us
in years that have ended,
still lift upon us the light of your face!

496 © Michael Perry†

1 God our Father, bless your people
that we may be one;
one in heart and one in worship,
love's communion.

2 Christ our Saviour, keep your people
that we may be one;
one in prayer and one in service,
joyful union.

3 Holy Spirit, guide your people
that we may be one;
one in faith and one in purpose,
truth's dominion.

4 Praise together God the Father,
serving Christ alone;
in the Spirit be united:
God is Three in One!

497 from Psalm 133, J. E. Seddon
© Mrs. M. Seddon†

1 How good a thing it is,
how pleasant to behold,
when all God's people live at one,
the law of love uphold!

2 As perfume, by its scent,
breathes fragrance all around,
so life itself will sweeter be
where unity is found.

3 And like refreshing dew
that falls upon the hills,
true union sheds its gentle grace,
and deeper love instils.

4 God grants his choicest gifts
to those who live in peace;
to them his blessings shall abound
and evermore increase.

498 © Timothy Dudley Smith

1 Look, Lord, in mercy as we pray,
on tasks as yet undone;
fire us anew to seek the day
that makes our churches one:
heirs to one work of grace divine –
one Spirit freely given,
one pledge in sacrament and sign,
one cross the hope of heaven.

2 One living faith be ours to learn
with saints in every age,
one timeless word of truth discern
in scripture's sacred page:
make us, with new resolve, begin
one common call to own;
to be one church one world to win,
and make one saviour known.

3 Hear us who join in praise and prayer
one act of faith to bring,
children who own one Father's care,
soldiers who serve one king:
your kingdom come, O Lord, we pray,
your will on earth be done;
our sins and errors purge away
and make our churches one.

499 © Timothy Dudley-Smith

1 Lord of the church,
we pray for our renewing:
Christ over all, our undivided aim.
Fire of the Spirit, burn for our enduing,
wind of the Spirit, fan the living flame!
We turn to Christ amid our fear and failing,
the will that lacks the courage to be free,
the weary labours, all but unavailing,
to bring us nearer what a church should be.

2 Lord of the church,
we seek a Father's blessing,
a true repentance and a faith restored,
a swift obedience and a new possessing,
filled with the Holy Spirit of the Lord!
We turn to Christ from all our restless striving,
unnumbered voices with a single prayer –
the living water for our souls' reviving,
in Christ to live, and love and serve and care.

3 Lord of the church, we long for our uniting,
true to one calling, by one vision stirred;
one cross proclaiming
and one creed reciting,
one in the truth of Jesus and his word!
So lead us on; till toil and trouble ended,
one church triumphant
one new song shall sing,
to praise his glory, risen and ascended,
Christ over all, the everlasting king!

500 © David Mowbray†

1 Risen Lord, whose name we cherish,
all the stars are in your hand!
Walk today among your people,
light each candle on its stand;
look in mercy, not in judgement,
on your church in every land.

2 For, divided in your service,
we have chosen selfish ways,
lived in bitterness of spirit,
quickly let our anger blaze;
often blindly followed leaders,
sought our glory, not your praise.

3 Yet your church has also triumphed,
   told of love's great offering,
   in its life shown forth your goodness,
   drawn from death its cruel sting;
   wakened to the needs of many,
   soothed the sorrows life can bring.

4 So, we pray, that by your Spirit
   all your scattered flock may find
   that deep unity you prayed for
   and would share with all mankind;
   by this gift our fears and envies
   shall in truth be left behind.

5 Risen Lord, your hand is knocking
   at each church's bolted door!
   Enter now, and dwell within us,
   trust and fellowship restore;
   that your Father's joys together
   all may taste for evermore.

501 S. J. Stone

1 The church's one foundation
   is Jesus Christ her Lord;
   she is his new creation
   by water and the word:
   from heaven he came and sought her
   to be his holy bride;
   with his own blood he bought her
   and for her life he died.

2 Called out from every nation,
   yet one through all the earth;
   her charter of salvation –
   one Lord, one faith, one birth:
   one holy name she blesses,
   and shares one holy food;
   as to one hope she presses
   with every grace endued.

3 We see her long divided
   by heresy and sect;
   yet she by God is guided –
   one people, one elect:
   her vigil she is keeping,
   her cry goes up, 'How long?'
   and soon the night of weeping
   shall be the dawn of song.

4 In toil and tribulation,
   and tumult of her war,
   she waits the consummation
   of peace for evermore:
   till with the vision glorious
   her longing eyes are blessed;
   at last the church victorious
   shall be the church at rest!

5 Yet she on earth has union
   with God the Three-in-One;
   and mystic, sweet communion
   with those whose rest is won:
   O happy ones and holy!
   Lord, grant to us your grace,
   with them the meek and lowly,
   in heaven to see your face.

502

after T. T'ing Fang Lew
in © Christian Conference of Asia Hymnal
and in this version Jubilate Hymns

1 O Christ the great foundation
      on which your people stand
   to preach your true salvation
      in every age and land:
   pour out your Holy Spirit
      to make us strong and pure,
   to keep the faith unbroken
      as long as worlds endure.

2 Baptized in one confession,
      one church in all the earth,
   we bear our Lord's impression,
      the sign of second birth:
   one fellowship united
      in love beyond our own –
   by grace we were invited,
      by grace we make you known.

3 Where tyrants' hold is tightened,
      where strong devour the weak,
   where innocents are frightened
      and righteous fear to speak,
   there let your church awaking
      attack the powers of sin
   and, all their ramparts breaking,
      with you the victory win.

4 The gates of hell are yielding,
      the hordes of Satan fly,
   for Christ the Lord is wielding
      the sword of victory:
   this is the moment glorious
      when he who once was dead
   shall lead his church victorious,
      their champion and their head.

5 He comes with acclamation
      to claim his holy bride;
   she stands in exultation,
      the Bridegroom at her side:
   the Lord of all creation
      his Father's kingdom brings –
   the final consummation,
      the glory of all things.

503
© Christopher Idle†

1 Now let us learn of Christ:
   he speaks, and we shall find
   he lightens our dark mind;
   so let us learn of Christ.

2 Now let us love in Christ
   as he has first loved us;
   as he endured the cross,
   so let us love in Christ.

3 Now let us grow in Christ
   and look to things above,
   and speak the truth in love;
   so let us grow in Christ.

4 Now let us stand in Christ
   in every trial we meet,
   in all his strength complete;
   so let us stand in Christ.

504
from 1 Peter 2, J. E. Seddon
© Mrs. M. Seddon†

1 Church of God, elect and glorious,
   holy nation, chosen race;
   called as God's own special people,
   royal priests and heirs of grace:
   know the purpose of your calling,
   show to all his mighty deeds;
   tell of love which knows no limits,
   grace which meets all human needs.

2 God has called you out of darkness
   into his most marvellous light;
   brought his truth to life within you,
   turned your blindness into sight.
   Let your light so shine around you
   that God's name is glorified;
   and all find fresh hope and purpose
   in Christ Jesus crucified.

3 Once you were an alien people,
   strangers to God's heart of love;
   but he brought you home in mercy,
   citizens of heaven above.
   Let his love flow out to others,
   let them feel a Father's care;
   that they too may know his welcome
   and his countless blessings share.

4 Church of God, elect and holy,
   be the people he intends;
   strong in faith and swift to answer
   each command your master sends:
   royal priests, fulfil your calling
   through your sacrifice and prayer;
   give your lives in joyful service –
   sing his praise, his love declare.

505
J. E. Seddon
© Mrs. M. Seddon†

1 Go forth and tell! O church of God, awake!
   God's saving news to all the nations take;
   proclaim Christ Jesus, saviour, Lord, and king,
   that all the world his worthy praise may sing.

2 Go forth and tell! God's love embraces all;
   he will in grace respond to all who call:
   how shall they call if they have never heard
   the gracious invitation of his word?

3 Go forth and tell where still the darkness lies;
   in wealth or want, the sinner surely dies:
   give us, O Lord, concern of heart and mind,
   a love like yours which cares for all mankind.

4 Go forth and tell! The doors are open wide:
   share God's good gifts – let no one be denied;
   live out your life
         as Christ your Lord shall choose,
   your ransomed powers for his sole glory use.

5 Go forth and tell! O church of God, arise!
   go in the strength
         which Christ your Lord supplies;
   go till all nations his great name adore
   and serve him, Lord and king for evermore.

506
J. Marriott

1 God, whose almighty word
   chaos and darkness heard,
   and took their flight:
   hear us, we humbly pray,
   and where the gospel day
   sheds not its glorious ray,
      let there be light!

2 Saviour, who came to bring
   on your redeeming wing
   healing and sight,
   health to the sick in mind,
   sight to the inly blind:
   O now to all mankind
      let there be light!

3 Spirit of truth and love,
   life-giving, holy dove,
   speed on your flight!
   move on the water's face
   bearing the lamp of grace
   and, in earth's darkest place,
      let there be light!

4 Gracious and holy Three,
   glorious Trinity,
   wisdom, love, might:
   boundless as ocean's tide
   rolling in fullest pride
   through the world far and wide,
      let there be light!

507
from Romans 10
© Michael Perry†

1 How shall they hear the word of God
unless his truth is told;
how shall the sinful be set free,
the sorrowful consoled?
  To all who speak the truth today
  impart your Spirit, Lord, we pray.

2 How shall they call to God for help
unless they have believed;
how shall the poor be given hope,
the prisoner reprieved?
  To those who help the blind to see
  give light and love and clarity.

3 How shall the gospel be proclaimed
that sinners may repent;
how shall the world find peace at last
if heralds are not sent?
  So send us, Lord, for we rejoice
  to speak of Christ with life and voice.

508
G. W. Kitchin and M. R. Newbolt
© Hymns Ancient & Modern Ltd
and in this version Jubilee Hymns

  Lift high the cross,
  the love of Christ proclaim
  till all the world
  adores his sacred name!

1 Come, Christians,
    follow where the captain trod,
  the king victorious, Christ the Son of God:
  Lift high the cross . . .

2 Each new-born soldier of the crucified
is signed with the cross,
    the seal of him who died:
  Lift high the cross . . .

3 This is the sign that Satan's armies fear
and angels veil their faces to revere:
  Lift high the cross . . .

4 Saved by the cross
    on which their Lord was slain,
  see Adam's children their lost home regain:
  Lift high the cross . . .

5 From north and south,
    from east and west they raise
  in growing unison their songs of praise:
  Lift high the cross . . .

6 Let every race and every language tell
of him who saves our souls from death
    and hell!
  Lift high the cross . . .

7 O Lord, once lifted on the tree of pain,
draw all the world to seek you once again:
  Lift high the cross . . .

8 Set up your throne,
    that earth's despair may cease
  beneath the shadow of its healing peace:
  Lift high the cross . . .

509
J. Montgomery
© in this version Jubilate Hymns†

1 Lift up your heads, you gates of brass! –
you bars of iron, yield,
and let the King of glory pass:
the cross is in the field.

2 The armies of the living God,
the warriors of his host,
where Christians yet have never trod
take their appointed post.

3 His servants wage a holy war,
a fierce and awesome strife,
as heaven and hell contend for more
than either death or life.

4 Obedient to their Lord's command,
and strong within his strength,
they fight for him in every land –
all must be his at length.

5 Rejoice then, Christians, fear not now,
in Jesus' name, be strong!
to him shall all the nations bow
and sing the triumph song.

6 Uplifted are the gates of brass,
the bars of iron yield
to let the King of glory pass:
the cross has won the field!

510
Frances R. Havergal

1 Lord, speak to me that I may speak
in living echoes of your tone;
as you have sought, so let me seek
your wandering children, lost, alone.

2 O lead me, Lord, that I may lead
the stumbling and the straying feet;
and feed me, Lord, that I may feed
your hungry ones with manna sweet.

3 O teach me, Lord, that I may teach
the precious truths which you impart;
and wing my words that they may reach
the hidden depths of many a heart.

4 O fill me with your fulness, Lord,
until my heart shall overflow
in kindling thought and glowing word,
your love to tell, your praise to show.

5 O use me Lord, use even me,
just as you will, and when, and where;
until at last your face I see,
your rest, your joy, your glory share.

511 © Hugh Sherlock and Michael Saward†

1 Lord, your church on earth is seeking
power and wisdom from above:
teach us all the art of speaking
with the accents of your love.
We will heed your great commission
sending us to every place –
'Go, baptize, fulfil my mission;
serve with love and share my grace!'

2 You release us from our bondage,
lift the burdens caused by sin;
give new hope, new strength and courage,
grant release from fears within.
Light for darkness, joy for sorrow,
love for hatred, peace for strife –
these and countless blessings follow
as the Spirit gives new life.

3 In the streets of every city
where the bruised and lonely live,
we will show the saviour's pity
and his longing to forgive.
In all lands and with all races
we will serve, and seek to bring
all the world to render praises
Christ, to you, redeemer king.

512 J. Armstrong © in this version Jubilate Hymns†

1 Lord, you can make our spirits shine
with light from brighter worlds above,
and cause the dew of grace divine
to fall on those who seek your love.

2 Now to the church your blessing give
on all who teach and all who learn;
that both in you may holier live
and every light more brightly burn.

3 Give those who learn a listening ear,
a godly heart and humble mind:
such gifts can help the poorest here
the riches of your truth to find.

4 Let those who teach, themselves be taught
faith, hope and love, with zeal to pray;
make pure their hearts and wise their thought
as true disciples of your way.

5 O bless the shepherd, bless the sheep,
that guide and guided may be one;
one in the faithful watch they keep
until this earthly life is done.

6 O Lord, let grace to us be given
in you to live, in you to die;
and so, before we rise to heaven,
we taste our immortality.

513 J. Montgomery

1 O Spirit of the living God,
in all the fulness of your grace,
wherever human feet have trod,
descend upon our fallen race:

2 Give tongues of fire and hearts of love
to preach the reconciling word;
anoint with power from heaven above
whenever gospel truth is heard:

3 Let darkness turn to radiant light,
confusion vanish from your path;
those who are weak inspire with might:
let mercy triumph over wrath!

4 O Spirit of our God, prepare
the whole wide world the Lord to meet;
breathe out new life, like morning air,
till hearts of stone begin to beat:

5 Baptize the nations; far and near
the triumphs of the cross record;
till Christ in glory shall appear
and every race declare him Lord! (Amen.)

514 J. E. Seddon © Mrs. M. Seddon†

1 One holy apostolic church,
the body of the Lord:
our task, to witness to his name
in full and glad accord –
one Lord confessed, one faith believed,
one baptism its sign;
one God and Father over all,
one fellowship divine.

2 By Christ redeemed, in Christ renewed,
from every tongue and race,
we live to share with all the world
the wonder of his grace:
as God is holy, we must be
above reproach and blame;
for royal service set apart,
his gospel to proclaim.

3 With apostolic faith and zeal,
the church in every land
must bring God's love to every life
as Jesus gave command:
his partners in a common task
uniting east and west,
we serve as one to make Christ known
in him shall all be blessed!

515 A. Midlane
© in this version Jubilate Hymns†

1 Revive your church, O Lord,
in grace and power draw near;
speak with the voice that wakes the dead,
and make your people hear!

2 Revive your church, O Lord,
disturb the sleep of death;
give life to smouldering embers now
by your almighty breath.

3 Revive your church, O Lord,
exalt your precious name;
and by your Holy Spirit come
and set our love aflame.

4 Revive your church, O Lord,
give us a thirst for you,
a hunger for the bread of life
our spirits to renew.

5 Revive your church, O Lord,
and let your power be shown;
the gifts and graces shall be ours,
the glory yours alone!

516 I. Watts
© in this version Jubilate Hymns†

1 Jesus shall reign where'er the sun
does his successive journeys run;
his kingdom stretch from shore to shore
till moons shall rise and set no more.

2 People and realms of every tongue
declare his love in sweetest song,
and children's voices shall proclaim
their early blessings on his name.

3 Blessings abound where Jesus reigns –
the prisoner leaps to lose his chains,
the weary find eternal rest,
the hungry and the poor are blessed.

4 To him shall endless prayer be made,
and princes throng to crown his head;
his name like incense shall arise
with every morning sacrifice.

5 Let all creation rise and bring
the highest honours to our king;
angels descend with songs again
and earth repeat the loud 'Amen!'

517 H. E. Fox
© in this version Jubilate Hymns†

1 Send out the gospel! Let it sound
northward and southward, east and west;
tell all the world Christ died and lives –
he gives us pardon, life and rest.

2 Send out the gospel, mighty Lord!
Out of this chaos bring to birth
your own creation's promised hope:
the coming days of heaven on earth.

3 Send out your gospel, gracious Lord!
Yours was the blood for sinners shed;
your voice still pleads in human hearts –
let all the world to you be led.

4 Send out your gospel, holy Lord!
Kindle in us love's sacred flame;
love giving all with heart and mind,
for Jesus' sake, in Jesus' name.

5 Send out the gospel! Make it known!
Christians, obey your master's call;
sing out his praise! he comes to reign,
the King of kings and Lord of all.

518 J. E. Seddon
© Mrs. M. Seddon†

1 To him we come –
Jesus Christ our Lord,
God's own living Word,
his dear Son:
in him there is no east and west,
in him all nations shall be blessed;
to all he offers peace and rest –
loving Lord!

2 In him we live –
Christ our strength and stay,
life and truth and way,
friend divine:
his power can break the chains of sin,
still all life's storms without, within,
help us the daily fight to win –
living Lord!

3 For him we go –
    soldiers of the cross,
    counting all things loss
    him to know;
    going to every land and race,
    preaching to all redeeming grace,
    building his church in every place –
        conquering Lord!

4 With him we serve –
    his the work we share
    with saints everywhere,
    near and far;
    one in the task which faith requires,
    one in the zeal which never tires,
    one in the hope his love inspires –
        coming Lord!

5 Onward we go –
    faithful, bold, and true,
    called his will to do
    day by day
    till, at the last, with joy we'll see
    Jesus, in glorious majesty;
    live with him through eternity –
        reigning Lord!

520 C. Wesley

1 You servants of God, your master proclaim,
    and publish abroad his wonderful name;
    the name all-victorious of Jesus extol,
    his kingdom is glorious, and rules over all.

2 God rules in the height, almighty to save –
    though hid from our sight,
        his presence we have;
    the great congregation his triumph shall sing,
    ascribing salvation to Jesus our king.

3 'Salvation to God who sits on the throne!'
    let all cry aloud, and honour the Son;
    the praises of Jesus the angels proclaim,
    fall down on their faces
        and worship the Lamb.

4 Then let us adore and give him his right:
    all glory and power, all wisdom and might,
    all honour and blessing – with angels above –
    and thanks never ceasing, and infinite love.

519 © Edward Burns

1 We have a gospel to proclaim,
    good news for all throughout the earth;
    the gospel of a saviour's name:
    we sing his glory, tell his worth.

2 Tell of his birth at Bethlehem,
    not in a royal house or hall
    but in a stable dark and dim:
    the Word made flesh, a light for all.

3 Tell of his death at Calvary,
    hated by those he came to save;
    in lonely suffering on the cross
    for all he loved, his life he gave.

4 Tell of that glorious Easter morn:
    empty the tomb, for he was free;
    he broke the power of death and hell
    that we might share his victory.

5 Tell of his reign at God's right hand,
    by all creation glorified;
    he sends his Spirit on his church
    to live for him, the lamb who died.

6 Now we rejoice to name him king:
    Jesus is Lord of all the earth;
    this gospel-message we proclaim:
    we sing his glory, tell his worth.

521 J. E. Seddon
© Mrs. M. Seddon†

1 Tell all the world of Jesus,
    our saviour, Lord and king;
    and let the whole creation
    of his salvation sing:
    proclaim his glorious greatness
    in nature and in grace;
    creator and redeemer,
    the Lord of time and space.

2 Tell all the world of Jesus,
    that everyone may find
    the joy of his forgiveness –
    true peace of heart and mind:
    proclaim his perfect goodness,
    his deep, unfailing care;
    his love so rich in mercy,
    a love beyond compare.

3 Tell all the world of Jesus,
    that everyone may know
    of his almighty triumph
    defeating every foe:
    proclaim his coming glory,
    when sin is overthrown,
    and he shall reign in splendour –
    the King upon his throne!

522 © Christopher Idle†

1 Christ's church shall glory in his power
and grow to his perfection;
he is our rock, our mighty tower,
our life, our resurrection:
   so by his skilful hand
   the church of Christ shall stand;
   the master-builder's plan
   he works, as he began,
   and soon will crown with splendour.

2 Christ's people serve his wayward world
to whom he seems a stranger;
he knows its welcome from of old,
he shares our joy, our danger:
   so strong, and yet so weak,
   the church of Christ shall speak;
   his cross our greatest need,
   his word the vital seed
   that brings a fruitful harvest.

3 Christ's living lamp shall brightly burn,
and to our earthly city
forgotten beauty shall return,
and purity and pity:
   to give the oppressed their right
   the church of Christ shall fight;
   and though the years seem long
   he is our strength and song,
   and he is our salvation.

4 Christ's body triumphs in his name;
one Father, sovereign giver,
one Spirit, with his love aflame,
one Lord, the same for ever:
   to you, O God our prize,
   the church of Christ shall rise
   beyond all measured height,
   to that eternal light,
   where Christ shall reign all-holy.

523 after M. Luther
© Michael Perry†

1 God is our fortress and our rock,
our mighty help in danger;
he shields us from the battle's shock
and thwarts the devil's anger:
   for still the prince of night
   prolongs his evil fight;
   he uses every skill
   to work his wicked will –
   no earthly force is like him.

2 Our hope is fixed on Christ alone,
the Man, of God's own choosing;
without him nothing can be won
and fighting must be losing:
   so let the powers accursed
   come on and do their worst,
   the Son of God shall ride
   to battle at our side,
   and he shall have the victory.

3 The word of God will not be slow
while demon hordes surround us,
though evil strike its cruellest blow
and death and hell confound us:
   for even if distress
   should take all we possess,
   and those who mean us ill
   should ravage, wreck, or kill,
   God's kingdom is immortal!

524 H. K. White
© in this version Jubilate Hymns†

1 Christian soldiers, onward go!
Jesus' triumph you shall know;
fight the fight, maintain the strife,
strengthened with the bread of life.

2 Join the war and face the foe!
Christian soldiers, onward go;
boldly stand in danger's hour,
trust your captain, prove his power.

3 Let your drooping hearts be glad,
march in heavenly armour clad;
fight, nor think the battle long –
soon shall victory be your song.

4 Sorrow must not dim your eye,
soon shall every tear be dry;
banish fear, you shall succeed –
great your strength if great your need.

5 Onward, then, in battle move!
more than conquerors you shall prove;
though opposed by many a foe
Christian soldiers, onward go!

525 J. Edmeston, © in this version Jubilate Hymns†
(see also traditional version, 595)

1 Lead us, heavenly Father, lead us
through this world's tempestuous sea;
guard us, guide us, keep us, feed us,
now and to eternity:
here possessing every blessing
if our God our Father be.

2 Saviour, by your grace restore us –
all our weaknesses are plain;
you have lived on earth before us,
you have felt our grief and pain:
tempted, taunted, yet undaunted,
from the depths you rose again.

3 Spirit of our God, descending,
fill our hearts with holy peace;
love with every passion blending,
pleasure that can never cease:
thus provided, pardoned, guided,
ever shall our joys increase.

526 J. S. B. Monsell

1 Fight the good fight with all your might,
Christ is your strength, and Christ your right;
lay hold on life, and it shall be
your joy and crown eternally.

2 Run the straight race through God's good
grace,
lift up your eyes, and seek his face:
life with its way before you lies,
Christ is the path and Christ the prize.

3 Cast care aside, lean on your guide,
his boundless mercy will provide;
trust, and your trusting soul shall prove
Christ is its life, and Christ its love.

4 Faint not, nor fear, his arms are near;
he does not change, and you are dear;
only believe and Christ shall be
your all-in-all eternally.

527 from Psalm 46
© Richard Bewes†

1 God is our strength and refuge,
our present help in trouble;
and we therefore will not fear,
though the earth should change!
Though mountains shake and tremble,
though swirling floods are raging,
God the Lord of hosts is with us evermore!

2 There is a flowing river,
within God's holy city;
God is in the midst of her –
she shall not be moved!
God's help is swiftly given,
thrones vanish at his presence –
God the Lord of hosts is with us evermore!

3 Come, see the works of our maker,
learn of his deeds all-powerful:
wars will cease across the world
when he shatters the spear!
Be still and know your creator,
uplift him in the nations –
God the Lord of hosts is with us evermore!

528 after W. Williams
P. Williams and others

1 Guide me, O my great Redeemer,
pilgrim through this barren land;
I am weak, but you are mighty,
hold me with your powerful hand:
Bread of heaven, bread of heaven,
feed me now and evermore!

2 Open now the crystal fountain
where the healing waters flow;
let the fiery, cloudy pillar
lead me all my journey through:
Strong Deliverer, strong Deliverer,
ever be my strength and shield.

3 When I tread the verge of Jordan
bid my anxious fears subside;
Death of death, and hell's Destruction,
land me safe on Canaan's side:
songs of praises, songs of praises,
I will ever sing to you.

529 after M. A. von Löwenstern
P. Pusey

1 Lord of our life, and God of our salvation,
star of our night, and hope of every nation:
hear and receive your church's supplication,
Lord God almighty!

2 See round your church
the angry tides are swirling,
see how your foes their banners are unfurling;
Lord, while their darts envenomed
they are hurling,
you can preserve us.

3 Lord, you can help
when earthly armour fails us,
Lord, you can save
when deadly sin assails us:
Lord, when at last that solemn trumpet
hails us,
keep and protect us!

4 Grant us your help
   till foes are backward driven,
grant them your truth,
   that they may be forgiven;
grant peace on earth
   and, after we have striven,
peace in your heaven.

530
J. M. Neale
© in this version Jubilate Hymns†

1 O happy band of pilgrims,
   if onward you will tread
   with Jesus as your brother
   and Jesus as your head!

2 O happy if you labour
   as Jesus did for all;
   O happy if you hunger
   and follow at his call!

3 The cross that Jesus carried,
   he carried as your due;
   the crown that he is wearing
   he wears it now for you.

4 The faith by which you see him,
   the hope which bravely burns,
   the love that through all troubles
   to Jesus always turns:

5 What are they but his jewels
   of true celestial worth;
   what are they but a ladder
   set up to heaven on earth?

6 The trials that afflict you,
   the sorrows you endure:
   what are they but the testing
   that makes your calling sure?

7 O happy band of pilgrims,
   look upward to the skies –
   beyond your earthly journey
   stands Jesus as your prize!

531
J. E. Bode

1 O Jesus, I have promised
   to serve you to the end –
   be now and ever near me,
   my Master and my Friend:
   I shall not fear the battle
   if you are by my side,
   nor wander from the pathway
   if you will be my guide.

2 O let me feel you near me,
   the world is ever near;
   I see the sights that dazzle,
   the tempting sounds I hear;
   my foes are ever near me,
   around me and within;
   but Jesus, draw still nearer
   and shield my soul from sin!

3 O let me hear you speaking
   in accents clear and still;
   above the storms of passion,
   the murmurs of self-will:
   O speak to reassure me,
   to hasten or control;
   and speak to make me listen,
   O Guardian of my soul.

4 O let me see your footmarks
   and in them place my own;
   my hope to follow truly
   is in your strength alone:
   O guide me, call me, draw me,
   uphold me to the end;
   and then in heaven receive me,
   my Saviour and my Friend.

532
S. Baring-Gould
© in this version Jubilate Hymns†

1 Onward, Christian soldiers!
      marching as to war,
   with the cross of Jesus going on before.
   Christ, the royal master, leads his armies on:
   forward into battle till the fight is won!
      Onward, Christian soldiers,
      marching as to war
      with the cross of Jesus going on before.

2 At the name of Jesus, Satan's armies flee:
   on then, Christian soldiers, on to victory!
   Hell's foundations tremble
      at the shout of praise –
   sing the song of triumph!
      loud your voices raise!
      Onward, Christian soldiers . . .

3 Like a mighty army moves the church of God:
   we are humbly treading
      where the saints have trod;
   Christ is not divided – all one body we,
   one in hope and calling, one in charity.
      Onward, Christian soldiers . . .

4 Crowns and thrones may perish,
      kingdoms rise and wane,
   but the church of Jesus ever shall remain;
   death and hell and Satan never shall prevail –
   we have Christ's own promise
      and that cannot fail.
      Onward, Christian soldiers . . .

5 Onward then, you people!
    march in faith, be strong!
blend with ours your voices
    in the triumph song:
Glory, praise and honour
    be to Christ the king!
this through countless ages
    we with angels sing.
    Onward, Christian soldiers . . .

533   C. Wesley

1 Soldiers of Christ, arise
and put your armour on;
strong in the strength which God supplies
through his eternal Son.

2 Strong in the Lord of hosts,
and in his mighty power;
who in the strength of Jesus trusts
is more than conqueror.

3 Stand then in his great might,
with all his strength endued;
and take, to arm you for the fight,
the weapons of our God.

4 To keep your armour bright
attend with constant care,
still walking in your captain's sight
and keeping watch with prayer.

5 From strength to strength go on:
wrestle and fight and pray;
tread all the powers of darkness down
and win the well-fought day:

6 Till, having all things done
and all your conflicts past,
you overcome through Christ alone
and stand complete at last.

534   W. W. How
© in this version Jubilate Hymns†

1 Soldiers of the cross, arise
clothed in shining armour bright:
mighty are your enemies,
hard the battle you must fight.

2 In a faithless fallen world
raise your banner to the sky;
let it float there, wide unfurled,
bear it onward, lift it high.

3 Where the shadows darkest fall,
there display the saving sign;
where our shameful crimes appal,
let the light of Jesus shine.

4 Guard the helpless, seek the strayed,
comfort troubles, banish grief;
in the strength of God arrayed
scatter sin and unbelief.

5 Keep the banner still unfurled,
still unsheathed the Spirit's sword,
till the kingdoms of the world
are the kingdom of the Lord.

535   G. Duffield
© in this version Jubilate Hymns†

1 Stand up, stand up for Jesus,
you soldiers of the cross!
lift high his royal banner,
it must not suffer loss:
from victory on to victory
his army he shall lead
till evil is defeated
and Christ is Lord indeed.

2 Stand up, stand up for Jesus!
the trumpet-call obey;
then join the mighty conflict
in this his glorious day:
be strong in faith and serve him
against unnumbered foes;
let courage rise with danger,
and strength to strength oppose.

3 Stand up, stand up for Jesus!
stand in his power alone,
for human might will fail you –
you dare not trust your own:
put on the gospel armour,
keep watch with constant prayer;
where duty calls or danger
be never failing there.

4 Stand up, stand up for Jesus!
the fight will not be long,
this day the noise of battle,
the next the victor's song:
to everyone who conquers,
a crown of life shall be;
we, with the king of glory,
shall reign eternally.

536 E. H. Plumptre

1 Your hand, O God, has guided
your flock, from age to age;
your faithfulness is written
on history's every page.
They knew your perfect goodness,
whose deeds we now record;
and both to this bear witness:
 one church, one faith, one Lord.

2 Your heralds brought the gospel
to greatest as to least;
they summoned us to hasten
and share the great king's feast.
And this was all their teaching
in every deed and word;
to all alike proclaiming:
 one church, one faith, one Lord.

3 Through many days of darkness,
through many scenes of strife,
the faithful few fought bravely
to guard the nation's life.
Their gospel of redemption –
sin pardoned, hope restored –
was all in this enfolded:
 one church, one faith, one Lord.

4 And we, shall we be faithless?
shall hearts fail, hands hang down?
shall we evade the conflict
and throw away the crown?
Not so! In God's deep counsels
some better thing is stored;
we will maintain, unflinching,
 one church, one faith, one Lord.

5 Your mercy will not fail us
nor leave your work undone;
with your right hand to help us,
the victory shall be won.
And then by earth and heaven
your name shall be adored;
and this shall be their anthem:
 one church, one faith, one Lord.

537 after J. Bunyan, © Michael Saward†
(see also traditional version, 590)

1 Who honours courage here,
 who fights the devil?
who boldly faces fear,
 who conquers evil?
We're not afraid to fight!
 we'll scorn the devil's spite:
Christ gives to us the right
 to be his pilgrims.

2 Some may be terrified
 by Satan's testing,
but faith is verified
 when we're resisting.
There's no discouragement
 shall cause us to relent
our firm declared intent
 to be his pilgrims.

3 Though evil powers intend
 to break our spirit,
we know we at the end
 shall life inherit.
So, fantasies, away!
 why fear what others say?
We'll labour night and day
 to be his pilgrims.

538 from 2 Peter 1
© Christopher Idle†

1 Come, praise the name of Jesus
for all his gracious powers,
our only God and Saviour
who makes his goodness ours;
he calls us to his kingdom,
the Lord of life and death,
to see his face in glory
and know him now by faith.

2 His virtue and his wisdom,
endurance, self-control,
his godliness and kindness,
his love which crowns them all –
this is his royal nature
that we are called to share,
his robe of perfect beauty
that we are given to wear.

3 We see his shining splendour
in every sunless place
where Christ, the light of nations,
appears in truth and grace.
Transfigured by his likeness
we make the vision known,
reflecting in our faces
the radiance of his own.

4 The king of grace inspires us
to love him more and more,
to grasp our hope more firmly
and make our calling sure.
Christ Jesus, Lord and Saviour,
to this dark world you came;
and for the dawn of heaven,
we praise your holy name.

539 © David Mowbray†

1 Father of all, whose laws have stood
as signposts for our earthly good;
whose Son has come with truth and grace,
your likeness shining in his face:
    Give us Christ's love, its depth and length,
    its heart and soul and mind and strength.

2 The first and finest day is yours
to consecrate all other hours;
all other lords may we disown
and worship bring to you alone:
    Give us Christ's love . . .

3 Surround our homes with joy and peace,
with loyalty and cheerfulness;
let partners live without pretence
and children grow in confidence:
    Give us Christ's love . . .

4 May bitter hearts fresh mercy feel
and thieving hands no longer steal;
none damn their neighbour with a lie,
nor stoke the fires of jealousy:
    Give us Christ's love . . .

5 Father of all, whose laws have stood
as signposts for our earthly good;
whose Son has come with truth and grace,
your likeness shining in his face:
    Give us Christ's love . . .

540 after C. Wesley
© in this version Jubilate Hymns†

1 Help us to help each other, Lord,
each other's load to bear;
that all may live in true accord,
our joys and pains to share.

2 Help us to build each other up,
your strength within us prove;
increase our faith, confirm our hope,
and fill us with your love.

3 Together make us free indeed –
your life within us show;
and into you, our living head,
let us in all things grow.

4 Drawn by the magnet of your love
we find our hearts made new:
nearer each other let us move,
and nearer still to you.

541 H. Bonar

1 Fill now my life, O Lord my God,
in every part with praise;
that my whole being may proclaim
your being and your ways.

2 Not for the lip of praise alone,
nor yet the praising heart,
I ask, but for a life made up
of praise in every part.

3 Praise in the common things of life,
its goings out and in;
praise in each duty and each deed,
exalted or unseen.

4 Fill every part of me with praise;
let all my being speak
of you and of your love, O Lord,
poor though I be and weak.

5 Then, Lord, from me you shall receive
the praise and glory due;
and so shall I begin on earth
the song for ever new.

6 So shall no part of day or night
from sacredness be free;
but all my life, with you my God,
in fellowship shall be.

542 © James Quinn S.J.
reprinted by permission of Cassell Publishers Ltd

1 Forth in the peace of Christ we go;
Christ to the world with joy we bring:
Christ in our minds, Christ on our lips,
Christ in our hearts, the world's true king.

2 King of our hearts, Christ makes us kings;
kingship with him his servants gain:
with Christ, the Servant-Lord of all,
Christ's world we serve
        to share Christ's reign.

3 Priests of the world, Christ sends us forth
the world of time to consecrate,
our world of sin by grace to heal,
Christ's world in Christ to re-create.

4 Prophets of Christ, we hear his word:
he claims our minds, to search his ways,
he claims our lips, to speak his truth,
he claims our hearts, to sing his praise.

5 We are his church; he makes us one:
here is one hearth for all to find,
here is one flock, one Shepherd-King,
here is one faith, one heart, one mind.

543 after R. Pynson

1 God be in my head
and in my understanding.

2 God be in my eyes
and in my looking.

3 God be in my mouth
and in my speaking.

4 God be in my heart
and in my thinking.

5 God be at my end
and at my departing.

544 © Christopher Idle†

1 Freedom and life are ours
for Christ has set us free!
never again submit to powers
that lead to slavery:
Christ is the Lord who breaks
our chains, our bondage ends,
Christ is the rescuer who makes
the helpless slaves his friends.

2 Called by the Lord to use
our freedom and be strong,
not letting liberty excuse
a life of blatant wrong:
freed from the law's stern hand
God's gift of grace to prove,
know that the law's entire demand
is gladly met by love.

3 Spirit of God, come, fill,
emancipate us all!
speak to us, Word of truth, until
before his throne we fall:
glory and liberty
our Father has decreed,
and if the Son shall make us free
we shall be free indeed!

545 from the Irish, Mary E. Byrne and Eleanor H. Hull
© in this version Jubilate Hymns†

1 Lord, be my vision, supreme in my heart,
bid every rival give way and depart:
you my best thought in the day or the night,
waking or sleeping, your presence my light.

2 Lord, be my wisdom and be my true word,
I ever with you and you with me, Lord:
you my great father and I your true child,
once far away, but by love reconciled.

3 Lord, be my breastplate,
my sword for the fight:
be my strong armour, for you are my might;
you are my shelter and you my high tower –
raise me to heaven, O Power of my power.

4 I need no riches, nor earth's empty praise:
you my inheritance through all my days;
all of your treasure to me you impart,
high King of heaven, the first in my heart.

5 High King of heaven, when battle is done,
grant heaven's joy to me, bright heaven's sun;
Christ of my own heart, whatever befall,
still be my vision, O Ruler of all.

546 © Christopher Idle†

1 Lord, you need no house,
no manger now, nor tomb;
yet come, I pray, to make
my heart your home.

2 Lord, you need no gift,
for all things come from you;
receive what you have given –
my heart renew.

3 Lord, you need no skill
to make your likeness known;
create your image here –
my heart your throne.

547 J. C. Winslow
© Mrs. J. Tyrrell

1 Lord of all power, I give you my will,
in joyful obedience your tasks to fulfil;
your bondage is freedom,
your service is song,
and, held in your keeping,
my weakness is strong.

2 Lord of all wisdom, I give you my mind;
rich truth
that surpasses our knowledge to find,
what eye has not seen
and what ear has not heard
is taught by your Spirit
and shines from your word.

3 Lord of all bounty, I give you my heart;
I praise and adore you for all you impart –
your love to inspire me,
your counsel to guide,
your presence to cheer me, whatever betide.

4 Lord of all being, I give you my all;
for if I disown you I stumble and fall,
but, sworn in glad service your word to obey,
I walk in your freedom to the end of the way.

548
© Michael Saward†

1 Lord of the cross of shame,
set my cold heart aflame
with love for you, my saviour and my master;
who on that lonely day
bore all my sins away,
and saved me from the judgement
and disaster.

2 Lord of the empty tomb,
born of a virgin's womb,
triumphant over death, its power defeated;
how gladly now I sing
your praise, my risen king,
and worship you,
in heaven's splendour seated.

3 Lord of my life today,
teach me to live and pray
as one who knows the joy of sins forgiven;
so may I ever be,
now and eternally,
one with my fellow-citizens in heaven.

549
© Michael Perry†

1 Lord Jesus, let these eyes of mine
reflect your beauty and your grace;
so joyful and so tender shine
that other eyes shall seek your face.

2 Lord, use my ears, for I rejoice
to hear the word of life – with awe
I listen for the whispering voice
that calls beyond the thunder's roar.

3 And holy Jesus, set my mind
to search for truth and know your way;
to think upon the good I find,
to spurn the night and love the day:

4 And may my hands, which learned their skill
at your direction, by your love,
now deftly moving at your will
console, encourage and improve.

5 So to your throne, O Christ, again
my sense of sight and sound I bring;
and in my mind I let you reign,
and with my hands serve you, my king:

6 Speak through this voice that you have given,
your love and mercy to proclaim,
until we join the choirs of heaven
and sing the glory of your name!

550
Katie B. Wilkinson
© in this version Jubilate Hymns†

1 May the mind of Christ my saviour
live in me from day to day,
by his love and power controlling
all I do and say.

2 May the word of God enrich me
with his truth, from hour to hour,
so that all may see I triumph
only through his power.

3 May the peace of God my Father
in my life for ever reign,
that I may be calm to comfort
those in grief and pain.

4 May the love of Jesus fill me
as the waters fill the sea,
him exalting, self abasing –
this is victory!

5 May his beauty rest upon me
as I seek to make him known;
so that all may look to Jesus,
seeing him alone.

551
M. Bridges
© in this version Jubilate Hymns†

1 My God, accept my heart this day
and make it yours alone;
no longer let my footsteps stray
from your belovèd Son.

2 Before the cross of him who died
in awe and shame I fall:
let every sin be crucified
and Christ be all in all.

3 Anoint me with your heavenly grace
and seal me as your own,
that I may see your glorious face
and worship at your throne.

4 Let every thought and work and word
to you be ever given;
then life shall be your service, Lord,
and death the gate of heaven.

5 All glory to the Father be,
the Spirit and the Son;
all love and praise eternally
to God the Three-in-One.

552
C. Wesley, © in this version Jubilate Hymns†
(see also traditional version, 596)

1 O Lord, who came from realms above
the pure celestial fire to impart,
kindle a flame of sacred love
upon the altar of my heart.

2 There let it for your glory burn
with inextinguishable blaze,
and trembling to its source return
in humble prayer and fervent praise.

3 Jesus, confirm my heart's desire
to work and speak and think for you;
still let me guard the holy fire,
and still in me your gift renew.

4 Here let me prove your perfect will,
my acts of faith and love repeat,
till death your endless mercies seal
and make the sacrifice complete!

553
from the traditional prayer
© David Mowbray†

1 O Master Christ, draw near to take
your undisputed place;
my gifts and faculties remake,
form and re-fashion for your sake
an instrument of peace.

2 O Master Christ, I choose to sow
in place of hatred, love;
where wounds and injuries are now
may healing and forgiveness grow
as gifts from God above.

3 O Master Christ, I choose to plant
hope where there is despair;
a warmth of joy, a shaft of light
where darkness has diminished sight,
where sorrow leaves its scar.

4 O Master Christ, make this my goal –
less to receive than give;
to sympathise – and to make whole,
to understand and to console
and so, through death, to live.

554
Frances R. Havergal
© in this version Jubilate Hymns†

1 Take my life and let it be
all you purpose, Lord, for me;
consecrate my passing days,
let them flow in ceaseless praise.

2 Take my hands, and let them move
at the impulse of your love;
take my feet, and let them run
with the news of victory won.

3 Take my voice, and let me sing
always, only, for my King;
take my lips, let them proclaim
all the beauty of your name.

4 Take my wealth – all I possess,
make me rich in faithfulness;
take my mind that I may use
every power as you shall choose.

5 Take my motives and my will,
all your purpose to fulfil;
take my heart – it is your own,
it shall be your royal throne.

6 Take my love – my Lord, I pour
at your feet its treasure-store;
take myself, and I will be
yours for all eternity.

555
H. Bonar
© in this version Jubilate Hymns†

1 Your way, not mine, O Lord,
whatever it may be:
lead me by your own hand,
choose out the path for me.

2 Smooth let it be or rough,
it will be still the best;
by winding paths or straight
it leads me to your rest.

3 I dare not choose my life,
I would not if I might:
O choose for me, my God;
your choice is sure and right.

4 Then fill my cup, O Lord,
according to your will,
with sorrow or with joy:
you choose my good or ill.

5 Not mine but yours the choice
in things both great and small!
for you shall be my guide,
my wisdom and my all.

556
Mary F. Maude
© in this version Jubilate Hymns†

1 Yours for ever! God of love,
hear us from your throne above;
yours for ever let us be,
here and in eternity.

2 Yours for ever! Lord of life,
shield us through our earthly strife;
Christ the life, the truth, the way:
guide us to the realms of day.

3 Yours for ever! O, how blessed
those who find in you their rest!
Saviour, Guardian, heavenly Friend:
O defend us to the end.

4 Yours for ever! You our guide;
all our needs by you supplied,
all our sins by you forgiven:
lead us, Lord, from earth to heaven.

557 Frances R. Havergal

1 In full and glad surrender
I give myself to you;
to love and serve you only
and all your will to do.

2 O Son of God, you love me;
I will be yours alone,
and all I have and am, Lord,
from now shall be your own.

3 Reign over me, Lord Jesus,
O make my heart your throne;
it shall be yours, my Saviour,
it shall be yours alone.

4 O come and reign, Lord Jesus,
rule over everything;
and keep me always loyal
and true to you, my king.

558 W. Bullock and H. W. Baker
© in this version Jubilate Hymns†

1 We love the place, O God,
in which your honour dwells:
the joy of your abode,
all earthly joy excels.

2 We love the house of prayer:
for where Christ's people meet,
our risen Lord is there
to make our joy complete.

3 We love the word of life,
the word that tells of peace,
of comfort in the strife
and joys that never cease.

4 We love the cleansing sign
of life through Christ our Lord,
where with the name divine
we seal the child of God.

5 We love the holy feast
where, nourished with this food,
by faith we feed on Christ,
his body and his blood.

6 We love to sing below
of mercies freely given,
but O, we long to know
the triumph-song of heaven.

7 Lord Jesus, give us grace
on earth to love you more,
in heaven to see your face
and with your saints adore.

559 from the Latin, J. M. Neale
© in this version Jubilate Hymns†

1 Christ is made the sure foundation,
Christ the head and corner-stone
chosen of the Lord and precious,
binding all the Church in one;
holy Zion's help for ever,
and her confidence alone.

2 All within that holy city
dearly loved of God on high,
in exultant jubilation
sing, in perfect harmony;
God the One-in-Three adoring
in glad hymns eternally.

3 We as living stones implore you:
Come among us, Lord, today!
with your gracious loving-kindness
hear your children as we pray;
and the fulness of your blessing
in our fellowship display.

4 Here entrust to all your servants
what we long from you to gain –
that on earth and in the heavens
we one people shall remain,
till united in your glory
evermore with you we reign.

5 Praise and honour to the Father,
praise and honour to the Son,
praise and honour to the Spirit,
ever Three and ever One:
one in power and one in glory
while eternal ages run.

560 F. Pratt Green
© Stainer & Bell Ltd

1 God is here! As we his people
meet to offer praise and prayer,
may we find in fuller measure
what it is in Christ we share:
here, as in the world around us,
all our varied skills and arts
wait the coming of his Spirit
into open minds and hearts.

2 Here are symbols to remind us
of our lifelong need of grace;
here are table, font and pulpit,
here the cross has central place:
here in honesty of preaching,
here in silence as in speech,
here in newness and renewal
God the Spirit comes to each.

3 Here our children find a welcome
in the Shepherd's flock and fold;
here, as bread and wine are taken,
Christ sustains us as of old:
here the servants of the Servant
seek in worship to explore
what it means in daily living
to believe and to adore.

4 Lord of all, of church and kingdom,
in an age of change and doubt,
keep us faithful to the gospel,
help us work your purpose out:
here, in this day's dedication,
all we have to give, receive;
we who cannot live without you,
we adore you! we believe!

562 © Christopher Idle†

1 God our Father and creator,
over all the earth you reign;
God of cities, nations, planets,
whom the heavens cannot contain:
Come among your children here,
come to bless this house of prayer.

2 Christ, whose undefended body
human hands destroyed and killed;
three days buried, till the moment
God had chosen to rebuild:
Raise your people from the dead,
we your body, you our head.

3 Holy Spirit, wind of heaven,
breaking earthly barriers down,
pouring out your gifts and graces –
life the seed, and love the crown:
Fill us all, till all become
your pure temple, your true home.

4 Living Lord of past and future,
now through us your word fulfil;
changing scenes and times of crisis
prove that you are with us still.
From one church, all praises be,
praise to you, one Trinity!

561 from 1 Kings 8
© Michael Perry†

1 God of light and life's creation,
reigning over all supreme,
daunting our imagination,
prospect glorious yet unseen:
Lord, whom earth and heaven obey,
turn towards this house today!

2 God of alien, God of stranger,
named by nations of the earth;
poor and exile in a manger,
God of harsh and humble birth:
let us all with love sincere
learn to welcome strangers here.

3 God of justice in our nation,
fearing neither rich nor strong,
granting truth its vindication,
passing sentence on all wrong:
Lord, by whom we die or live,
hear, and as you hear, forgive.

4 God the Father, Son, and Spirit,
Trinity of love and grace,
through your mercy we inherit
word and worship in this place:
let our children all their days
to this house return with praise!

563 © Timothy Dudley-Smith

1 Here within this house of prayer
all our Father's love declare;
love that gave us birth, and planned
days and years beneath his hand:
praise to God whose love and power
bring us to this present hour!

2 Here, till earthly praises end,
tell of Christ the sinner's friend;
Christ whose blood for us was shed,
Lamb of God and living bread,
life divine and truth and way,
light of everlasting day.

3 Here may all our faint desire
feel the Spirit's wind and fire,
souls that sleep the sleep of death
stir to life beneath his breath:
may his power upon us poured
send us out to serve the Lord!

4 Here may faith and love increase,
flowing forth in joy and peace
from the Father, Spirit, Son,
undivided, Three-in-One:
his the glory all our days
in this house of prayer and praise!

1 Christ is our corner-stone,
on him alone we build;
with his true saints alone
the courts of heaven are filled;
    on his great love
    our hopes we place
    of present grace
    and joys above.

2 With psalms and hymns of praise
this holy place shall ring;
our voices we will raise,
the Three-in-One to sing;
    and thus proclaim
    in joyful song
    both loud and long,
    that glorious name.

3 Here, gracious God, draw near
as in your name we bow;
each true petition hear,
accept each faithful vow;
    and more and more
    on all who pray
    each holy day
    your blessings pour.

4 Here may we gain from heaven
the grace which we implore;
and may that grace, once given,
be with us evermore,
    until that day
    when all the blessed
    to endless rest
    are called away.

565 S. Crossman
© in this version Jubilate Hymns†

1 Jerusalem on high
my song and city is;
my home when I shall die,
the centre of my bliss:
    O happy place!
    when shall I be
    with God, to see
    him face to face?

2 There reigns my Lord, my king,
judged here unfit to live;
there angels to him sing,
and lowly homage give:
    O happy place . . .

3 The patriarchs of old
there from their travels cease;
the prophets there behold
the longed-for prince of peace:
    O happy place . . .

4 Sweet place, sweet place alone,
the home of God most high;
the Heaven of heavens, the throne
of holiest majesty:
    O happy place . . .

566 J. Cennick

1 Children of the heavenly king,
as you journey, sweetly sing;
sing your saviour's worthy praise,
glorious in his works and ways.

2 We are travelling home to God
in the way our fathers trod;
they are happy now, and we
soon their happiness shall see.

3 Lift your eyes and walk in light –
God's own city is in sight;
there our endless home shall be,
there our Lord we soon shall see.

4 Never fear, but boldly stand
on the borders of your land;
Christ, the everlasting Son,
gives you strength to journey on.

5 Lord, obediently we go,
gladly leaving all below:
Master, be our guide indeed –
we shall follow where you lead.

567 W. W. How
© in this version Jubilate Hymns†

1 For all the saints, who from their labours rest;
who to the world
        by faith their Lord confessed,
your name, O Jesus, be for ever blessed:
    Alleluia, alleluia!

2 You were their rock, their fortress,
        and their might;
you, Lord, their captain
        in the well-fought fight,
and in the darkness their unfailing light.
    Alleluia, alleluia!

3 So may your soldiers, faithful, true and bold,
fight as the saints who nobly fought of old
and win with them the victor's crown of gold.
    Alleluia, alleluia!

4 One holy people, fellowship divine!
we feebly struggle, they in glory shine –
in earth and heaven
        the saints in praise combine:
    Alleluia, alleluia!

5 And when the fight is fierce, the warfare long,
far off we hear the distant triumph-song;
and hearts are brave again,
    and arms are strong.
Alleluia, alleluia!

6 The golden evening brightens in the west:
soon, soon to faithful warriors
    comes their rest,
the peaceful calm of paradise the blessed.
Alleluia, alleluia!

7 But look! –
    there breaks a yet more glorious day;
saints all-triumphant rise in bright array –
the king of glory passes on his way!
Alleluia, alleluia!

8 From earth's wide bounds,
    from dawn to setting sun,
through heaven's gates to God
    the Three-in-One
they come, to sing the song on earth begun:
Alleluia, alleluia!

568
from Ecclesiasticus 44
© Christopher Idle†

1 Give praise for famous men
from history's open page,
by whom our God unfolds his plan
for each succeeding age.

2 Some wore a kingdom's crown
and made themselves a name;
some by God's word brought kingdoms down
and with his judgement came.

3 Some fashioned wisest laws
to guard our liberty;
some champions of a lonely cause
set slaves and prisoners free.

4 Some gave their land its songs
of love and hope and faith;
some fought against malignant wrongs
unceasingly till death.

5 Some preached to courts and kings
a Saviour's sovereign claim;
some paid the price his service brings
through torture, blood, and flame.

6 Let us pursue the prize
and praise their deeds and words;
the life is theirs that never dies,
the glory is their Lord's.

569
F. B. P. (sixteenth-seventeenth century)
© in this version Jubilate Hymns†

1 Jerusalem, my happy home,
name ever dear to me!
when shall my sorrows have an end,
your joys when shall I see?

2 When shall I leave this dying world
and to that city rise;
when shall those mighty walls and gates
delight my wondering eyes?

3 That glorious hope, Jerusalem!
in faith I make my prayer:
O God, that all my grief might end,
O God, that I were there!

4 Apostles, martyrs, prophets, saints
around my saviour stand,
and all I love in Christ below
await his clear command.

5 Jerusalem, my happy home,
when shall that glory be
when all my labours have an end
and all your joys I see?

6 Lord Jesus Christ, prepare me now
for that dear home above;
to see, and know, and worship you
in your eternal love.

570
from *Glory and Honour* (Revelation 4–5)
© Timothy Dudley-Smith

1 Heavenly hosts in ceaseless worship
'Holy, holy, holy!' cry;
'He who is, who was and will be,
God almighty, Lord most high.'
Praise and honour, power and glory,
be to him who reigns alone!
we, with all his hands have fashioned,
fall before the Father's throne.

2 All creation, all redemption,
join to sing the saviour's worth;
Lamb of God whose blood has bought us,
kings and priests, to reign on earth.
Wealth and wisdom, power and glory,
honour, might, dominion, praise,
now be his from all his creatures
and to everlasting days!

571 from Revelation 7
© Christopher Idle†

1 Here from all nations, all tongues,
      and all peoples,
   countless the crowd but their voices are one;
   vast is the sight and majestic their singing –
   'God has the victory:
      he reigns from the throne!'

2 These have come
      out of the hardest oppression,
   now they may stand in the presence of God,
   serving their Lord day and night in his temple,
   ransomed and cleansed
      by the Lamb's precious blood.

3 Gone is their thirst
      and no more shall they hunger,
   God is their shelter, his power at their side;
   sun shall not pain them,
      no burning will torture,
   Jesus the Lamb is their shepherd and guide.

4 He will go with them to clear living water
   flowing from springs
      which his mercy supplies;
   gone is their grief and their trials are over –
   God wipes away every tear from their eyes.

5 Blessing and glory and wisdom and power
   be to the Saviour again and again;
   might and thanksgiving and honour for ever
   be to our God: Alleluia! Amen.

572 from Revelation 7, after I. Watts and W. Cameron
© in this version Jubilate Hymns†

1 How bright these glorious spirits shine;
   whence all their white array?
   how have they come to this fair place
   of everlasting day?

2 These have endured through sufferings great
   and come to realms of light,
   and through the blood of Christ the Lamb
   their robes are pure and white.

0 Humble they stand before the throne,
   palm-branches in their hands;
   here they are serving him they love,
   fulfilling his commands.

4 No more can hunger hurt them now,
   nor shall they thirst again;
   no scorching heat can do them harm
   nor sun shall cause them pain.

5 For at the centre of the throne,
   Jesus the Lamb who died
   feeds them with nourishment divine,
   their shepherd and their guide.

6 In pastures green he'll lead his flock
   where living streams appear,
   and God the Lord from every eye
   shall wipe away each tear.

573 after Bernard of Cluny, J. M. Neale
© in this version Jubilate Hymns†

1 Jerusalem the golden
   in glory high above;
   O city of God's presence,
   O vision of God's love:
   how wonderful the pleasures
   and joys awaiting there;
   what radiancy of glory,
   what peace beyond compare!

2 They stand, those halls of Zion,
   all jubilant with song;
   and bright with many an angel,
   and all the martyr throng:
   the Prince is ever in them,
   the daylight is serene;
   the tree of life and healing
   has leaves of richest green.

3 There is the throne of David;
   and there from pain released,
   the shout of those who triumph,
   the song of those who feast:
   and all who with their leader
   have conquered in the fight,
   are garlanded with glory
   and robed in purest white.

4 How lovely is that city!
   the home of God's elect;
   how beautiful the country
   that eager hearts expect!
   Jesus, in mercy bring us
   to that eternal shore
   where Father, Son and Spirit
   are worshipped evermore.

574 C. Wesley
© in this version Jubilate Hymns†

1 Let saints on earth together sing
   with those whose work is done;
   for all the servants of our king
   in earth and heaven, are one.

2 One family, we live in him,
   one church above, beneath,
   though now divided by the stream,
   the narrow stream of death.

3 One army of the living God,
to his command we bow;
part of his host have crossed the flood
and part are crossing now.

4 But all unite in Christ their head,
and love to sing his praise:
Lord of the living and the dead,
direct our earthly ways!

5 So we shall join our friends above
who have obtained the prize;
and on the eagle wings of love
to joys celestial rise.

575 I. Watts
© in this version Jubilee Hymns†

1 There is a land of pure delight
where saints immortal reign,
eternal day excludes the night
and pleasures banish pain.

2 There everlasting spring abides,
and never-withering flowers;
death, like a narrow stream, divides
this heavenly land from ours.

3 Sweet fields beyond the rolling flood
stand dressed in living green,
as once to Israel Canaan stood
while Jordan flowed between.

4 But trembling mortals fear, and shrink
to cross the narrow sea;
they linger shivering on the brink,
afraid to launch away.

5 If only we could all remove
those gloomy doubts that rise,
and see the Canaan that we love
with clear unclouded eyes!

6 If we could climb where Moses stood
and fear that view no more,
not Jordan's stream, nor death's cold flood,
would keep us from the shore.

576 H. Alford
© in this version Jubilee Hymns†

1 Ten thousand times ten thousand
give glory to the Lamb;
the angel hosts around the throne
praise God, the great I AM.
Triumphant alleluias
fill earth and sea and sky,
as countless voices join the song
and worship God on high.

2 O day, for which creation
and all its tribes were made!
O joy, for all its former grief
a thousandfold repaid!
The armies of the ransomed
have fought with death and sin:
fling open wide the mighty gates
to let the victors in!

3 Bring near your great salvation,
O Lord, return again
to gather all your chosen flock –
then take your power and reign!
Appear, Desire of Nations,
your exiles long for home:
show in the heavens your promised sign,
then, Prince and Saviour, come!

577 R. Heber
© in this version Michael Saward†

1 The Son of God rides out to war
the ancient foe to slay;
his blood-red banner streams afar –
who follows him today?
Who bears his cross? who shares his grief?
who walks his narrow way?
who faces rampant unbelief?
who follows him today?

2 The martyr Stephen's eagle eye
could pierce beyond the grave;
he saw his master in the sky
and called on him to save.
By zealots he was stoned to death
and, as he knelt to pray,
he blessed them with his final breath –
who follows him today?

3 The valiant twelve, the chosen few,
on them the Spirit fell;
and faithful to the Lord they knew
they faced the hosts of hell.
They died beneath the brandished steel,
became the tyrant's prey,
yet did not flinch at their ordeal –
who follows them today?

4 A noble army – young and old –
from every nation came;
some weak and frail, some strong and bold,
to win the martyr's fame.
Eternal joy to all is given
who trust you and obey:
O give us strength, great God of heaven,
to follow them today!

578 from Isaiah 6, R. Mant
© in this version Jubilate Hymns†

1 Bright the vision that delighted
once Isaiah bowed in fear;
sweet the countless tongues united
to entrance the prophet's ear.

2 Round the Lord in glory seated,
cherubim and seraphim
filled his temple and repeated
each to each the alternate hymn:

3 'Lord, your glory fills the heaven,
earth is with its fulness stored;
to your name be glory given:
Holy, holy, holy Lord!'

4 Heaven is still with glory ringing,
earth takes up the angels' cry:
'Holy, holy, holy' singing,
'Lord of hosts, the Lord most high!'

5 With his seraphim before him,
with his holy church below,
thus united, we adore him –
let our glorious anthem flow:

6 'Lord, your glory fills the heaven,
earth is with its fulness stored;
to your name be glory given:
Holy, holy, holy Lord!'

579 H. B. George

1 By every nation, race and tongue,
worship and praise be ever sung;
     praise the Father: Alleluia!
For pardoned sin, death overcome,
and hopes that live beyond the tomb:
     Alleluia, alleluia;
     alleluia, alleluia, alleluia!

2 Saints who on earth have suffered long,
for Jesus' sake enduring wrong,
     ever-faithful: Alleluia!
Where faith is lost in sight, rejoice
and sing with never-wearied voice:
     Alleluia . . .

3 Let earth and air and sea unite
to celebrate his glorious might,
     their creator: Alleluia!
Sun, moon and stars in endless space
echo the song of every race:
     Alleluia . . .

580 from Psalm 118
I. Watts

1 From all who live beneath the skies
let the Creator's praise arise!
let the Redeemer's name be sung
through every land, by every tongue!

2 Eternal are your mercies, Lord,
eternal truth attends your word;
your praise shall sound from shore to shore
till suns shall rise and set no more.

581 from *Gloria in Excelsis*
© Michael Perry†

1 Glory be to God in heaven,
peace to those who love him well;
on the earth let all his people
speak his grace, his wonders tell:
Lord, we praise you for your glory,
mighty Father, heaven's king;
hear our joyful adoration
and accept the thanks we bring.

2 Only Son of God the Father,
Lamb who takes our sin away,
now with him in triumph seated –
for your mercy, Lord, we pray:
Jesus Christ, most high and holy,
Saviour, you are God alone
in the glory of the Father
with the Spirit: Three-in-One!

582 from *Gloria in Excelsis*
© Christopher Idle†

1 Glory in the highest
     to the God of heaven!
Peace to all your people
     through the earth be given!
Mighty God and Father,
     thanks and praise we bring,
singing Alleluia
     to our heavenly king.

2 Jesus Christ is risen,
     God the Father's Son!
With the Holy Spirit,
     you are Lord alone!
Lamb once killed for sinners,
     all our guilt to bear,
show us now your mercy,
     now receive our prayer.

3 Christ the world's true Saviour,
    high and holy one,
seated now and reigning
    from your Father's throne:
Lord and God, we praise you!
    Highest heaven adores:
in the Father's glory,
    all the praise be yours!

583 anonymous
Foundling Hospital Collection

1 Praise the Lord, you heavens, adore him;
  praise him, angels in the height;
sun and moon, rejoice before him;
  praise him, all you stars and light.
Praise the Lord, for he has spoken,
  worlds his mighty voice obeyed;
laws which never shall be broken
  for their guidance he has made.

2 Praise the Lord, for he is glorious,
  never shall his promise fail;
God has made his saints victorious,
  sin and death shall not prevail.
Praise the God of our salvation!
  hosts on high, his power proclaim;
heaven and earth and all creation
  praise and glorify his name!

584 Frances J. van Alstyne

1 To God be the glory!
    great things he has done;
so loved he the world that he gave us his Son
who yielded his life an atonement for sin,
and opened the life-gate that all may go in.
  Praise the Lord, praise the Lord!
  let the earth hear his voice;
  praise the Lord, praise the Lord!
  let the people rejoice:
  O come to the Father
  through Jesus the Son
  and give him the glory;
    great things he has done.

2 O perfect redemption, the purchase of blood!
To every believer the promise of God:
the vilest offender who truly believes,
that moment from Jesus a pardon receives.
  Praise the Lord! . . .

3 Great things he has taught us,
    great things he has done,
and great our rejoicing through Jesus the Son:
but purer and higher and greater will be
our wonder, our gladness,
    when Jesus we see!
  Praise the Lord! . . .

585 after T. Ken, © in this version Jubilate Hymns†
(see also traditional version, 586)

Praise God from whom all blessings flow,
in heaven above and earth below;
one God, three persons, we adore –
to him be praise for evermore!

586 T. Ken
(see also revised version, 585)

Praise God from whom all blessings flow:
praise him, all creatures here below,
praise him above, ye heavenly host –
praise Father, Son, and Holy Ghost.

587 E. Perronet and J. Rippon
(see also revised version, 203)

1 All hail the power of Jesus' name!
  let angels prostrate fall;
bring forth the royal diadem
  to crown him Lord of all.

2 Crown him, you morning stars of light,
  who fixed this floating ball;
now hail the Strength-of-Israel's might
  and crown him Lord of all.

3 Crown him, you martyrs of our God,
  who from his altar call;
extol the Stem-of-Jesse's rod
  and crown him Lord of all.

4 You seed of Israel's chosen race
  and ransomed from the fall,
hail him who saves you by his grace
  and crown him Lord of all.

5 Hail him, you heirs of David's line,
  whom David 'Lord' did call,
the God incarnate, Man divine –
  and crown him Lord of all.

6 Sinners, whose love cannot forget
  the wormwood and the gall,
go spread your trophies at his feet
  and crown him Lord of all.

7 O that with every tribe and tongue
  we at his feet may fall,
lift high the universal song
  and crown him Lord of all.

588 C. Wesley
(see also revised version, 452)

1 And can it be that I should gain
an interest in the Saviour's blood?
Died he for me, who caused his pain;
for me, who him to death pursued?
Amazing love! – how can it be
that thou, my God, shouldst die for me?

2 'Tis mystery all! – the Immortal dies, –
who can explore his strange design?
In vain the first-born seraph tries
to sound the depths of love divine!
'Tis mercy all! – Let earth adore;
let angel minds inquire no more.

3 He left his Father's throne above –
so free, so infinite his grace –
emptied himself of all but love,
and bled for Adam's helpless race.
'Tis mercy all, immense and free;
for, O my God, it found out me.

4 Long my imprisoned spirit lay
fast bound in sin and nature's night:
thine eye diffused a quickening ray;
I woke – the dungeon flamed with light.
My chains fell off, my heart was free;
I rose, went forth, and followed thee.

5 No condemnation now I dread;
Jesus, and all in him, is mine!
Alive in him, my living head,
and clothed in righteousness divine,
bold I approach the eternal throne
and claim the crown through Christ my own.

589 after R. Maurus, J. Cosin
(see also revised version, 232)

1 Come, Holy Ghost, our souls inspire,
and lighten with celestial fire:
thou the anointing Spirit art,
who dost thy sevenfold gifts impart.

2 Thy blessèd unction from above
is comfort, life, and fire of love:
enable with perpetual light
the dulness of our blinded sight.

3 Anoint and cheer our soilèd face
with the abundance of thy grace:
keep far our foes, give peace at home –
where thou art guide no ill can come.

4 Teach us to know the Father, Son,
and thee of both to be but One:
that, through the ages all along,
this may be our endless song:
  'Praise to thy eternal merit,
  Father, Son, and Holy Spirit.' Amen

590 after J. Bunyan, P. Dearmer
(see also revised version, 537)

1 He who would valiant be
  'gainst all disaster,
let him in constancy
  follow the Master:
there's no discouragement
  shall make him once relent
his first avowed intent
  to be a pilgrim.

2 Who so beset him round
  with dismal stories
do but themselves confound –
  his strength the more is:
no foes shall stay his might,
  though he with giants fight;
he will make good his right
  to be a pilgrim.

3 Since, Lord, thou dost defend
  us with thy Spirit,
we know we at the end
  shall life inherit:
then, fancies, flee away!
  I'll fear not what men say,
I'll labour night and day
  to be a pilgrim.

591 from Psalm 23, W. Whittingham and others
(see also revised version, 45)

1 The Lord's my shepherd: I'll not want;
he makes me down to lie
in pastures green: he leadeth me
the quiet waters by.

2 My soul he doth restore again,
and me to walk doth make
within the paths of righteousness,
e'en for his own name's sake.

3 Yea, though I walk through death's dark vale,
yet will I fear no ill;
for thou art with me, and thy rod
and staff me comfort still.

4 My table thou hast furnishèd
in presence of my foes;
my head with oil thou dost anoint
and my cup overflows.

5 Goodness and mercy all my life
shall surely follow me;
and in God's house for evermore
my dwelling-place shall be.

592 unknown
(see also revised version, 326)

1 God save our gracious Queen,
long live our noble Queen,
God save the Queen!
Send her victorious,
happy and glorious,
long to reign over us:
God save the Queen!

2 Thy choicest gifts in store
on her be pleased to pour:
long may she reign!
May she defend our laws,
and ever give us cause
to sing with heart and voice:
God save the Queen!

593 A. M. Toplady
(see also revised version, 444)

1 Rock of ages, cleft for me,
let me hide myself in thee;
let the water and the blood
from thy riven side which flowed,
be of sin the double cure,
cleanse me from its guilt and power.

2 Not the labours of my hands
can fulfil thy law's demands;
could my zeal no respite know,
could my tears for ever flow,
all for sin could not atone:
thou must save, and thou alone.

3 Nothing in my hand I bring,
simply to thy cross I cling;
naked, come to thee for dress,
helpless, look to thee for grace;
foul, I to the fountain fly:
wash me, Saviour, or I die!

4 While I draw this fleeting breath,
when my eyelids close in death,
when I soar through tracts unknown,
see thee on thy judgement throne:
Rock of ages, cleft for me,
let me hide myself in thee.

594 R. Heber
(see also revised version, 7)

1 Holy, holy, holy, Lord God almighty!
early in the morning
our song shall rise to thee:
Holy, holy, holy! – merciful and mighty,
God in three persons, blessèd Trinity.

2 Holy, holy, holy! All the saints adore thee,
casting down their golden crowns
around the glassy sea;
cherubim and seraphim
falling down before thee:
God from of old who evermore shall be!

3 Holy, holy, holy! –
though the darkness hide thee,
though the eye of sinful man
thy glory may not see;
only thou art holy, there is none beside thee
perfect in power, in love and purity.

4 Holy, holy, holy, Lord God almighty!
all thy works shall praise thy name,
in earth and sky and sea:
Holy, holy, holy! – merciful and mighty,
God in three persons, blessèd Trinity.

595 J. Edmeston
(see also revised version, 525)

1 Lead us, heavenly Father, lead us
o'er the world's tempestuous sea;
guard us, guide us, keep us, feed us –
for we have no help but thee,
yet possessing every blessing
if our God our Father be.

2 Saviour, breathe forgiveness o'er us:
all our weakness thou dost know,
thou didst tread this earth before us,
thou didst feel its keenest woe;
through the dreary desert, weary,
in obedience thou didst go.

3 Spirit of our God, descending,
fill our hearts with heavenly joy,
love with every passion blending,
pleasure that can never cloy:
thus provided, pardoned, guided,
nothing can our peace destroy.

596 C. Wesley
(see also revised version, 552)

1 O thou who camest from above
the pure celestial fire to impart,
kindle a flame of sacred love
on the mean altar of my heart!

2 There let it for thy glory burn
with inextinguishable blaze;
and trembling to its source return,
in humble prayer and fervent praise.

3 Jesus, confirm my heart's desire
to work and speak and think for thee;
still let me guard the holy fire,
and still stir up thy gift in me:

4 Ready for all thy perfect will,
  my acts of faith and love repeat,
  till death thy endless mercies seal
  and make the sacrifice complete.

597 after J. F. Wade, F. Oakeley and others
(see also revised short version, 65)

1 O come, all ye faithful,
  joyful and triumphant;
  O come ye, O come ye to Bethlehem;
  come and behold him,
        born the king of angels!
  O come, let us adore him,
  O come, let us adore him,
  O come, let us adore him, Christ the Lord!

2 God from God,
  Light from light –
  lo, he abhors not the virgin's womb!
  Very God, begotten, not created.
  O come . . .

3 See how the shepherds
  summoned to his cradle,
  leaving their flocks,
        draw nigh with lowly fear:
  we too will thither bend our joyful footsteps.
  O come . . .

4 Led by the starlight,
  Magi, Christ adoring,
  offer him incense, gold, and myrrh;
  we to the Christ-child
        bring our hearts' oblations.
  O come . . .

5 Child, for us sinners,
  poor and in the manger,
  we would embrace thee with love and awe:
  who could not love thee, loving us so dearly?
  O come . . .

6 Sing, choirs of angels,
  sing in exultation!
  Sing, all ye citizens of heaven above,
  'Glory to God in the highest!'
  O come . . .

7 Yea, Lord, we greet thee,
  born for our salvation;
  Jesus, to thee be glory given!
  Word of the Father now in flesh appearing.
  O come . . .

OR on Christmas morning:
7 Yea, Lord, we greet thee,
  born this happy morning;
  Jesus, to thee be glory given!
  Word of the Father now in flesh appearing.
  O come . . .

598 from Luke 12, P. Doddridge
© in this version Word & Music†

1 You servants of the Lord
  who for his coming wait:
  observe with care his heavenly word –
  be watchful at his gate.

2 Let all your lamps be bright
  and guard the living flame;
  be ready always in his sight,
  for awesome is his name.

3 Await your Lord's command:
  the bridegroom shall appear,
  for his returning is at hand,
  and while we speak he's near.

4 O happy servants they
  who wide awake are found
  to greet their master on that day,
  and be with honour crowned!

5 Christ shall the banquet spread
  with his own royal hand,
  and raise each faithful servant's head
  amid the angelic band.

599 from *Benedictus* (Luke 1)
© Michael Perry†

1 O bless the God of Israel
        who comes to set us free;
  who visits and redeems us,
        with love for all to see.
  The prophets spoke of mercy,
        of rescue and release:
  God shall fulfil his promise
        and bring our people peace.

2 He comes! the Child of David,
        the Son whom God has given;
  he comes to live among us
        and raise us up to heaven:
  before him goes his servant –
        forerunner in the way,
  the prophet of salvation,
        the herald of the Day.

3 Where once were fear and darkness,
        the sun begins to rise –
  the dawning of forgiveness
        upon the sinner's eyes.
  He guides the feet of pilgrims
        along the paths of peace:
  O bless our God and Saviour,
        with songs that never cease!

600 Christina Rossetti

1 In the bleak mid-winter
　　frosty wind made moan,
earth stood hard as iron,
　　water like a stone;
snow had fallen, snow on snow,
　　snow on snow,
in the bleak mid-winter
　　long ago.

2 Heaven cannot hold him,
　　nor the earth sustain;
heaven and earth shall flee away
　　when he comes to reign:
in the bleak mid-winter
　　a stable-place sufficed
God, the Lord almighty,
　　Jesus Christ.

3 Enough for him whom cherubim
　　worship night and day –
a breastful of milk
　　and a manger full of hay;
enough for him whom angels
　　fall down before –
the wise men and the shepherds
　　who adore!

4 What can I give him,
　　poor as I am?
If I were a shepherd
　　I would give a lamb,
if I were a wise man
　　I would do my part;
yet what I can I give him –
　　give my heart.

601 after C. Coffin, J. Chandler
© in this version Word & Music†

1 On Jordan's bank the Baptist's cry
announces that the Lord is nigh:
awake and listen for he brings
glad tidings of the King of kings.

2 Let every heart be cleansed from sin,
make straight the way for God within,
and so prepare to be the home
where such a mighty guest may come.

3 For you are our salvation, Lord,
our refuge and our great reward;
without your grace we waste away
like flowers that wither and decay.

4 To heal the sick, stretch out your hand,
and make the fallen sinner stand;
shine out, and let your light restore
earth's own true loveliness once more.

5 To you, O Christ, all praises be,
whose advent sets your people free;
whom with the Father we adore
and Holy Spirit evermore!

602 © Timothy Dudley-Smith

1 We come as guests invited
when Jesus bids us dine,
his friends on earth united
to share the bread and wine;
the bread of life is broken,
the wine is freely poured
for us, in solemn token
of Christ our dying Lord.

2 We eat and drink, receiving
from Christ the grace we need,
and in our hearts believing
on him by faith we feed;
with wonder and thanksgiving
for love that knows no end,
we find in Jesus living
our ever-present friend.

3 One bread is ours for sharing,
one single fruitful vine,
our fellowship declaring
renewed in bread and wine –
renewed, sustained and given
by token, sign and word,
the pledge and seal of heaven,
the love of Christ our Lord.

603 G. Herbert
© in this version Word & Music†

1 King of glory, king of peace
　　I will love you;
since your mercies never cease,
　　faith shall prove you!
You have granted my request,
　　you have heard me;
though my sinful soul transgressed,
　　you have spared me.

2 Praises with my utmost art
　　I will bring you;
songs of triumph from my heart
　　I will sing you.
Though my sins against me cried,
　　this shall cheer me:
God in Christ has justified
　　and will clear me.

3 Seven whole days – not one in seven –
    I will praise you;
  worship lifts the heart to heaven,
    love obeys you!
  Once you died, when no-one sought
    to console you;
  now eternity's too short
    to extol you!

604 from *A Song of Creation/Benedicite*
© Timothy Dudley-Smith

1 Bless the Lord, creation sings;
  earth and sky his hand proclaim.
  Praise him, all created things;
  angel hosts, exalt his Name.

2 Bless the Lord! To heaven's throne
  songs of endless glory rise;
  in the clouds his praise be shown,
  sun and moon and starry skies.

3 Bless the Lord with ice and snow,
  bitter cold and scorching blaze,
  floods and all the winds that blow,
  frosty nights and sunlit days.

4 Bless the Lord in mist and cloud,
  lightnings shine to mark his way;
  thunders speak his name aloud,
  wind and storm his word obey.

5 Bless the Lord who brings to birth
  life renewed by sun and rain;
  flowing rivers, fruitful earth,
  bird and beast on hill and plain.

6 Bless the Lord! From earth and sky,
  ocean depths and furthest shore,
  all things living bear on high
  songs of praise for evermore.

7 Bless the Lord! His name be blessed,
  worshipped, honoured, loved, adored;
  and with holy hearts confessed,
  saints and servants of the Lord.

8 Bless the Lord! The Father, Son,
  and the Holy Spirit, praise;
  high exalt the Three-in-One,
  God of everlasting days!

605 from *Great and Wonderful* (Revelation 15)
© Christopher Idle†

1 Great and wonderful your deeds,
  God from whom all power proceeds:
  true and right are all your ways –
  who shall not give thanks and praise?
    To your name be glory!

2 King of nations, take your crown!
  every race shall soon bow down:
  holy God and Lord alone,
  justice in your deeds is shown;
    all have seen your glory.

3 To the one almighty God,
  to the Lamb who shed his blood,
  to the Spirit now be given
  by the hosts of earth and heaven;
    love and praise and glory!

606 from *Gloria in Excelsis*
© Timothy Dudley-Smith

1 All glory be to God on high,
  his peace on earth proclaim;
    to all his people tell abroad
    the grace and glory of the Lord,
  and bless his holy Name.

2 In songs of thankfulness and praise
  our hearts their homage bring
    to worship him who reigns above
    almighty Father, Lord of love,
  our God and heavenly King.

3 O Christ, the Father's only Son,
  O Lamb enthroned on high,
    O Jesus, who for sinners died
    and reigns at God the Father's side,
  in mercy hear our cry.

4 Most high and holy is the Lord,
  most high his heavenly throne;
    where God the Father, God the Son,
    and God the Spirit, ever One,
  in glory reigns alone.

607 from *Saviour of the World*
© Christopher Idle†

1 Jesus, Saviour of the world,
  you have bought your people's freedom
  by your cross, your life laid down·
  now bring in your glorious kingdom:
    Come to help us!

2 Christ, who once on Galilee
  came to your disciples' rescue:
  we, like them, cry out for help –
  free us from our sins, we ask you.
    Come to save us!

3 Lord, make known your promised power;
  show yourself our strong deliverer:
  so our prayer shall turn to praise –
  hear us, stay with us for ever:
    Come to rule us!

4 When you come, Lord Jesus Christ,
  filling earth and heaven with wonder,
  come to make us one with you –
  heirs of life, to reign in splendour:
      Alleluia!

608 from Psalm 134
© Timothy Dudley-Smith

1 Bless the Lord as day departs;
  let your lamps be brightly burning,
  lifting holy hands and hearts
  to the Lord, till day's returning.

2 As within the darkened shrine,
  faithful to their sacred calling,
  sons and priests of Levi's line
  blessed the Lord as night was falling:

3 So may we who watch or rest
  bless the Lord of earth and heaven;
  and by him ourselves be blessed,
  grace and peace and mercy given.

609 from Psalm 134
© Christopher Idle†

1 Come, praise the Lord, all you his servants,
  who stand within his house by night!
  Come, lift your hands and hearts in worship;
  make him your praise and your delight:

2 Come, bless the Lord, all those who love him,
  who serve within his holy place:
  may God who made both earth and heaven
  grant us the blessings of his grace.

610 from *Bless the Lord*
© Christopher Idle†

1 Bless the Lord, our fathers' God,
  bless the name of heaven's king;
  bless him in his holy place,
  tell his praise, his glories sing.

2 Bless the Lord who reigns on high
  throned between the cherubim;
  bless the Lord who knows the depths,
  show his praise and worship him.

3 Bless the Lord for evermore;
  bless the Holy Trinity:
  bless the Father, Spirit, Son,
  sing his praise eternally!

611 from *Nunc Dimittis* (Luke 2), J. E. Seddon
© Mrs. M. Seddon†

1 Lord, now let your servant
  go his way in peace;
  your great love has brought me
  joy that will not cease:

2 For my eyes have seen him
  promised from of old –
  saviour of all people,
  shepherd of one fold:

3 Light of revelation
  to the gentiles shown,
  light of Israel's glory
  to the world made known.

612 from *The Song of Christ's Glory* (Philippians 2)
© Brian Black and Word & Music†

1 Before the heaven and earth
  were made by God's decree,
  the Son of God all-glorious dwelt
  in God's eternity.

2 Though in the form of God
  and rich beyond compare,
  he did not stay to grasp his prize;
  nor did he linger there.

3 From heights of heaven he came
  to this world full of sin,
  to meet with hunger, hatred, hell,
  our life, our love to win.

4 The Son became true Man
  and took a servant's role;
  with lowliness and selfless love
  he came, to make us whole.

5 Obedient to his death –
  that death upon a cross,
  no son had ever shown such love,
  nor father known such loss.

6 To him enthroned on high,
  by angel hosts adored,
  all knees shall bow, and tongues confess
  that Jesus Christ is Lord.

S.1
from Luke 24
© Michael Perry†

(Alleluia, alleluia!)

1 As we walk along beside you,
and we hear you speak of mercy,
then it seems our hearts are burning
for we find you in the sharing of the word.

2 As we ask that you stay with us
and we watch what you are doing,
then our eyes begin to open
for we see you in the breaking of the bread.

3 As we reach for you believing
and we go to love and serve you,
then our lives will be proclaiming
that we know you in the rising from the dead.

(Lord, alleluia!)

S.2
unknown

1 Come into his presence singing,
Alleluia, alleluia, alleluia!

2 Come into his presence singing
Jesus is Lord, Jesus is Lord, Jesus is Lord!

3 Come into his presence singing,
Worthy the Lamb, worthy the Lamb,
worthy the Lamb!

4 Come into his presence singing,
Glory to God, glory to God, glory to God!

S.3
Don Fishel
© 1973 and arranged © 1982 by The Word of God,
P.O. Box 8617, Ann Arbor, Michigan 48107, USA.

Alleluia, alleluia,
give thanks to the risen Lord!
Alleluia, alleluia,
give praise to his name!

1 Jesus is Lord of all the earth,
he is the king of creation:
Alleluia . . .

2 Spread the good news o'er all the earth –
Jesus has died and has risen:
Alleluia . . .

3 We have been crucified with Christ;
now we shall live for ever:
Alleluia . . .

4(5) Come let us praise the living God;
joyfully sing to our saviour:
Alleluia . . .

S.4
Bob Gillman, © 1977 Thankyou Music, P.O. Box 75,
Eastbourne BN23 6NW.

Bind us together, Lord,
bind us together
with cords that cannot be broken;
bind us together, Lord,
bind us together,
O bind us together in love!

There is only one God,
there is only one King,
there is only one Body –
that is why we sing:
Bind us together . . .

S.5
Terrye Coelho
© 1972 Maranatha! Music/Word Music (UK) Ltd
9 Holdom Avenue, Bletchley, Milton Keynes

1 Father, we adore you,
lay our lives before you:
how we love you!

2 Jesus, we adore you,
lay our lives before you:
how we love you!

3 Spirit, we adore you,
lay our lives before you:
how we love you!

S.6
Janet Lunt, © 1978/9 Mustard Seed Music
9 Holdom Avenue, Bletchley, Milton Keynes

Broken for me, broken for you,
the body of Jesus broken for you.

1 He offered his body, he poured out his soul,
Jesus was broken that we might be whole:
Broken for me . . .

2 Come to my table and with me dine,
eat of my bread and drink of my wine:
Broken for me . . .

3 This is my body given for you,
eat it remembering I died for you:
Broken for me . . .

4 This is my blood I shed for you,
for your forgiveness, making you new:
Broken for me . . .

S.7
from Philippians 2
© Marvin Frey

He is Lord, he is Lord,
he is risen from the dead, and he is Lord!
Every knee shall bow, every tongue confess
that Jesus Christ is Lord.

S.8 unknown

1 Come and praise the Lord our king,   Alleluia,
  come and praise the Lord our king.   alleluia!

2 Christ was born in Bethlehem,   Alleluia,
  Son of God and Son of Man.   alleluia!

3 He grew up an earthly child   Alleluia,
  in the world, but undefiled.   alleluia!

4 He who died at Calvary   Alleluia,
  rose again triumphantly.   alleluia!

5 He will cleanse us from our sin   Alleluia,
  if we live by faith in him.   alleluia!

6 Come and praise the Lord our king,   Alleluia,
  come and praise the Lord our king.   alleluia!

S.9 Peter Jackson, © 1980 Word Music (UK)
9 Holdom Avenue, Bletchley, Milton Keynes

Sovereign Lord, Sovereign Lord,
you made all things by your word;
my creator, redeemer, my King of kings adored,
sovereign Lord, sovereign Lord!

S.10 after Suzanne Toolan
© Michael Baughen
and GIA Publications Incorporated

1 Come, let us worship Christ
  to the glory of God the Father,
  for he is worthy of all our love;
  he died and rose for us!
  praise him as Lord and saviour.
      And when the trumpet shall sound
      and Jesus comes in great power,
      then he will raise us to be with him
      for evermore!

2 'I am the bread of life;
  he who comes to me shall not hunger:
  and all who trust in me shall not thirst' –
  this is what Jesus said:
  praise him as Lord and saviour.
      And when the trumpet . . .

3 'I am the door to life;
  he who enters by me is saved,
  abundant life he will then receive' –
  this is what Jesus said:
  praise him as Lord and saviour.
      And when the trumpet . . .

4 'I am the light of the world;
  if you follow me, darkness ceases,
  and in its place comes the light of life' –
  this is what Jesus said:
  praise him as Lord and saviour.
      And when the trumpet . . .

5 Lord, we are one with you;
  we rejoice in your new creation:
  our hearts are fired by your saving love –
  take up our lives, O Lord,
  and use us for your glory.
      And when the trumpet . . .

S.11 unknown

1 Give me joy in my heart, keep me praising;
  give me joy in my heart, I pray:
  give me joy in my heart, keep me praising –
  keep me praising till the break of day.
      Sing hosanna, sing hosanna,
      sing hosanna to the King of kings;
      sing hosanna, sing hosanna,
      sing hosanna to the King.

2 Give me peace in my heart, keep me resting;
  give me peace in my heart, I pray:
  give me peace in my heart, keep me resting –
  keep me resting till the break of day.
      Sing hosanna . . .

3 Give me love in my heart, keep me serving;
  give me love in my heart, I pray:
  give me love in my heart, keep me serving –
  keep me serving till the break of day.
      Sing hosanna . . .

S.12 from *Come Together* by Jimmy and Carol Owens
© 1972 Lexicon Music Inc./Word Music (UK)
9 Holdom Avenue, Bletchley, Milton Keynes

1 God forgave my sin in Jesus' name;
  I've been born again in Jesus' name,
  and in Jesus' name I come to you
  to share his love as he told me to.
  He said:
      Freely, freely you have received,
      freely, freely give;
      go in my name and because you believe,
      others will know that I live.

2 All power is given in Jesus' name,
  in earth and heaven in Jesus' name;
  and in Jesus' name I come to you
  to share his power as he told me to.
  He said . . .

S.13 © 1966 by Willard Jabusch

God has spoken to his people,   Alleluia,
and his words are words of wisdom.   alleluia!

1 Open your ears, O Christian people,
  open your ears and hear good news;
  open your hearts, O royal priesthood,
  God has come to you, God has come to you.
    God has spoken . . .

2 They who have ears to hear his message,
  they who have ears, then let them hear;
  they who would learn the way of wisdom,
  let them hear God's word,
    let them hear God's word!
  God has spoken . . .

3 Israel comes to greet the saviour,
  Judah is glad to see his day;
  from east and west the peoples travel,
  he will show the way, he will show the way.
    God has spoken . . .

from *Come Together* by Jimmy and Carol Owens
© 1972 Lexicon Music Inc./Word Music (UK)
9 Holdom Avenue, Bletchley, Milton Keynes

S.14

1 Holy, holy, holy, holy,
  holy, holy, Lord God Almighty!
  and we lift our hearts before you
  as a token of our love:
  holy, holy, holy, holy!

2 Gracious Father, gracious Father,
  we're so glad to be your children,
    gracious Father;
  and we lift our heads before you
  as a token of our love,
  gracious Father, gracious Father.

3 Precious Jesus, precious Jesus,
  we're so glad that you've redeemed us,
    precious Jesus;
  and we lift our hands before you
  as a token of our love,
  precious Jesus, precious Jesus.

4 Holy Spirit, Holy Spirit,
  come and fill our hearts anew, Holy Spirit!
  and we lift our voice before you
  as a token of our love,
  Holy Spirit, Holy Spirit.

Max Dyer
© 1974, 1975 Celebration Services/Thankyou Music
PO Box 75, Eastbourne BN23 6NW

S.15

1 I will sing, I will sing a song unto the Lord,
  I will sing, I will sing a song unto the Lord,
  I will sing, I will sing a song unto the Lord:
  Alleluia, glory to the Lord:
    Allelu, alleluia, glory to the Lord,
    allelu, alleluia, glory to the Lord,
    allelu, alleluia, glory to the Lord,
    alleluia, glory to the Lord!

2 We will come, we will come
    as one before the Lord . . .
  Alleluia, glory to the Lord!
    Allelu, alleluia . . .

3 If the Son, if the Son shall make you free . . .
  you shall be free indeed:
    Allelu, alleluia . . .

4 They that sow in tears shall reap in joy . . .
  Alleluia, glory to the Lord!
    Allelu, alleluia . . .

S.16 © C. Simmonds and others

1 I want to walk with Jesus Christ
  all the days I live of this life on earth;
  to give to him complete control
  of body and of soul.
    Follow him, follow him,
    yield your life to him –
    he has conquered death,
    he is King of kings;
    accept the joy which he gives to those
    who yield their lives to him!

2 I want to learn to speak to him,
  to pray to him, confess my sin,
  to open my life and let him in,
  for joy will then be mine.

3 I want to learn to speak of him –
  my life must show that he lives in me;
  my deeds, my thoughts, my words
    must speak
  of his great love for me.

4 I want to learn to read his word,
  for this is how I know the way
  to live my life as pleases him,
  in holiness and joy.

5 O Holy Spirit of the Lord,
  now enter into this heart of mine;
  take full control of my selfish will
  and make me yours alone!
    Follow him . . .

David Mansell
© 1979 Springtide/Word Music (UK)
9 Holdom Avenue, Bletchley, Milton Keynes

S.17

1 Jesus is Lord! creation's voice proclaims it,
  for by his power each tree and flower
    was planned and made.
  Jesus is Lord! the universe declares it –
  sun, moon and stars in heaven cry:
    'Jesus is Lord!'
  Jesus is Lord, Jesus is Lord!
  Praise him with alleluias,
  for Jesus is Lord!

2 Jesus is Lord! yet from his throne eternal
   in flesh he came to die in pain
      on Calvary's tree.
   Jesus is Lord! from him all life proceeding –
   yet gave his life a ransom thus setting us free.
   Jesus is Lord, Jesus is Lord!
   Praise him with alleluias,
   for Jesus is Lord!

3 Jesus is Lord! o'er sin the mighty conqueror;
   from death he rose and all his foes
      shall own his name.
   Jesus is Lord! God sends his Holy Spirit
   to show by works of power that Jesus is Lord.
   Jesus is Lord . . .

S.18 J. E. Seddon
© Mrs. M. Seddon†

1 Let us praise God together,
      let us praise;
   let us praise God together
      all our days:
   he is faithful in all his ways,
   he is worthy of all our praise,
      his name be exalted on high!

2 Let us seek God together,
      let us pray;
   let us seek his forgiveness
      as we pray:
   he will cleanse us from all our sin,
   he will help us the fight to win,
      his name be exalted on high!

3 Let us serve God together,
      him obey;
   let our lives show his goodness
      through each day:
   Christ the Lord is the world's true light –
   let us serve him with all our might,
      his name be exalted on high!

S.19 from the traditional prayer, Sebastian Temple
© 1975 Franciscan Communications Center
Los Angeles, CA 90015, USA.

1 Make me a channel of your peace:
   where there is hatred let me bring your love,
   where there is injury, your pardon, Lord,
   and where there's doubt, true faith in you:
      O Master, grant that I may never seek
      so much to be consoled as to console;
      to be understood as to understand,
      to be loved, as to love with all my soul!

2 Make me a channel of your peace:
   where there's despair in life
      let me bring hope,
   where there is darkness, only light,
   and where there's sadness, ever joy:
      O Master grant . . .

3 Make me a channel of your peace:
   it is in pardoning that we are pardoned,
   in giving of ourselves that we receive,
   and in dying that we're born to eternal life.

S.20 after Mother Teresa

1 Make us worthy, Lord,
   to serve our neighbour's need
   throughout the world,
   who live in poverty and hunger,
      in poverty and hunger,
      in poverty and hunger.

2 Give them through our hands
   this day their daily bread
   and, by our understanding love,
   give peace and joy,
      give peace and joy,
      give peace and joy!

S.21 unknown
© in this version Jubilate Hymns†

1 Praise him, praise him,
   everybody praise him –
   he is love, he is love;
   praise him, praise him,
   everybody praise him –
   God is love, God is love!

2 Thank him, thank him,
   everybody thank him –
   he is love, he is love;
   thank him, thank him,
   everybody thank him –
   God is love, God is love!

3 Love him, love him,
   everybody love him –
   he is love, he is love;
   love him, love him,
   everybody love him –
   God is love, God is love!

4 Alleluia,
   glory, alleluia;
   he is love, he is love;
   alleluia,
   glory, alleluia!
   God is love, God is love!

S.22

1 Sing alleluia to the Lord,
   sing alleluia to the Lord,
   sing alleluia, sing alleluia,
   sing alleluia to the Lord!

2 Jesus is risen from the dead,
   Jesus is risen from the dead,
   Jesus is risen, Jesus is risen,
   Jesus is risen from the dead!

3 Jesus is Lord of heaven and earth,
   Jesus is Lord of heaven and earth,
   Jesus is Lord, Jesus is Lord,
   Jesus is Lord of heaven and earth!

4 Jesus is coming for his own,
   Jesus is coming for his own,
   Jesus is coming, Jesus is coming,
   Jesus is coming for his own.

S.23

Spirit of the living God, fall afresh on me;
Spirit of the living God, fall afresh on me:
break me, melt me, mould me, fill me –
Spirit of the living God, fall afresh on me!

S.24 © Michael Baughen†

Spirit of the living God, move among us all;
make us one in heart and mind,
      make us one in love:
humble, caring, selfless, sharing –
Spirit of the living God, fill our lives with love!

S.25 West Indian carol
© collected Boosey & Hawkes Inc.

1 The virgin Mary had a baby boy,
   the virgin Mary had a baby boy,
   the virgin Mary had a baby boy
   and they say that his name is Jesus.
      He come from the glory,
      he come from the glorious kingdom;
      he come from the glory,
      he come from the glorious kingdom:
      O yes, believer!
      O yes, believer!
      He come from the glory,
      he come from the glorious kingdom.

2 The angels sang when the baby was born,
   the angels sang when the baby was born,
   the angels sang when the baby was born
   and they sang that his name is Jesus.
      He come from the glory . . .

3 The shepherds came
      where the baby was born,
   the shepherds came
      where the baby was born,
   the shepherds came
      where the baby was born
   and they say that his name is Jesus.
      He come from the glory . . .

S.26 from John 13

The new commandment that I give to you
   is to love one another as I have loved you;
   is to love one another as I have loved you.
By this shall people know you are my disciples:
   if you have love one for another;
by this shall people know you are my disciples:
   if you have love one for another.

S.27 © Michael Baughen†

1 There's no greater name than Jesus,
   name of him who came to save us;
   in that saving name so gracious
   every knee shall bow.

2 Let everything that's beneath the ground,
   let everything in the world around,
   let everything exalted on high
   bow at Jesus' name!

3 In our minds, by faith professing,
   in our hearts, by inward blessing,
   on our tongues, by words confessing,
   Jesus Christ is Lord.

S.28 from Psalm 118

1 This is the day, this is the day,
   that the Lord has made,
      that the Lord has made;
   we will rejoice, we will rejoice,
   and be glad in it, and be glad in it:
      This is the day that the Lord has made,
      we will rejoice and be glad in it;
      this is the day, this is the day
      that the Lord has made.

2 This is the day, this is the day
  when he rose again . . .
      This is the day that the Lord has made,
      we will rejoice and be glad in it;
      this is the day, this is the day
      that the Lord has made.

3 This is the day, this is the day
  when the Spirit came . . .

S.29
Bruce Ballinger, © 1976 Sound III Incorporated, 2712 West 104th Terrace, Leawood, Kansas 66206, USA.

We have come into this house
and gathered in his name
    to worship him;
we have come into this house
and gathered in his name
    to worship him;
we have come into this house
and gathered in his name
    to worship Christ the Lord,
worship him, Christ the Lord.

S.30
from Revelation 4, Pauline Michael Mills
© 1963 Fred Bock Music Company.

You are worthy, you are worthy,
you are worthy, O Lord;
you are worthy to receive glory,
glory and honour and power:
for you have created, have all things created,
for you have created all things
and for your pleasure they are created:
you are worthy, O Lord!

S.31
from Psalm 148
© Richard Bewes†

1 Praise the Lord our God, praise the Lord;
  praise him from the heights, praise the Lord;
  praise him, angel throngs, praise the Lord –
  praise God, all his host!

2 Praise him, sun and moon, all the stars;
  praise him, sky and clouds, wind and rain;
  let them praise his name, works of God –
  all creatures, praise the Lord!

3 Praise him, wind and storm, mountains steep;
  praise him, fruitful trees, cedars tall;
  beasts and cattle herds, birds that fly –
  all creatures, praise the Lord!

4 Kings of earth, give praise, rulers all;
  all young men and girls, praise the Lord;
  old men, children small, praise the Lord –
  all people, praise the Lord!

S.32
from *A Song of Creation/Benedicite*
© Michael Perry†

1 Angels, praise him,
  heavens, praise him,
  waters, praise him,
      Alleluia!
  creatures of the Lord,
  all praise him
      for evermore:

2 Sun, praise him,
  moon, praise him,
  stars, praise him,
      Alleluia!
  showers, praise him,
  dews, praise him
      for evermore:

3 Wind, praise him,
  fire, praise him,
  heat, praise him,
      Alleluia!
  winter, praise him,
  summer, praise him
      for evermore:

4 Nights, praise him,
  days, praise him,
  light, praise him,
      Alleluia!
  lightnings, praise him,
  clouds, praise him
      for evermore:

5 Earth, praise him,
  mountains, praise him,
  hills, praise him,
      Alleluia!
  green things, praise him,
  wells, praise him
      for evermore:

6 Seas, praise him,
  rivers, praise him,
  fish, praise him,
      Alleluia!
  birds, praise him,
  beasts, praise him
      for evermore:

7 Nations, praise him,
  churches, praise him,
  saints, praise him,
      Alleluia!
  all his people,
  join to praise him
      for evermore!

HYMNS: FIRST LINES

Italics indicate former first line.

A debtor to mercy alone – 449
A great and mighty wonder – 49
A messenger named Gabriel – 73
A mighty fortress is our God – God is our fortress and our rock – 523
A new commandment – The new commandment – S.26
A purple robe – 122
A safe stronghold our God is still – God is our fortress and our rock – 523
A song was heard at Christmas – 75
Abide with me – 425
Ah, holy Jesus, how have you offended – 123
Alas! and did my saviour bleed – 124
All creation join to say – 150
All creatures of our God and King – 13
All for Jesus, all for Jesus – 469
All glory be to God on high – 606
All glory, praise and honour – 120
All hail the power of Jesus' name (revised version) – 203
All hail the power of Jesus' name (traditional version) – 587
All my heart this night rejoices – 76
All my hope on God is founded – 451
All people that on earth do dwell – 14
All praise to Christ, our Lord and king divine – 204
All shall be well – 149
All things bright and beautiful – 283
All-creating heavenly Giver – 489
All-holy Father, king of endless glory – 391
Alleluia, alleluia! As we walk along beside you – S.1
Alleluia, alleluia, give thanks to the risen Lord – S.3
Alleluia, alleluia! hearts to heaven – 151
Alleluia! raise the anthem – 205
Alleluia, sing to Jesus – 170
Almighty Lord, the holy One – 373
Amazing grace – 28
And can it be (revised version) – 452
And can it be (traditional version) – 588
And now, O Father, mindful of the love – 392
Angel voices ever singing – 307
Angels from the realms of glory – 77
Angels, praise him – S.32
As sons of the day and daughters of light – 490
As water to the thirsty – 470
As we break the bread – 393
As with gladness men of old – 99
Ascended Christ – 171
At evening, when the sun had set – 315
At the name of Jesus – 172
At the supper, Christ the Lord – 394
Author of life divine – 395
Awake, my soul, and with the sun – 264
Away in a manger – 72
Away with our fears – 224

Come all you good people – 80
Come and praise the Lord our king – S.8
Come and see the shining hope – 188
Come and sing the Christmas story – 81
Come down, O Love divine – 231
Come, Holy Ghost, our souls inspire – 589
   (also: Creator Spirit, come, inspire – 232)
Come into his presence singing – S.2
Come let us join our cheerful songs – 206
Come, let us with our Lord arise – 375
Come, let us worship Christ – S.10
Come, let us worship the Christ of creation – 207
Come, most Holy Spirit, come – 227
Come, O Fount of every blessing – 337
Come, O long-expected Jesus – 52
Come, praise the Lord – 609
Come, praise the name of Jesus – 538
Come, rejoice before your maker – 17
Come, risen Lord, as guest – 399
Come sing the praise of Jesus – 208
Come, thou Holy Spirit, come – Come, most Holy Spirit, come – 227
Come, thou long-expected Jesus – Come, O long-expected Jesus – 52
Come to us, creative Spirit – 308
Come with all joy to sing to God – 16
Come, worship God who is worthy of honour – 18
Come, ye faithful, raise the anthem – Alleluia! raise the anthem – 205
Come, ye faithful, raise the strain – Spring has come for us today – 160
Come, you thankful people, come – 284
Comes Mary to the grave – 152
Creator of the earth and skies – 320
Creator Spirit, come, inspire – 232
   (also: Come, Holy Ghost, our souls inspire – 589)
Crown him with many crowns – 174

Dear Lord and Father of mankind – 356
Deck yourself, my soul, with gladness – 400
Downtrodden Christ – 125
Draw near and take the body of the Lord – 401

Earth was waiting, spent and restless – 54
Empty he came – 127
Eternal Father, Lord of life – 806
Eternal Father, strong to save – 285
Eternal light, eternal light – 454
Eternal light, shine in my heart – 339

Fairest Lord Jesus – 209
Faithful shepherd, feed me – 29
Faithful vigil ended – 55
Father almighty, we your humble servants – 402
Father, although I cannot see – 455
Father and God, from whom our world derives – 357
Father eternal, Lord of the ages – 1
Father God in heaven, Lord most high – 358
Father, hear the prayer we offer – 360
Father in heaven, grant to your children – 2
Father, let us dedicate – 257

Father most holy, merciful and loving – 3
Father, now behold us – 384
Father of all, whose laws have stood – 539
Father of heaven, whose love profound – 359
Father of mercies, in your word – 247
Father on high to whom we pray – 296
Father, we adore you – S.5
Fight the good fight – 526
Fill thou my life – Fill now my life – 541
Fill your hearts with joy and gladness – 30
Filled with the Spirit's power – 233
Fire of God, titanic Spirit – 234
Firmly I believe and truly – 429
First of the week and finest day – 376
For all the saints – 567
For the beauty of the earth – 298
For the bread which you have broken – 403
For the fruits of his creation – 286
For your mercy and your grace – 258
Forgive our sins as we forgive – 111
Forth in the peace of Christ we go – 542
Forth in your name, O Lord, I go – 306
Forty days and forty nights – 103
Freedom and life are ours – 544
From all who live beneath the skies – 580
From you all skill and science flow – 310

Give me joy in my heart – S.11
Give praise for famous men – 568
Give to our God immortal praise – 31
Glad music fills the Christmas sky – 82
Glorious things of you are spoken – 494
Glory be to God in heaven – 581
Glory be to Jesus – 126
Glory in the highest to the God of heaven – 582
Glory to you, my God, this night – 274
Go forth and tell – 505
God be in my head – 543
God forgave my sin in Jesus' name – S.12
God has spoken – by his prophets – 248
God has spoken to his people – S.13
God is here! As we his people – 560
God is love – his the care – 311
God is our fortress and our rock – 523
God is our strength and refuge – 527
God is working his purpose out – 191
God made me for himself, to serve him here – 361
God of eternity, Lord of the ages – 495
God of God, the uncreated – 56
God of gods, we sound his praises – 340
God of grace and God of glory – 324
God of light and life's creation – 561
God of mercy, God of grace – 293
God our Father and creator – 562
God our Father, bless your people – 496
God rest you merry, gentlemen – 84
God save and bless our nation – 325

Lord Jesus Christ, you have come to us – 417
Lord Jesus, for my sake you come – 133
Lord Jesus, let these eyes of mine – 549
Lord Jesus, once you spoke to men – 112
Lord Jesus, think of me – 316
Lord Jesus, when your people meet – 371
Lord, make your word my rule – 250
Lord, now let your servant – 611
Lord of all hopefulness, Lord of all joy – 101
Lord of all power, I give you my will – 547
Lord of our growing years – 259
Lord of our life, and God of our salvation – 529
Lord of the changing year – 261
Lord of the church, we pray for our renewing – 499
Lord of the cross of shame – 548
Lord, speak to me that I may speak – 510
Lord, teach us how to pray aright – 367
Lord, thy word abideth – Lord your word shall guide us – 251
Lord, who left the highest heaven – 97
Lord, you can make our spirits shine – 512
Lord, you need no house – 546
Lord, you were rich beyond all splendour – 63
Lord, your church on earth is seeking – 511
Lord your word shall guide us – 251
Love came down at Christmas – 62
Love divine, all loves excelling – 217
Love is his word, love is his way – 481
Loved with everlasting love – 482
Love's redeeming work is done – All creation join to say – 150
Loving Shepherd of your sheep – 305
Low in the grave he lay – 158

Make me a channel of your peace – S.19
Make us worthy, Lord – S.20
Man of sorrows! what a name – 130
May God be gracious to us – 330
May the grace of Christ our saviour – 370
May the mind of Christ my saviour – 550
May we, O Holy Spirit, bear your fruit – 236
Morning has broken – 265
My Father, for another night – 269
My God, accept my heart this day – 551
My God, how wonderful you are – 369
My God, I love you – 479
My God, now is your table spread – 418
My hope is built on nothing less – 462
My Lord, I did not choose you – 107
My Lord of light – 4
My Lord, you wore no royal crown – 118
My song is love unknown – 136
My trust I place in God's good grace – 387

Name of all majesty – 218
New every morning is the love – 270
New songs of celebration render – 343
No weight of gold or silver – 138
Not all the blood of beasts – What offering shall we give – 439

Now let us from this table rise – 419
Now let us learn of Christ – 503
Now lives the Lamb of God – 159
Now praise the protector of heaven – 19
Now thank we all our God – 33
Now through the grace of God – 390

O bless the God of Israel – 599
O bless the Lord, my soul – 34
O Breath of life, come sweeping through us – 237
O changeless Christ, for ever new – 108
O Christ, at your first eucharist – 420
O Christ of all the ages, come – 262
O Christ the great foundation – 502
O Christ, the Master Carpenter – 135
O Christ the same, through all our story's pages – 263
O come, all ye faithful (long, traditional version) – 597
O come, all you faithful (short, revised version) – 65
O come, O come, Emmanuel – 66
O come, our all-victorious Lord – 441
O dearest Lord, your sacred head – 134
O for a closer walk with God – 368
O for a heart to praise my God – 483
O for a thousand tongues to sing – 219
O God beyond all praising – 36
O God of Jacob, by whose hand – 35
O God, our help in ages past – 37
O God, unseen yet ever near – 421
O God, you give to all mankind – 313
O happy band of pilgrims – 530
O happy day that fixed my choice   442
O Holy Spirit, come to bless – 238
O Holy Spirit, giver of life – 239
O Jesus, I have promised – 531
O Jesus, king most wonderful – 484
O joy of God, we seek you in the morning – 422
O little town of Bethlehem – 88
O Lord my love, my strength, my tower   485
O Lord of every shining constellation – 314
O Lord of heaven and earth and sea   287
O Lord our guardian and our guide – 374
O Lord, who came from realms above – 552
   (also: O thou who camest from above – 596)
O Lord, you gave in love divine – 410
O Love that will not let me go – 486
O Master Christ, draw near to take – 553
O praise ye the Lord – Sing praise to the Lord – 354
O Prince of peace whose promised birth – 89
O sacred head surrounded – 139
O Sacrifice of Calvary – 424
O Spirit of the living God – 513
O thou who at thy eucharist didst pray – O Christ, at your first eucharist – 420
O thou who camest from above – 596
   (also: O Lord, who came from realms above – 552)
O thou who makest souls to shine – Lord, you can make our spirits shine – 512
O Trinity, O Trinity – 6
O worship the King all glorious above – 24

O worship the Lord in the beauty of holiness – 344
Of the Father's love begotten – God of God, the uncreated – 56
Oft in danger, oft in woe – Christian soldiers, onward go – 524
Oh the bitter shame and sorrow – 487
Oh the deep, deep love of Jesus – 465
On Jordan's bank the Baptist's cry – 601
Once in royal David's city – 67
One holy apostolic church – 514
Onward, Christian soldiers – 532
Our great Redeemer, as he breathed – 241
Our Saviour Christ once knelt in prayer – 116
Out of darkness let light shine – 447

Peace, perfect peace – 467
Powerful in making us wise to salvation – 252
Praise be to Christ in whom we see – 220
Praise for the mighty love – 488
Praise God for the harvest of farm and of field – 288
Praise God from whom all blessings flow (revised version) – 585
Praise God from whom all blessings flow (traditional version) – 586
Praise him, praise him, everybody praise him – S.21
Praise him, praise him, praise him – 25
Praise, my soul, the king of heaven –˙38
Praise the Father, God of justice – 8
Praise the Lord, his glories show – 345
Praise the Lord our God – S.31
Praise the Lord, you heavens, adore him – 583
Praise to the Holiest in the height – 140
Praise to the Lord, the almighty – 40
Praise we offer, Lord of glory – 346
Prayer is the soul's supreme desire – 372

Rejoice, O land, in God your Lord – 331
Rejoice, the Lord is king – 180
Rejoice today with one accord – 347
Remember, Lord, the world you made – 332
Restless souls, why do you scatter – 443
Revive your church, O Lord – 515
Ride on, ride on in majesty – 119
Ring from your steeple – 378
Risen Lord, whose name we cherish – 500
Roar the waves – 289
Rock of ages, cleft for me (revised version) – 444
Rock of ages, cleft for me (traditional version) – 593
Round me falls the night – 279

Safe in the shadow of the Lord – 445
Saviour, again to your dear name we raise – 281
Saviour Christ, in praise we name him – 216
See, amid the winter snow – 90
See, Christ was wounded for our sake – 137
See him lying on a bed of straw – 91
See the conqueror mounts in triumph – 181
Send out the gospel! Let it sound – 517
Shepherds came, their praises bringing – 74
Shout for joy, loud and long – 348
Silent night! holy night – 95

The Confession

Almighty God, our heavenly Father,
we have sinned against you
in thought and word and deed,
through negligence, through weakness,
through our own deliberate fault.
We are truly sorry
and repent of all our sins,
For the sake of your Son Jesus Christ,
    who died for us,
forgive us all that is past;
and grant that we may serve you
    in newness of life
to the glory of your name.   Amen.

The Apostles' Creed

I believe in God, the Father almighty,
creator of heaven and earth.
I believe in Jesus Christ, his only Son,
    our Lord.
He was conceived by the power of the
    Holy Spirit,
and born of the Virgin Mary.
He suffered under Pontius Pilate,
was crucified, died, and was buried.
He descended to the dead.
On the third day he rose again.
He ascended into heaven,
and is seated at the right hand
    of the Father.
He will come again to judge
    the living and the dead.
I believe in the Holy Spirit,
the holy catholic Church,
the communion of saints,
the forgiveness of sins,
the resurrection of the body,
and the life everlasting.   Amen.

The Lord's Prayer

Our Father in heaven,
hallowed be your name,
your kingdom come,
your will be done,
on earth as in heaven.
Give us today our daily bread.
Forgive us our sins
as we forgive those who sin against us.
Lead us not into temptation
but deliver us from evil.
For the kingdom, the power, and the glory
    are yours
now and for ever.   Amen.

The Grace

The Grace of our Lord Jesus Christ,
and the love of God,
and the fellowship of the Holy Spirit
be with us all evermore.   Amen.